KT-469-534

Change in British Society

A. H. HALSEY

Third Edition

Oxford   New York

OXFORD UNIVERSITY PRESS

Oxford University Press, Walton Street, Oxford OX2 6DP

Oxford New York Toronto
Delhi Bombay Calcutta Madras Karachi
Petaling Jaya Singapore Hong Kong Tokyo
Nairobi Dar es Salaam Cape Town
Melbourne Auckland

and associated companies in
Berlin Ibadan

Oxford is a trade mark of Oxford University Press

First published 1978
Second edition 1981
Third edition 1986
Reprinted 1986, 1987, 1988, 1989

British Library Cataloguing in Publication Data
Halsey, A. H.
Change in British society.—3rd ed.—(OPUS)
1. Great Britain—Social conditions—20th century
I. Title II. Series
941.082 HN385
ISBN 0–19–289200–2

Library of Congress Cataloging in Publication Data
Halsey, A. H.
Change in British society
(An OPUS Book)
Bibliography: p. Includes index.
1. Great Britain—Social conditions—20th century
Addresses, essays, lectures. 2. Great Britain—
Economic conditions—20th century—Addresses, essays,
lectures. 3. Social change—Case studies. I. Title.
II. Series: OPUS
HN390.H3 1986 303.4'0941 85–15544
ISBN 0–19–289200–2

Printed in Great Britain by
Biddles Ltd.
Guildford and King's Lynn

For Norman Dennis
True friend and exemplary citizen

Acknowledgements

My thanks are due to the *Oxford Review of Education* for allowing me to incorporate part of my article 'Authority, Bureaucracy, and Education' from Vol. 3, No. 3, 1977; to the *Listener* for permission to reprint part of my essay on Liverpool, first published there on 24 February 1983; to Routledge and Kegan Paul for allowing me to use a table from M. Young and P. Willmott, *The Symmetrical Family*; and to HMSO for allowing me to use tables from the *Report* of the Royal Commission on the Distribution of Income and Wealth.

An OPUS book

CHANGE IN BRITISH SOCIETY

Preface to the third edition

This book has its origins in my Reith Lectures of 1977. A second edition was published in 1981 in response to an invitation from the Open University to revise it as a set book for the Social Sciences Foundation Course. In a third edition it is now possible to take advantage of the experience of students in using the book as a general introduction to the social sciences. Few authors have the enlightening, if painful, experience of learning directly about the difficulties they impose on their readers by unclarity or other faults of composition. I am grateful to the Open University tutors and their students for their detailed candour in criticizing my earlier versions. I am especially grateful to Andy Northedge, whose introduction, signpostings, and summaries written for the students about the book have been an invaluable guide in my rewriting.

Professor Stuart Hall and John Clark have also put me in their particular debt by their own contributions to the Open University foundation course. Their expositions have obliged me to be clearer about my theoretical and political position.

A third edition also gives me the opportunity to take account of social change in the 1980s. In the past six years a new concept has been bequeathed to social science—Thatcherism. It has also become clear that in the mid-seventies the post-war period came to an end. My intention is to give meaning to these remarks and, more broadly, to provide students of all ages with a short but comprehensive introduction to the information needed in order to form a view of the direction of twentieth-century social history in Britain, and to offer a sociological interpretation of that history. In a short concluding chapter I have deliberately trespassed beyond sociology to a moral and political interpretation. This I have done mainly in the hope that the reader may thereby be helped and encouraged to form his or her own view and to appreciate both the separation of and the link between the social sciences and social action.

I have acknowledged my many debts to friends and colleagues

in previous prefaces. The debts are now greater, and I must particularly thank David Coleman for bringing my demography up to date in Chapter 5.

Nuffield College,   A. H. HALSEY
Oxford

April 1985

Contents

List of figures and tables

1

To know ourselves

Britain has changed immensely in the twentieth century. The vast majority of its people have had no direct experience of Victorian society. The tiny minority of $\frac{3}{4}$ million who are over 85 began their lives in a society without radio, the Labour party, plastics, or airlines. They have survived into a world without trams or Sunday suits and with television, computers, the Open University, the closed shop, and the nuclear bomb. Yet it is, in a similar range of trivial and serious senses, the same country. Fish and chips and Sheffield Wednesday and Cambridge and the monarchy are still parts of the social continuity which is Britain.

I want to describe these changes and continuities, and even to explain them. The explanations will be limited and partial, partly because there could be no full explanation without careful comparison with other countries, and more fundamentally because a comprehensive and accepted theory of social change does not exist. By the end of the book I hope to have moved towards a convincing interpretation. But on the way it will become evident that social scientists do not agree as to what causes changes and continuity or even what are the significant features, changing or unchanging, which require either notice or explanation. Accordingly I shall be arguing along the way about the disagreements between sociologists, as well as about the society they wish to explain. And the argument will also raise the question of how far people have it in their power to determine for themselves change in the society in which they live.

On the last issue, and on most of the issues of continuity and change, my own position is opposed to both orthodox or 'mainstream' Marxism and to orthodox or economic liberalism. Both these doctrines, in my view, give too much weight to 'structure' as against 'agency'—Marxism conceiving of class struggle and economic liberals discovering the market to be the engine of social change. In arguing otherwise I shall find myself closer to those liberals or socialists who look to democratic institutions as vehicles of change, and closer to the earlier writings of Karl Marx in which he insisted not only that people 'make their own history' but also 'under circumstances directly encountered, given and transmitted from the past'.

Britain is, of course, a Western European capitalist society which has evolved into a capitalist Welfare State governed politically by parliamentary democracy. Its commitment to both state welfare and a free market results in conflicts and accommodations which are to be found in all the Western countries. The present shape of the international world, with its aggressive multinational capitalism and its state communisms, adds to these difficulties. But Britain's past is also distinctive. First it has had a millennium of territorial integrity, which culminated in the nineteenth century in a far-flung empire. Second it has a pre-industrial as well as an industrial past which, while bequeathing it a continuous structure of inequality, has also profoundly marked and modified the class structure which is basic to capitalist development. The analysis of persistent inequality in British society requires therefore a more complex analysis than that which is afforded by a simple class theory. British nationalism and the social hierarchy are intertwined.

Third, and most fundamentally, British culture is deeply individualistic. It is no accident that Hume and Locke are its philosophers rather than Hegel or Marx. The deeply embedded cultural assumption is that ultimate values are individual, that society is in no sense superior to the sum of the people who make it up; that collectivism can only be instrumental and that the state is best when minimal. Not that ordinary British men and women or their politicians have ever had much taste for such abstractions: it is just that individualism is built into 'custom and practice', into local work places and community organizations, into all commonsensical explanations of why people do what they do.

Inequality has lived through centuries of this culture. The ruling minority has survived all the transformations from medieval to modern society by a long series of concessions and assimilations to successive demands of the excluded and underprivileged, always provided that incorporation has accepted the limitation of not seriously challenging established privileges and rights of property. Those who have aspired to challenge the existing order of inequality, whether as 'left' revolutionaries or as 'right' reactionaries, have been successfully excluded and with remarkably little bloodshed. British violence has been characteristically naval rather than military.

Yet the question of social disorder has never and could never be finally solved. Conflicting interests whether from without or within must always threaten any establishment. So finally that question must be raised in the context of present conditions. The new Conservatism which gained power in 1979 has set out, at least rhetorically, to revitalize the movement towards an order of economic liberalism which made its first bid for dominance in the first half of the nineteenth century. Most twentieth-century observers (of the Left and the Right) had believed this type of conservatism to be buried by the evolved consensus of traditional conservative, political liberal, and ethical socialist forces. So we live, as the Chinese say, in interesting times.

Continuity and change

Given that change is the central theme of the book, we could start by putting the problem in biological terms. You and I are the same in that we belong to the same species—*Homo sapiens*—which has existed on earth for something like two million years. We are therefore the product of roughly 100,000 generations. But these reproductions have never been exact replications. The complexity of genetic transmission is so great that it is a reasonable guess that no two persons alive (identical twins excepted) carry the same genes. So you and I are both alike and different.

Moreover our sameness and difference are more than genetic. We are creatures of cultural as well as genetic reproduction. Culture is the sum of the skills by which we live, which are passed down the generations by means other than genetic transmission —our language, science, religion, art, and practical knowledge, as well as our material artefacts and social organizations. These too exhibit continuity and change in interaction with genetic evolution. Just as you and I share differentially a genetic inheritance, so too we are variant products of a common human culture.

As to continuity and change, we must appreciate that the country experienced by Britons now was made and continues to be modified for them by forces beyond their own encounters—by its geology, topography, latitude and longitude, and by the activity of their ancestors, labouring incessantly down the ages to master their environment. The unfinished result is their cultural inheritance. Whether they see it as a 'green and pleasant land', or as the cradle of 'dark, Satanic mills', or both, what they see and, indeed, how they learn to see it, is rooted in a long process of human history and cultural evolution.

Much of all this we must simply take for granted, appealing to what every mythical schoolboy knows, for example, that the Phoenicians dug tin in the mines of Cornwall, that Derby, given its name, must have been founded by the Danes, or that 30.8 per cent of the inhabitants of Wales were Welsh-speaking in 1921. The lessons of history are no doubt numberless but, quite apart from sifting them out of the lessons of historians, they do not foreclose the future. A story about Scotland can illustrate both points. Edward Gibbon, writing in the eighteenth century, noted that the Romans failed to conquer northern Scotland.

The native Caledonians preserved in the northern extremity of the island their wild independence, for which they were not less indebted to their poverty than to their valour. Their incursions were frequently repelled and chastised; but their country was never subdued. The masters of the fairest and most wealthy climates of the globe turned with contempt from gloomy hills assailed by the winter tempest, from lakes concealed in a blue mist, and from cold and lonely heaths, over which the deer of the forest were chased by a troop of naked Barbarians.[1]

If we are listening here to a faithful echo of the Roman voice, we are bound to remark that the Romans could not have anticipated Gibbon's Scottish contemporaries like David Hume, or John Millar,[2] or Adam Smith,[3] who made their universities the leading centres of European thought in their day; and, if we are listening to Gibbon's amiable prejudices, we can at least remark that he could not have anticipated North Sea oil.

When sociologists or historians consider continuity and change they must also start from the commonplace generalization that man is to be distinguished from the brutes, not so much by his desire for a better life as by the range of his conception of what that life might be, and the complexity of the language in which he is able to express his hope. Our period in the twentieth century can be thought of as one of unprecedented advance in the capacity of mankind to realize dreams—at least in that one-third of the world to which Britain belong where, in the past generation, the natural sciences have been harnessed to spectacular new dominance over nature. The power of productive systems, whether for peace or war, has transformed the significance of the age-old debate over the ends towards which society may be directed. Such clichés of political discussion as 'the revolution of rising expectations' point to that significance. Dreams have come to earth and ends are secularized. An aerial view of the island shows the motorway and the church spire as the ubiquitous monuments of human aspiration. But the spires point to otherworldly vision, and were built over centuries of a passing civilization in which the attainment of bliss was seen to belong to the next world. The road, by contrast, seems to hold out the promise of satisfaction, tomorrow if not today, but *on this earth* as it busily connects factory to town to suburb to coastal resort. So, for example, in the older world, poverty was accepted as inevitable, and morality was addressed to the endurance of it and its relief. In the twentieth century, the moral objective has switched from endurance to protest, and from relief to abolition. Equality is to be realized among men, not only found before God. Liberty is for the lords of the earth, not the angels in heaven.

There are, of course, those who prophesy that these dreams come true will shortly turn into living nightmares. The twentieth century in Britain and throughout the so-called first and second worlds of industrial capitalism and communism, is thought by some critics to be an interlude of materialist fantasy. The earthly paradise is a miasma and the modern secular '-isms' doomed to fail. So Mr Muggeridge, with a journalist's genius for self-caricature, expresses the traditionalist opposition to modernity when he tells us that if he were Pope he would form an underground church, organized to survive through the new Dark Ages we are about to enter, until the time when the world can again be given the eternal verities hitherto preserved, albeit imperfectly and with gross infidelity, by the Catholic Church.[4]

So ends remain in question and this must not be forgotten even though my purpose in this book is to consider means, that is, the changes in social organization of the past fifty years through which people in Britain have co-operated and argued in pursuit of their interests. Sociology cannot prescribe ends, but it can help us to argue about them more intelligently by describing accurately the social conditions under which people act, and the intended and unintended consequences of their actions.

Older studies of continuity, and particularly the study of national character by cultural anthropologists and historians, were posited essentially on the existence of a modal personality in each nation. The last such anthropological book on Britain (actually more narrowly focused on England) was Geoffrey Gorer's *Exploring English Character* (1953). Such works are out of fashion now: but one of them is especially remarkable. Writing as a German for Germans, Wilhelm Dibelius tell us that he conceived of his book on *England* during the First World War out of an 'overwhelming sense of a people giving its best in fighting an enemy which it did not know'.[5] He wrote in a spirit of high European liberalism, and evoked the essential manners and outlook of the British with the clarity—perhaps false clarity—which can sometimes appear from off the coast of Dover of what is held in common, but unnoticed, between the natives.

He was neither the first nor the last observer to insist on the extraordinary combination of solidarity and hierarchy in British society. And his basic explanation is the long-established, always dominant, force of English aristocracy. 'To the great surprise of the Continental student of England', says Dibelius, 'this matter-of-fact, practical, and conservative English character appears wherever the Anglo-Saxon is met with: the differentiation between different geographical sub-types of the race is astonishingly small.' He then goes on to put stress on the early establishment of royal absolutism in England by the Norman kings. Real variations from the type appear in Britain only outside England and the Norman sphere of influence.

Thus, the Scot was affected neither by Norman centralization, nor by a civilization based upon the Anglican Church. So, under Calvinist influences, he developed a profound habit of thought, and a one-sidedly religious character, while the wildness of his nature, half-English and half-Celtic, never fully submitted to the surface polish of an Anglo-Saxon court. The Irish, even after the loss of their language, went their own way. Visionary dreamers, capable of swift, passionate excitement, prone to swift weariness and disillusionment, and richly endowed with artistic gifts, they also have their full share of the peasant inheritance of coarse materialism, and at the centre of their inner life, in the sphere of religion and national feeling, are capable of an amazing endurance, that centuries of disappointment proved powerless to break.

In England itself, Dibelius insists that there was a homogeneous national character, even across classes. 'Apart from Scotland, English national life contrasted with the rich variations of the Continent, presents a picture of drab uniformity, fatally congenial to the creation of a featureless and spineless urban population.'[6]

These sketches of national character are amusing: they may even be true. They speak to us of stubborn historical persistence and uniformity. But what of conflict and change?

Continuity normally presupposes consensus. Change typically results from conflict. We must, therefore, explore the sources of consensus and conflict. How are differences between classes, sexes, generations, and ethnic groups to be depicted, how have they been changing, and how controlled? The answers are to be found, I think, in the relation between means and ends. The means are social organizations and movements, and these we shall consider in the following chapters. The ends are the ideals which dominate modern social thought—what I have referred to as the dreams of the modern age.

Continuity is no accident. Social customs, like personal habit, economize human effort. They store knowledge, pre-arrange decisions, save us the trouble of weighing every choice afresh. In this way the world is ordered; but, in the same way, control in the interest of the status quo is more or less powerfully embodied in any society. Maintenance of that control then depends on a stable environment of which one important element is external security. In this respect British history is distinctive by contrast with the history of the European continent. The towns and villages of the island have peaceable traditions over many centuries. The last battle on British soil took place at Culloden in 1746; every other European country has known violent and bitter warfare with foreigners on its own territory. Britain has exported its bloodshed. But above all, continuity is a matter of social control and this brings with it its puzzles. For example, many have noted and praised Britain as a land of tolerance and liberty, while at the same time wondering at its capacity to resist the claims of egalitarian movements without resort to overt force.

The issue of freedom and control was raised in a moment of dramatic debate when the Russian leader Gorbachev visited London in 1984 and was challenged by the Conservative MP Norman St John-Stevas about the persecution of Christians in the Soviet Union. Gorbachev replied by asking whether Britain was not persecuting its three-and-a-quarter million unemployed. Questions of liberty and equality can be put or evaded in ways which reveal alternative assumptions about human priorities and social controls.

Personal knowledge

Any number of questions can be put about persistence and change. My answers will be those of a sociologist. This you may immediately find an imprisonment of method, especially if I add that just by living and learning to the point of reading this book, you already know practically all the sociology that is to be known. But that is a misleading truth—a play on the verb 'to know'. Sixth-form boys and girls setting out on an A level science course are frequently told that they already know 95 per cent of all known physics. It is true: but the other 5 per cent transforms the meaning and the power of knowing.

Yet personal knowledge is by no means to be disregarded as a traditional and commonly shared method of cultural understanding. An immense store of information about a country is lodged in the minds and memories of its inhabitants. The collective store, including as it does visual, auditary, olfactory, and tactile knowledge, is vastly greater than that of any conceivable data set stored from a survey into a computer file. Any British native has accordingly acquired by nurture a formidable battery of, so to say, tests of significance which he or she may readily apply to the findings of sociological research.

To elaborate the point I will cite my own version of this accumulation of personal knowledge: for it happens that I recently tried to sketch the condition of Britain by making a series of excursions out of Oxford and London with the object of preparing a series of talks for the BBC. The idea was to use personal knowledge. I tried to eschew official statistics, Blue Books, or analyses of British social structure. I could not be wholly successful, for professional knowledge inevitably becomes personal. Nevertheless, in anyone of middle age, memory is more than adequate to a mere 160 minutes of talk; and the journeys could easily be contrived to lift the dust from stored recollections. So I planned my excursions to repeat my own biography, and thus to construct one slender strand in British experience from the early 1920s to the 1980s.

The professional sociologist will shudder at the imperfections of such a method. The encounters of the traveller are not random: a sample cannot be a scientific basis for assertion about a population without specified probabilities of representing it. Indeed, the people to whom I talked were not even a sample in any scientific sense. I did not choose them in relation to the British population. They were chosen for me by my passage through the restricted circumstances of the street, the railway compartment, or the pub, to which the traveller is confined: or if they were private contacts they were my friends and acquaintances and thus a refraction of public life through the peculiar network of my personal associates.

On the other hand, personal knowledge, however unsystematically, covers a vastly larger territory than any specialized professional knowledge. A man may be no architect, but buildings evoke periods and people he has never known. A woman may be no paediatrician yet spend half her life tending children: people may be innocent of theology but can scarcely avoid coming to terms with life and death. In any case I was committed on this occasion to the method of personal encounter and encouraged in it by awareness of my predecessors. The genre is well known and thoroughly understood. Journeying through the island is a tradition. Every child learns the phrase 'from Land's End to John o' Groats'. There is a large library of books where the author has projected his personal knowledge on to the national screen and called it England. Daniel Defoe, William Cobbett, and J. B. Priestley are only a few famous names in a multitude. George Orwell justified them all in the introductory section of his *The Lion and the Unicorn* to which he gave the subtitle 'England your England'.

above all, it is *your* civilisation, it is *you*. However much you hate or laugh at it, you will never be happy away from it for any length of time. The suet puddings and the red pillar boxes have entered into your soul. Good or evil, it is yours, you belong to it, and this side of the grave you will never get away from the marks that it has given you.[7]

I pondered this passage before setting out on my summer travels, knowing that I was a patriot and fearing that I was a sentimentalist. So I asked myself in advance what fragments in my memory would put a stamp of interpretation on the journeys I was preparing to make. Slowly the confused recollections ordered themselves into four themes as personal perceptions of my country and my compatriots. You might care to compare them with your own as a prelude to reading the sociological analysis in the chapters which follow.

The first is an age-old tension between urban and rural life. I was born among the dirty brick, smoky streets, little men in baggy trousers, and shapeless women with shopping baskets that made up Kentish Town in the early 1920s. Then I was transported to Liddington in Rutland. A railway journey from the grandiose grime of Gothic St Pancras through the more domestic Victorian elegance of Kettering Station, with its neat platforms and its decorated iron stanchions, gave way finally to a horse-and-cart ride across the Welland Valley into a rural world of medieval sleepiness. Stone and thatch, huge skies, vast woods, and unending open fields were my first memories of the English countryside.

None the less, I retained a cockney snobbishness towards the 'country bumpkin'. When I first read the *Communist Manifesto of 1848* the phrase which leapt out of that strident pamphlet of vulgarized Marxism was 'the idiocy of rural life'. Marx gave historical credit to the bourgeoisie for our escape from rural stagnation. I had to give the credit to the London Midland and Scottish Railway, which gave railway servants periodic free passes to go anywhere in the country. We always went back to St Pancras. The tension never ceased, and I came to accept it as not only a private experience but as an integral part of the national psyche. In the end it gave me two patriotisms, the one of the soil, the other of the Cenotaph.

The second theme was a kaleidoscope in memory of continuous variation of colour, sound, and smell. England is a Jacob's coat of a country. The black splendour of Liverpool Town Hall, white hawthorn everywhere in the spring, the red mud of Devon, the golden stone of villages scattered from Banbury to Peterborough, and the innumerable greens encircling and shrouding all human settlements.

The ear of the traveller too is assailed by a great variety of sound if only from what is called common speech. Shaw's *Pygmalion* is not a caricature. A man from Sunderland has only to say 'good morning' to distinguish his origins from the Newcastle man twelve miles away. I remember the two languages which I learned in order to survive the day in a grammar school and the evening in the village street. Scents also linger, persistently pervading my recollections. Coal fires, crushed grass, road tarmac, and pigsties. I can still smell the clammy stink of urine and stale vegetables in the kitchens at the wrong end of the street by contrast with the odour of the carbolic soap and boot polish of the respectable families.

Then, third, there was the hierarchy. A sociologist may refine it into abstractions, but no one could grow up in England without acquiring a deep personal-cum-anthropological knowledge of class and status. Two memories are enough to evoke it. On one occasion in the 1930s the tram from Kentish Town was slow. My mother, the latest baby, my sister, my brother, and I rushed into the vault of St Pancras Station and bundled with our impedimenta into the corridor of a first-class carriage, seconds before the train drew out. A large, florid-faced man in a pin-striped suit flung open a compartment door to demand of my mother whether she had a first-class ticket. Some years later I was youth hostelling through Bath, and idling beside the entrance to a hotel in one of the stately crescents of classical architecture, when I heard the female version of the same arrogant voice demanding coffee at the reception desk. A mumbling, apologetic, but stubborn West Country voice replied that the kitchens were closed: the lady stormed out with the disdainful judgement of English metropolitan snobbery, 'these damned provinces'.

Fourth, and finally, there is the sense of tension between change and changelessness in English society. The London townscape has been transformed in my lifetime—invaded by the international architecture of Corbusier and modern brutalism. New towns appear and old industrial development falls into decay. But underneath lies the never defeated countryside, and English sentiment refuses to give up its rural nostalgia. The Victorian hierarchy has virtually collapsed and generations of 'class abatement' have changed poverty from the common experience of the working class into the misfortunes of the old, the sick, and the deprived areas. Yet the House of Lords, the public schools, the phoney farms of the millionaires, and the shabby back streets of Toxteth and Brixton remain.

Sociological knowledge: positivism

How then can we proceed from personal to sociological questions and answers? One approach, borrowing from the natural sciences, is to strive for objectivity and value-neutrality: to study ourselves as objects, to record the pattern and regularities of our behaviour and to explain what we observe by theories which are tested to ensure that they 'fit the facts'. This is the method called positivism. At the risk of caricature we can appreciate its force by imaging ourselves as visitors from some other planet, as Martian anthropologists, possessed of belief in science and of the intelligence to use it, but without the understanding which enables us to interpret our neighbour through the fact of our own humanity. What would the interplanetary visitor see? Even without human understanding, his computer picture would reveal order rather than chaos, regularity rather than randomness. A guarded boundary of British society would be as clear to him as the physical coastline. He would notice that there are two ways of entering this society, either through the wombs of mothers and the records of the Registrar of Births, Marriages, and Deaths, or from other countries overseas and via the desk of the immigration officer. Exit is similarly marked and rule-bound. Births, deaths, and migrations are governed not only by physical laws, but also by social mechanisms: there are both legitimate and illegitimate births and deaths. Further inspection, again unaided by any kind of human empathy, would reveal patterns and continuities of relations inside the boundary. Our Martian would quickly conceptualize pair-bonding in what we call marriage, courtship, and friendship, class structure in the social relations of production, scientific organizations in the social relations of discovery, status systems in the relations of dominance and submission, and so on. Without doubt, considerable inhuman sense could be made of British society and its history.

Sociological knowledge: humanism

But why not seek for human rather than inhuman sense? Why cannot men and women be the subject rather than the object of social science? Various modern schools of sociological thought take this humanistic view. Whatever their differences (denoted by such labels as phenomenological, ethnomethodological, idealist, existentialist, etc.) they agree on defining sociology as a way of interpreting the meanings created by people in their relations with one another. Society is to be understood through these meanings. Men and women are conceived as active makers of society; their intentions move the world.

On this view our own social knowledge is both less and more than Martian. Less, because human involvement makes us creatures of our time and place, hampering us with preconceptions and prejudices, and restricting the range of our imagination. More, and it is a crucial more, because we can turn understanding to the service of scholarship. You might, therefore, think of the social sciences as striving simultaneously both to understand so as to interpret human activity, and also to achieve Martian objectivity so as to remove from it adulterating passion. This, at all events, is the intellectual posture I will adopt in my attempt to interpret recent generations of British social experience.

This is a considerable task. A single book could not hope to reproduce more than the most minute fraction of the social action and perception of a single hour in British society. Moreover, the fact that to understand other human beings is an indispensable tool to sociological explanation also constitutes a peculiar handicap in exposition because it makes sociologists of us all. Words like 'class' or 'status' are common to 'folk sociology' as well as to professional sociology, but their meanings differ (and, in the case of this particular pair of words, are usually reversed as between a newspaper and a learned article). Hence the struggle to rescue scholarship and science from gossip, which the physicist has largely won, is much harder for the social scientist, for the paradoxical reason that he more readily 'knows' and is known to the 'object' of his study.

The posture I have described as proper to sociologists, its difficulty apart, is not the only possible one for understanding society; nor is it either confined to or always adopted by sociologists. Much of our collective self-knowledge comes from fiction or books and essays in persuasion. It is arguable whether we learn more about the social circumstances of childhood at the beginning of the present century from Arthur Morrison's *A Child of the Jago*, or from Charles Booth's *London Survey* of that time. Yet there can be no doubt that accuracy of perspective is more likely to be obtained by use of the sociological method. The novel seeks drama before balance. As it happens, both of the works cited are excellent examples of their genre. But the Jago was the worst of slums, and therefore Morrison's novel tells us about childhood in that environment only, while Booth's Survey not only described but quantified the population living in a much wider range of environments. From him we receive a quantified description not only of the 'lowest class of occasional labourers, loafers and semi-criminals', but also of 'the very poor' and 'the poor', those on 'regular standard earnings', 'higher-class labour', and so on. Booth estimated the lowest class to number 11,000 out of 900,000. But this was the class, the lumpenproletariat so heartily detested by Marx, which has constantly attracted the attention and caught the imagination of research workers, reformer, and journalists. The resulting descriptions make good copy, but they tempt romantic minds to identify the working class as a whole with a distinctive and unrepresentative segment of it.

Structure and agency

Whether or not a sociology can combine positivist and humanist approaches, it will still have essential features distinguishing it from other kinds of writing about social life. If I again ask a native of our chosen country—'Who are you?'—he or she might reply with the title of one of Graham Greene's entertainments, *England Made Me*. The sociologist would then ask, 'How?' Or he might quote Sir Harry Smith's mother who took leave of him saying 'If you ever meet your enemy, remember you are born a true Englishman.'[8] The sociologist would want to ask who, apart from a traditional matriarch, advances a definition of the true Englishman, what other definitions are available, from whom, and who knows them, follows them, or defies them. Sociology is about social relations—relations of individuals and groups in work and in play, war and peace, transient encounters and enduring bonds. Sociologists seek regularity and pattern in these relations. Hence they summarize them in abstractions as relations of production and reproduction, of kinship and affinity, of authority and freedom, power and advantage. They assume that the social world is not a universe of random changes and exchanges but, on the contrary, that the successful study of social relations will yield general rules governing their persistence and their rupture—rules which are by no means necessarily known to the social actors themselves.

Now I realize I have already taken us into deep water. To go further would be to navigate those oceans in which are to be found the question of free will, and whether there are laws of social motion, historical necessities, propelling us towards a determined fate.

Sociologists are no more agreed on this issue than are philosophers. There have been deterministic theories of many kinds to which humanistic sociology is opposed. Structural Marxism is one such theory—that the history of man and society is ultimately determined by the mode of production. But there are non-Marxist determinisms attributing guiding force to climate or race or culture. And there is Marxist humanism as well as the voluntaristic humanism usually associated with liberal traditions of thought. In other words there remains unresolved debate as to whether and to what degree human beings are made by or make their own history. The debate over 'structure' and 'agency' is tied to any interpretation of the problem of continuity and change. The dispute cuts across that between Marxists and non-Marxists. I cannot promise to settle it in this book. Indeed I doubt whether it can be resolved by social science. What will emerge from an attempt at objectivity of method is my belief that men and women have been relatively more constrained by 'structure' in the past than their age-old aspiration to 'agency' need be in the future.

The search for objectivity through social science has another characteristic feature. Sociology, as I have said, is essentially a set of propositions about social relations, about characteristic tendencies and variations in social conditions and social consciousness. Sociological reference is thus to the role, not to the person. Even references to groups should normally be taken as statements about a structure of relations rather than an aggregate of people. For example, if we speak of the British working class, it is more often than not misleading to take this to mean a summary label for the enumeration of men and women in manual employment in Britain at a point of time. So the sociologist Colin

Crouch is faithful to his calling when he begins a book with a firm reminder to the reader that 'class is treated here as an analytical relationship rather than as the identification of empirical groups of persons'. And he goes on to point out that where this usage is carried to its logical conclusion, as in the writings of Marxists like Poulantzas, human beings are seen 'as simply the "bearers" of structural variables'.[9] At first reading, this may seem a weird distortion of language. Certainly it runs risks. It can lead to what is called the over-socialized conception of man which, in its crude form, portrays people as mere social puppets so that the Britons we study in this book are depicted as nothing but the expression of, say, bureaucratization, or class conflict, or secularization. But the method is justified precisely to distinguish and analyse such social forces. That is what sociology is. It does not set out to describe and explain some total 'human condition'. It narrows the beam to intensify the light: and the world it thus illuminates is far from being the whole world.

Liberty, equality, and fraternity

Our task, then, is to use sociology to explain cultural continuity and social change. The sociological method intrinsically draws our attention to structures of social relations. One way to keep 'agency' in view is to phrase questions in terms of the ideals sought by people through social action. Three ends or ideals have dominated European thought since the eighteenth century and the transition out of agrarian into industrial society. In the popular slogan of the French Revolution they are liberty, equality, and fraternity. They are the dreams of radicals and reformers. They are, so to say, courts of appeal before which policy and practice appear as plaintiffs or defendants in an evolving trial of promise and performance. As society develops, it is through various combinations of these three ideals that scholars abstractly, and ordinary people concretely, assess the quality of that development. And in this complex interplay of social action and reflections upon it, we can discern two contending traditions of reform—the one liberal, evolutionist, and giving highest priority to liberty; the other socialist, revolutionary, critical, and giving highest priority to equality. What is most clearly evident from the British experience, in my opinion, is an unresolved problem of fraternity or basis for social order beneath the clash of egalitarian and libertarian argument. This argument is central to political debate. Fraternity, for all its relevance, is somehow left to moralists and theologians.

To the contemporary ear fraternity is an unsatisfactory concept if only because of its male connotation. I shall therefore revise the terminology in the last chapter. Meanwhile, accepting its historical meaning, as I understand it, fraternity is sociologically prior to liberty and equality. All three principles are difficult to define. All three have a subjective as well as an objective aspect: they are all, in other words, both abstractions about the experience of people in their dealings with others as well as phenomena which can be observed by our Martian visitor as behaviour. But the priority of fraternity is that it is the principle which defines the *group* within which certain social *values* are to be applied. These values are essentially those of recognizing a common humanity: quintessentially they consist for each individual in recognizing the value of life for the other and the common fate of death for all. But the totality of social morality covers many more features of social life. Social moralities may be restricted with respect to either the group within which they are applied or in the extent that others are treated as equivalent to self. The moral community is bounded by these restrictions. Primitive man, characteristically, made linguistic distinctions at the boundary of the tribe to exclude the outsider from access to the humanity attributed to the insider. Every case of racism or sexism, or class or status distinction is to some greater or lesser extent such a restriction. The subjective feeling of fraternity is that of brotherhood: the objective behaviour is that of altruism. But this brotherhood may be exclusive or universal. The mark of the world religions is that they discovered and proclaimed the species as the only group boundary. As St Paul put it in the famous letter to the Ephesians (4: 25), 'We are members one of another.' The code of conduct enjoined by universal fraternalism is expressed most graphically in the story of the Samaritan. Sociologically, then, we mean by fraternity that, objectively, a collectivity in which the fraternal principle operates is one in which the members are integrated in their relations to one another by a set of distributional rules in which all are implicated and in which all share. Yet a fraternal society need be neither liberal nor egalitarian. Fraternity may be linked to liberty in that the liberty in question may be held to be a right for, and an obligation upon all. Fraternity may be linked to equality in that the values to be distinguished are held, in some sense, to be everyone's equal due. But liberty and equality can operate as social principles only within the bounds set by fraternity.

Equality, by contrast with fraternity, occupies an extensive place in sociological writing. There is broad agreement that society always and everywhere, though it constitutes a powerful apparatus of survival for its members, is also a structure of inequality. But sociologists differ as to the origin and development of inequality, and therefore draw different conclusions as to how it persists, and to what extent it can be modified, if not eliminated.

The sources of inequality are of two fundamental kinds. On the one hand, individuals have *interests* in life. If we assume, as we must, that there is scarcity in the means available to satisfy wants, desires, or appetites, then interests potentially imply conflict. On the other hand, human beings are, whatever else they are, *evaluating* animals: they have preferences; they distinguish between better or worse in all things, and thus continually judge themselves and others with respect to all human attributes and behave accordingly towards each other. It thus comes about that there are hierarchies of virtue, taste, sexual attractiveness, occupational skill, artistic talent, sporting prowess, and so on. Social relations reflect these as invidious comparisons, deference and disrespect, admiration and contempt. Evaluation, given scarcity, also implies conflict.

Sociological thought tends to divide according to the emphasis put on interest as distinct from evaluation, in explaining the social origins of inequality. We shall elaborate this division as class (interest) and status (evaluation) analysis in Chapters 2 and 3. The fact that both interests and evaluations are created and maintained by society itself is not in question. Nor is the fact of scarcity. The capacity of human beings to consume or hoard is unlimited, and the thirst for honour and power may be insatiable. As Thomas Hobbes said:

Felicity is a continuall progresse of desire, from one object to the other; the attaining of the former being still but the way to the later. . . So that in the first place, I put as the general inclination of all mankind, a perpetual and restlesse desire of Power after power, that ceaseth onely in

Death . . . because he cannot assure the power and means to live well, which he hath present, without the acquisition of more . . . and when that is done, there succeedeth a new desire; in some, of Fame from new Conquest; in others, of ease and sensuall pleasure; in others of admiration, or being flattered for excellence in some art, or other ability of the mind.[10]

If this is so, then the problem would appear to be not so much how conflict arises, but how civil society exists at all.

Marxism, liberalism, and social order

In this division of sociological thought, Marxists start from the primacy of interests, and liberals start from the primacy of evaluations. Their accounts of social change differ accordingly. For Marx and his followers, both continuity and change are systematically built into the history of all societies in the form of a class struggle. The social relations of people are fundamentally determined by their attachment to the means whereby they wrest a living from nature—that is, the productive system of their day. The ensuing principle of distribution is exploitation. The consequent view of British history in our time is of class struggles against inequality. There is no national or international fraternity, only class solidarity and such liberty as is consistent with maintaining the dominance of a capitalist class—a dominance which necessarily imposes unequal rewards and opportunities.

For liberals, by contrast, the maintenance of civil society, as well as its improvement, operates through tastes, preferences, and human values. Society changes through the inventive activity of individuals seeking to satisfy their preferences. The principle of distribution on this view is competition. The liberal version of historical experience emphasizes the expansion of liberty through the development of free economic and political activity. Expansion is the watchword, whether in markets, or education, or culture. Expansion gradually assimilates every man into the material and cultural privileges previously enjoyed by a minority. Expansion also equalizes, but by granting new opportunities, not by curtailing existing freedoms. Fraternity consists essentially in this universal offer of new opportunity.

Of course both Marxism and liberalism have complexities and internal debates within them: both are dynamic traditions of thought, transcending the simple characterization I give to them in this introduction. Both recognize both interests and evaluations. Moreover, for all its ideology of individualism, economic liberalism as distinct from political liberalism is tied to the concept of class because of its emphasis and support for market relations. Nevertheless, it is a distinctive Marxist assertion that social ideas and attitudes are controlled by the ruling class. Order is maintained, at least in the short run, by monolithic control. For the liberal, on the other hand, society is pluralistic and status groups, family, school, church, and voluntary organizations can play independent roles as bearers of socializing or civilizing influence. Socialization is the key in liberal thought about order and continuity. Economic liberalism, with its emphasis on market relations, makes strong, if tacit, assumptions that the family is capable of maintaining a stable moral order.

So we inherit two fundamentally opposed theories of history. One has set Eastern Europe on the path to communism. The other has been tested in our own time and in Western Europe. They are both, of course, children of the same historic European convulsion, but our immediate concern is with Britain. For Britons, the triad of social aspirations descends in popular imagination from the slogans carried across Europe by French revolutionary soldiers after the fall of the *ancien régime*. But a competent Chinese historian would pay scant attention to what he would see as the trivial tribal boundaries of European states. He would note that these political proclamations were to be heard in Manchester as well as in Paris in the 1790s—that is to say, in the heartland of the economic as distinct from the political territory of a Western Europe which was modernizing itself in the late eighteenth and early nineteenth centuries.

Professor Hobsbawm, adopting on this occasion an impeccably Chinese view, has graphically described all this in his book *The Age of Revolution*. The old society of hierarchy, order, duty, and reciprocity was to be replaced by one of democratic fellowship in a society of free men associating together on equal terms. True that two of the three principles—equality and freedom—could be shown in some ways to oppose and in more ways to limit each other in the actual social relations of people. These oppositions and limits have absorbed the attention of social scientists down to our own day. We still find them ranged from the aggressive libertarianism of Milton Friedman,[11] through the gentler accommodations to the egalitarianism of Isaiah Berlin,[12] or the 'new liberty' to which Ralf Dahrendorf devoted his Reith Lectures,[13] on through the argued egalitarian liberalism of John Rawls,[14] to the radical egalitarianism of R.H. Tawney.[15]

Liberalism has to face the problem of social order as an immediate problem of reconciling equality with freedom. Since the mid-1970s that reconciliation has become more difficult and the spectre of a Hobbesian disorder of 'every man's hand against every other man's' is raised by economic decline. Mrs Thatcher's economic and social policies divide the nation in class and sectional conflict over a smaller 'national cake'. Before 1979 the liberal solution was to increase the size of the cake; to promote economic growth.

Economic growth, of which Britain was the leader in the first half of the nineteenth century, might still appear to offer a way out of the Hobbesian tragedy. And modern political promises to enlarge and spread material abundance seem to reassert that promise. But it cannot be so. As Professor Hirsch argues, there are social limits to growth.[16]

We can see these limits if we follow Hirsch and distinguish two economies: one in *material* goods, and the other in *positional* goods. Material goods like tea or mugs can be expanded in their supply practically without limit. But positional goods are in more or less fixed supply. If we have a monarchy, only one of us can be queen: only 49 per cent can enjoy superior amenities. There is a range of positional goods such as old masters, suburban houses, and the Wardenship of Nuffield College which are fixed or scarce in some socially imposed sense or spoilt if more extensively used. The market for them is a zero-sum game—if you win I lose—or even a negative sum game, in that people consume resources in mutually cancelling efforts to gain market advantage. Hirsch's thesis is, then, a restatement of the Hobbesian problem applied to the special conditions of modern Britain, where economic liberalism, as he puts it, is 'the victim of its own success'. He argues that affluence presents a new form of the old problem of reconciling limited means to unlimited ends. 'The liberal capitalist order', he says, 'was associated with what can now be seen as transient inaugural conditions. First, full participation was confined to a minority—the minority that had reached material affluence before liberal capitalism had set the masses on the path

of material growth.' But the story of Britain in the twentieth
century, as in other industrial countries, is undoubtedly one of
gradually increasing demand for full participation in the 'good
life'.[17] And so it becomes increasingly clear that the economic
liberalism which encourages self-interest (or liberty) runs against
the no less pressing need for a social morality of obligation, if
markets are to be free and efficient. As Emile Durkheim argued,
'There is more to the contract than the contract.'

Here again, then, is the problem of fraternity. Its origin lie in
the intrinsic character of scarcity as an essential feature of society
which also gives rise to a perennial problem of inequality in the
distribution of power, and advantage. Scarcity will always bring
us back to the problem of fraternity. In present-day discussion,
the characteristic and confused expression of this problem is a
familiar and widely expressed fear of the fragility of our social
order. In that form it appears as the comprehensive proposition
that British society faces imminent disaster. The proposition is
that Britain has declined, is declining, and will shortly collapse.
There are many versions of it short of apocalyptic prophecy with
which no sociologist is equipped to deal. The secular versions
point to the threats to institutions which are necessary to ensure
our survival, banal as it may be to say so. Thus Britons must
produce and the economy is held to be faltering. And Britons
must reproduce, yet it is widely argued that their institutions of
kinship and upbringing are in increasing disarray.

Some Conservative politicians tend to describe current British
conditions in terms of the eleventh hour at which the country
must turn back, or give itself up to socialist tyranny. Mrs
Thatcher's government was swept to power in 1979 and was
returned in 1983 on precisely this rhetorical tide. Some Marxists
hail what they term 'contradictions' as evidence of the end of
capitalist society and the approaching revolution. Even the
Labour party, the main bearer of political cheerfulness in our
time, has tended to see North Sea oil as a last chance to modernize
the British economy and society. No industrial technology is
without a scientist to forecast its demise: no political party,
Labour, Conservative, Liberal, or Communist, is without a
political scientist to predict its break-up and the end of parliamentary institutions. Nor do anticipations of mortality stop at
the economy and the state. The institutions of reproduction,

that is, the family and the school, have collected to themselves a chorus of equally gloomy forecast over the past generation: and with them, according to many intellectuals, go the foundations of authority and the maintenance of cultural standards.

Here is Lord David Cecil's expression of the thesis: he is looking back in 1973 to the death of his grandfather, Lord Salisbury, in 1903.

My grandfather died that evening, as the sun was setting.

This sunset, as subsequently historians have not failed to point out, was symbolic; and not just of my grandfather's death. To the contemporary observer his career had remained to its close a success story. He died still a revered national figure, with his party in power and his policies apparently successful: he had been Prime Minister of England at the Diamond Jubilee of 1897, which celebrated the highest point of dominion and glory ever attained by the English. In fact Fate, in a spirit of irony which my grandfather would have appreciated, if grimly, had designed these triumphs as though to provide a contrasting prelude to a period of spectacular catastrophe, which entailed, incidentally, the decline of most of what my grandfather had stood for: British greatness, aristocractic government, individual liberty and international peace. Within fifty years of his death, British greatness had dwindled, aristocratic government had disappeared, individual liberty had lost its prestige and England had been involved in the two greatest wars in the history of mankind.[18]

Can all these authorities be wrong? Certainly it would be imprudent to ignore them. I want, therefore, to set out the main lines of argument in contemporary writing, and thus to arrive, if I can, at a more secure base for agreeing or disagreeing with what I take to be the dominant theme of current conventional wisdom.

Conclusion

The main lines of argument are concerned with the ends of liberty, equality, and fraternity, and they run between the two traditions of social thought to which I have referred, Marxism and liberalism. The fundamental question, as I understand it, is whether or to what extent these values can be realized in any society: and the approach to an answer is by examining twentieth-century experience of the basic institutions of one country, Britain. I have tried to illustrate the sociological method in this introductory chapter, emphasizing its focus on structures of social relations, its concern to explain both continuity and change, and its two opposed theories of history which are rooted in alternative liberal and Marxist views of the place of interests and evaluations as springs of human action.

The arrangement of the chapters which follow is guided by these themes. We begin, in Chapter 2, with the economy, asking first what is the outcome of work and how its fruits are distributed within the nation. Both economic growth and unequal distribution will be found as the main features of our description. With the facts of affluence and inequality before us, we can then ask how far inequality can be explained in terms of the class structure which has evolved in Britain as it developed from an agrarian to an advanced industrial nation.

We shall conclude from this analysis that not all inequality can be accounted for as a consequence of class. Accordingly, in Chapter 3, we shall turn to the history of status as distinct from class in Britain so as to refine our conception of stratification and to rest our explanation of inequality on a broader base.

Then, in Chapter 4, we can carry our class and status analysis further to include the power of organization or 'party' and in this way further strengthen our understanding of the changing distribution of power and advantage through economic, social, and political processes. Thus we shall have related the ends of liberty and equality to the means through which they have been sought in the institutions and organizations of class, status, and party.

At this point we will have completed our survey of Britain as a productive system—productive, that is, of material and psychic values—and we can turn, in the following Chapters 5 and 6, to the reproduction of the society and its culture through the family and education. These matters, from yet another point of view, confront us with the problem of explaining continuity and change over recent generations.

Finally, in Chapter 7, we shall attempt a composite picture of the changing state of British society, asking how liberty, equality, and fraternity interact as the underlying principles of the social order, how these interactions of consensus and conflict strengthen or weaken the integration of the United Kingdom, and what view we are to take of the widespread opinion that Britain is in decline. The answers to these questions will in turn guide our views on the further questions of policies for the future. The claim, and the aim, throughout the argument is that sociological analysis is an aid to more sophisticated analysis. But it cannot carry us to final views beyond political or moral challenge. I have not hesitated to end, in Chapter 8, with a brief statement of my own preferences. It is for you to decide whether and how far my interpretations are consistent with the arguments leading to them. More important is the hope that you may thereby arrive more confidently at your own.

2

A class-ridden prosperity

Our aim is to understand continuity and change. In this chapter we focus our attention on class. Class, I shall argue, is a key concept in analysing British history. If, as is now clear, the post-war period came to an end in the mid-1970s, giving way to a new period of deindustrialization, national economic decline, and Thatcherism as a strategy of attempted revival by policies of economic liberalism, then our new period must be one of increased class conflict. In the long and the short run class persists in continually changing forms.

'A class-ridden society'; that is the common judgement on Britain made by social observers, whether delivered as praise or condemnation. I heard this exact phrase from two foreign acquaintances, revisiting the island after an interval of ten years. Both sociologists, but the one a Russian Communist, and the other an American liberal. The Russian spoke of the continuing hegemony of a capitalist class with its power legally based on concentrated ownership of property and its control operating both through the direct employment of labour and through the state apparatus of budgetary manipulation of the level of employment, definition of welfare spending, domination of the mass media and, in the last resort, disposition of the means of violence through the armed forces and the police. He gave me, in short, a brief recital of Marxist orthodoxy in which every significant feature of social structure and the distribution of life-chances rests fundamentally on the present sovereignty and approaching overthrow of a capitalist class.

The American used the phrase with a tone and in a context which changed its meaning. Under the leadership of Mrs Thatcher the country was seeking to renew its economic growth by greater efficiency in private industry, which requires thorough reform of outdated class attitudes among both managers and employees. Nevertheless, class was still the outstanding feature of British society: neither the élite Establishment nor the attitudes of lower-class people had really changed. That, he added, is the reason why Britain still has the highest-quality television in the world: adaptations of Hardy's novels or Robert Graves's *I Claudius* would be impossible in mainstream America; and so would the Reith Lectures. Nowhere else in the Western world does the élite retain the confidence both to indulge its own cultural tastes and also to believe that these should be offered to or imposed didactically upon the mass of the population. The American upper class just doesn't have that status any more. He gave me, in short, a nostalgic anglophile expression of the liberalism which regrets what it sees as the inevitable sacrifice of quality when democracy is triumphant. Here then is the large theme for this second chapter. Why is it that, though Britain has become a rich country, social inequality is a continuing feature of its internal life?

A vocabulary of social inequality

In looking for an answer to this question, and noting the different words used by my American and Russian colleagues, we shall be carried to the centre of the debate about Britain among sociologists. Quite apart from the contrasting explanations of my visitors, their terminology is confusing. It includes references to upper, lower, capitalist, and working classes, to élites, the Establishment, status, mass, and power. My first task, therefore, is to assemble a clear vocabulary from modern sociological writing. It is a vocabulary which differs from common speech and derives mainly from the German sociologist, Max Weber, who may be said to have stood on the shoulders of Marx in order to reach a refinement of the language of stratification in general and of class in particular.

When sociologists speak of a structure of inequality they refer to the ways in which power and advantage form a stratified system of relations. By power they mean the resources which individuals or groups use to have their will, irrespective of the will of others. A board of directors can close a plant: a union can strike. By advantage, they mean control over things which are valued and scarce, such as the wealth of a millionaire, or the skill of a surgeon. Power and advantage are convertible. Together they define the character of strata and the relations between them in a stratification system. This system has three dimensions or forms of organization through which power and advantage are distributed.

The three dimensions are class, status, and party. Classes—for example, professional people or factory workers—are formed socially out of the division of labour. They make up more or less cohesive and socially conscious groups from those occupational groups and their families which share similar work and market situations. Status is formed out of the no less fundamental tendency of human beings to attach positive and negative values to human attributes, and to distribute respect or honour and contempt or derogation accordingly: status groups, for example peers of the realm or vagrants, form as social networks of those who share similar social prestige or life-style. Parties form out of the organized pursuit of social objectives; they are political parties, pressure groups, associations, and unions of those who consciously share a planned movement for the acquisition of power. In short, classes belong to the economic, status groups to the social, and parties to the political structure of society.[1]

Status and party will concern us in my third and fourth chapters. Here and now my task is to see how far inequality can be explained by class. But again, there is a welter of confusing terms. One thing is broadly agreed. Britain held a special historical place as the first industrial nation, which made it in the nineteenth century the classic home of an urbanized industrial working class or proletariat. But there agreement ends, and there is sharp debate about its older and its more recent history of a shifting balance of power and advantage.

A proletariat implies a bourgeois or capitalist class, and here it is essential to appreciate the long pre-industrial history of a landed aristocracy and gentry into which that capitalist class was absorbed. With due allowance for its sustained willingness and capacity to assimilate new elements, it may be said that an essentially hereditary medieval estate was slowly transformed into a fully developed class, retaining its hereditary character in a period stretching from late medieval times almost to our own day. There was no overt political revolution of the bourgeoisie. Control of state power and cultural advantage was virtually unbroken in the long journey from agrarian feudalism to industrial capitalism. The muddle of adjectives to denote classes comes from this history so that the terms upper, leisured, middle or middling, and lower are verbal deposits from the earlier pre-industrial age. It was the nineteenth-century analysts of industrial society who identified classes as capitalist, bourgeois, proletarian, and working. So the peculiarity of the British case is the mixture of confusing terms, reflecting history rather than logic. One consequence is that, in trying to name the classes which have evolved out of industrialism, Britons frequently divide themselves not into an upper and a lower but, absurdly, into a middle and a working class.

The class structure

The classical source of class analysis is Karl Marx. In some of his writings, for example in the *Eighteenth Brumaire of Louis Bonaparte* (1852), Marx distinguishes several classes for the purpose of refined analysis. But his main legacy is a two-class model of classes divided by ownership and non-ownership of the means of production (capital). This essential split determines the unequal distribution of power and advantage. Relations between the two great classes are exploitative and antagonistic. Capitalists in competitive pursuit of profit organize work in their own interests, seek to extend their control over all social institutions, especially the state, and extract surplus value (i.e. the value of products minus wages) from the proletariat. Society polarizes into two great warring camps as classes become more subjectively aware of their antagonisms. Classes form and develop from classes in themselves to classes for themselves through the experience of struggle against each other. The predicted outcome is revolution and eventually a conflict-free society without classes and with a voluntary division of labour.

History itself has been the severest critic of the theory of history to which the two-class model is tied. However, a two-class model, detached from this particular theory of the fate of industrial society, can be used as a simple starting-point for class analysis. The open questions are then whether power and advantage, especially state power and cultural advantage, may have sources other than or in addition to the class relations of production. Again following Max Weber and subsequent writers, most contemporary sociologists, and indeed most Britons, take a more pluralist view of the general system of stratification and the distribution of power and advantage.

On this more general view the importance of property is not denied but the elaboration of the division of labour is emphasized. As Frank Parkin puts it, 'the long-run tendency in Western Societies has been for the share of national income accruing to property steadily to diminish relative to income from employment'. The essential point is that in industrial society the anatomy of class is displayed in the occupational structure.[2] Groups and individuals differ first according to the terms on which they can sell their skills and their labour on the market, and second according to the actual conditions of their work—its autonomy, or lack of it, its intrinsic satisfactions, and its attendant amenities.

True, the British retain the archaic customs of an honours system through which they translate occupational achievement into feudal rank. They pretend, in other words, that power and advantage derive not from activity in the labour or capital markets, but from birth and breeding. True, too, that part of all social inheritance is immutable: birth gives us a family of origin, sex, race, and nationality. Some medieval estates—an extreme form of status—were legally hereditary. Class, too, in its fully developed form, shares this hereditary quality: but its foundation is in the market, not the law. An individual may move between classes in his own lifetime. The rise and fall of classes themselves is a broader and usually longer historical process through changes in the economy and polity which may be intended or unintended, violent or peaceful. Whether we follow the original Marxist orthodoxy and hold that legal ownership of the means of production is the crucial distinction or whether, with later writers like Dahrendorf,[3] we prefer to concentrate on authority in the organization of work, classes emerge out of occupational structure, and power and advantage are unequally distributed between them.

It is this definition of class in terms of occupation which is widely used in European sociology and which I use in this book. To do so implies adherence to no rigid orthodoxy as to the number of classes in twentieth-century Britain, nor to any preconception of their historical role, past or future. The number of classes that may be identified at any point of time is partly a matter of convenience directed towards the degree of refinement required for the analysis of occupational-based power and advantage. For our purposes in this book—the analysis of Britain within living memory—it will usually suffice to distinguish three classes—the middle, lower-middle, and working classes.

The first stratum can be taken to mean what most people mean by the *middle class*: professional, managerial, and administrative occupational groups and higher technicians, and their wives and children—the 'service class'. The second stratum is a hetero-geneous *lower-middle class* of non-manual employees, small proprietors, self-employed artisans—the petite bourgeoisie or lower-middle class—but also lower-grade technicians and super-visors of manual workers who might be thought of as a 'blue-collar élite'. The third stratum is the *working class*—industrial manual workers, and agricultural workers whether skilled, semi-skilled, or unskilled. Nevertheless, the reader should be aware that more refined class schema may be used, and indeed would be necessary, to identify groups with more homogeneous market and work situations.[4]

At the beginning of the century the occupational division of labour in Britain was such that over three-quarters of the employed and self-employed population were engaged in manual work. Of these, 28.7 per cent were skilled, 34.3 per cent semi-skilled, 9.6 per cent unskilled, and 1.8 per cent were self-employed artisans in 1911. Above these manual workers stood a white-collar and professional class, more confidently divided then than now into the upper-middle class and lower-middle class. And above these stood the tiny group of a few thousand—the group which Lord David Cecil, whom I quoted earlier, termed 'the governing class' of his grandfather's day. By mid-century the proportion of manual workers had fallen below two-thirds and since then it has fallen still further to roughly a third. So the first impression is of a gradual movement away from what might be called a proletarian society: and this transformation has been gathering pace in recent decades. Thus between the 1971 and 1981 Censuses the proportion of employed people in manual work fell from 62 to 56 per cent for men, and from 43 to 36 per cent for women.[5]

By 1971, as John Goldthorpe and Catriona Llewellyn have described it,[6] the occupational structure was more differentiated and more balanced. In the middle there were now three main blocks of comparable size, each accounting for one-fifth to one-quarter of the total. There were first the semi-skilled manual workers, second the skilled manual workers, and third the clerical and sales workers. Flanking these three groups were three other small groups, each between 7 and 15 per cent of the total—on the one side the unskilled workers, and on the other the professional and technical workers and the administrative, managerial, and supervisory staff.

These shifts of occupational structure in the first three-quarters of the twentieth century, from the shape of a pyramid to that of an electric light bulb, are characteristic of advanced industrial societies in general. They are shown for Britain in Table 2.1, which was constructed by Goldthorpe and Llewellyn. Behind them lies economic transformation: from small to large scale; from manufacturing to so-called tertiary-sector activity; from personal dealing to bureaucracy: from handling things to manipulating words and numbers; and from private to public organizations.

Some sociologists interpreted these trends as involving the development of a middle mass of technical and clerical employees with a consequent decline of class antagonisms, and with the spectre of polarized capitalist society in retreat.[7] We shall see below that the end of the post-war period and the resurgence of economic liberalism with high unemployment and privatization raise again the problem of class polarization.

But in any case, before drawing such inferences about Britain, it is prudent to notice what is perhaps the outstanding feature of occupational change, namely the growth of women's employment outside the home. Male and female involvement in the economy have run different courses over the period we are considering. As may be seen from Table 2.1, in 1911 both sexes were divided between manual and non-manual jobs three-quarters to one-quarter. Subsequently, the female labour force has both grown and shifted substantially into non-manual work, so that by 1981 three-fifths of the employed women were non-manual while over half of the men were still manual workers. And even the shift to non-manual jobs among men has mostly taken place since the Second World War. What is more important about it is that the increasing numbers of higher-level professional and managerial positions have largely gone to men, while women have filled the even faster expanding array of lower white-collar jobs.

This development of the pattern of male and female employment raises two important issues, one with respect to the Marxist two-class model, the other concerning the relation of women to the class structure. The two-class model has to be adapted to take account of the expansion of professional and managerial occupations. Marxists have argued that these middle classes are in a contradictory class position. They exercise control over the productive powers but most of them own no capital. Ralf Dahrendorf and other liberal analysts have called them the 'service class'—those who provide a bridge between the rulers (capitalists) and the masses (workers) by acting as the agents of public and private authorities.[8] From a Marxist standpoint these groups are explained as functionaries serving the owners of capital which has brought them into existence as a consequence of concentrations into larger enterprises. Large scale necessitates delegation of capitalist control to bureaucratic managers and professional experts. The capitalist development of production, on this view, determines the division of labour.

Women and the class structure

The second point—women and class—is still more important and has occasioned lively recent debate.[9] Are women a class? My answer is no; but explanation is needed. Married women's paid employment has certainly increased from about a tenth at the beginning of the century to roughly half now: but employment outside the home is not only largely treated as additional to retaining the major responsibilities for domestic work but is also characteristically intermittent, part-time, and secondary to male employment. The typical case remains that the 'head' of a family determines the class of its members, including wives, by his labour market role. The restricted and conditional nature of women's participation in the labour market also largely deprives them of the essential capacity for class action, i.e. the power to disrupt the productive process in any serious or effective manner. Instead, as Parkin has argued, women like other groups with status or 'party' disadvantages, 'are forced to rely far more heavily upon collective mobilisation of a purely social and expressive kind in order to press their claims'.[10]

Most certainly the evidence is overwhelmingly that women suffer systematic inequalities of power and advantage as against

Table 2.1[1] Distribution of economically active population by occupational category, Great Britain 1911–1971, males (M) and females (F) shown separately (percentages by column)

Standardized Census occupational category	1911 M	1911 F	1921 M	1921 F	1931 M	1931 F	1951 M	1951 F	1961 M	1961 F	1971 M	1971 F
Self-employed and higher-grade salaried professionals	1.5[a]	1.0[a]	1.6	0.9	1.7	1.0	2.8	1.0	4.5[b]	1.1[b]	6.1	1.4
Employers and proprietors	7.7	4.3	7.7	4.7	7.6	4.4	5.7	3.2	4.8[c]	3.0[c]	5.2	2.9
Administrators and managers	3.9	2.3	4.3	2.1	4.5	1.6	6.8	2.7	7.5[c]	2.6[c]	9.9	3.3
Lower-grade salaried professionals and technicians	1.4[a]	5.8[a]	1.8	6.3	1.8	6.0	3.0	7.9	4.0[b]	9.2[b]	5.5	10.8
Inspectors, supervisors, and foremen[d]	1.8	0.2	1.9	0.3	2.0	0.4	3.3	1.1	3.8	0.9	4.5	1.2
Clerical workers	5.1	3.3	5.1	9.8	5.1	10.3	6.0	20.3	6.5	25.5	6.1	28.0
Sales personnel and shop assistants[e]	5.0	6.4	4.1	7.5	5.9	8.2	4.0	9.6	3.9	10.0	3.9	9.4
Skilled manual workers (inc. self-employed artisans)	33.0	24.6	32.3	20.3	30.1	19.2	30.3	12.7	32.3	10.8	29.4	9.3
Semi-skilled manual workers[f]	29.1	47.0	24.5	40.0	23.4	41.4	24.3	33.6	22.8	30.9	21.2	27.3
Unskilled manual workers[f]	11.5	5.1	16.7	8.1	17.9	7.5	13.8	7.9	9.9	6.0	8.2	6.4
Total active population (Thousands)	12,926	5,424	13,635	5,698	14,760	6,263	15,584	6,930	15,992	7,649	15,609	8,762

[1] This table was constructed by J. H. Goldthorpe and Catriona Llewellyn

[a] Divided according to 1921 ratios. (The 1911 Census did not distinguish between self-employed and salaried professionals.)

[b] Divided on the assumption of a linear trend in the ratios from 1951–1966 (sample census),

i.e. $\dfrac{\times 61}{\text{Total } 61} = \dfrac{\times 51}{\text{Total } 51} + 2/3 \dfrac{\times 66}{\text{Total } 66} = \dfrac{\times 51}{\text{Total } 51}$

i.e. $P_{61} = P_{51} + 2/3(P_{66} - P_{51})$

(The 1961 Census did not distinguish between self-employed and salaried professionals.)

[c] Numbers in Groups 3 and 4 divided according to a ratio arrived at by plotting trend lines for these groups from 1951 to 1961, i.e. $P_{61} = P_{51} + 2/3(P_{66} - P_{51})$. (The 1961 Census did not distinguish between employers and managers.)

[d] Of manual workers.

[e] Includes supervisory personnel and also a small number of self-employed workers.

[f] Includes self-employed workers.

Sources: The basic source is the Occupational Tables of the Censuses of Population for England and Wales and Scotland. We have, however, drawn to a large extent on the reworking of Census data by earlier investigators although modifying their procedures somewhat, and correcting what appear to be several minor errors. In various respects, therefore, our figures differ from those of our predecessors where they might appear comparable, but not to any very significant degree.

For 1911 to 1951 we began with the work of Guy Routh, *Occupation and Pay in Great Britain, 1906–60*, Cambridge University Press, 1965, Table 1, pp. 4–5, taken together with the further information provided in Appendix A, pp. 155–7.

For 1961 we have drawn on the work of G. S. Bain, *The Growth of White Collar Unionism*, Oxford University Press, 1970, Table 2A.1, p. 191; and of Bain, Robert Bacon, and John Pimlott, 'The Labour Force', in A. H. Halsey (ed.), *Trends in British Society since 1900*, Macmillan, 1972, Tables 4.1 and 4.5, pp. 113–14.

men. But, while warranting full recognition, these inequalities are more adequately explained as inequalities of status, party (organization), and kinship than as class phenomena, even though their character is related to class. Accordingly their discussion is deferred to Chapters 3, 4, and 5. Nevertheless, it should be remarked at this point that sexual stratification is a fundamental feature of the social division of labour in all complex societies and that the increasing involvement of women in the occupational (i.e. labour market) division of labour in the twentieth century has had important consequences for class structure. Sexual inequality is a dimension of social stratification in its own right. But its impact on class inequality, as Westergaard and Resler have suggested, is to sharpen class division.[11] Socially assortative mating increases the spread of income and wealth *between* families 'headed' by individuals (usually males) of different occupational class. Significantly also there is a high correlation between husband's and wife's unemployment.

The wealth of the nation

So much for a preliminary view of stratification using a simple conception of class. Now let us look at collective prosperity. At the outset, the reader should be warned against taking official estimates of the national income or the gross national product—those modern talismans of national virility—as ultimate measures of the wealth of a nation. They are the gifts of bureaucracy rather than social science. These economists' sums tell us roughly what are the products of the *occupational* division of labour: but there is a larger *social* division of labour which includes the exchanges in families, and the services of the Samaritans, as well as the fiddles unrecorded by the Inland Revenue. There is, in short, another economy of vast dimension. It was, for example, only by the fiat of the Victorian economist Alfred Marshall that the paid labour of charwomen is counted as part of the national product, while the work of housewives is not.[12] If we were to reckon the whole output of the social division of labour it is most likely that our sterling numbers would be more than doubled. Nevertheless, if we assume that outputs from the two economies are in less than completely inverse relation, the official figures can be used to indicate trends. They tell us that since 1900 the United Kingdom has at least tripled its gross national product in real terms.[13]

In any case, there is general agreement that British levels of living rose throughout the century until the late 1970s and even in the 1980s for those in secure employment. If the word 'living' is taken quite literally, it may be noted that, compared with a hundred years ago, the average Briton lives thirty years longer, mainly because of a reduction in infantile mortality. In the childhood of the oldest readers the death of a baby in the house was a grim commonplace: now, less than two in a hundred die in infancy. A narrower and more conventional measurement of living standards, by income, yields a similar ameliorative story. The median earnings of male manual workers rose from just over £1.00 a week in 1905 to £122 a week in 1983. While it is difficult if not impossible to translate these money figures into real purchasing power by discounting for inflation, we can safely say that they also represent at least a tripling of real income. Nor can there be any doubt that the ordinary manual worker and his wife are very much less the slaves of toil than they were in Edwardian England. Their market freedoms, whether as earners or spenders, have been transformed.

One aspect of contemporary affluence is the length of time it is necessary for a married man on average earnings who has two children under 11 and whose wife is not earning to work in order to pay for various goods. Some examples in 1983 were:

- 1 large loaf   7 minutes
- 1 pint of fresh milk   4 minutes
- 1 dozen eggs   7 minutes
- 1 pint of beer   12 minutes
- 1 cwt. of coal   90 minutes

Hours of work have been steadily reduced (from 54 to 43 between 1900 and 1980). After the Second World War, paid holidays became common and four weeks is now the norm. The official statistics for 1983 record 48 million holidays by residents of Great Britain. This is a far cry from the experience of many, if not most, ordinary children between the wars—the annual charabanc trip to Blackpool or Skegness.

Yet inequality persists after a long period of economic growth. From this point of view the picture of prosperity looks very different, especially since the end of the 1970s and the arrival of a government determined to press policies of economic liberalism. The assumption of growing affluence is not beyond question. The old poverties of lack of property, low pay, poor health, inadequate education, and bad housing still disfigure, and many would say disgrace, the powerful engine of production which we call industrial society. The official rate of registered unemployment doubled from the beginning of the Thatcher administration to over 13 per cent of all employees in 1983 (Figure 2.1). Unemployment is heavily concentrated in the working class, and within that class among the young, the old, the sick, and the disabled. Over seven million Britons depend on the Supplementary Benefits Commission. In other words, over seven million are living on the government's own estimate of the poverty line. And there are more below it who do not claim their due.[14]

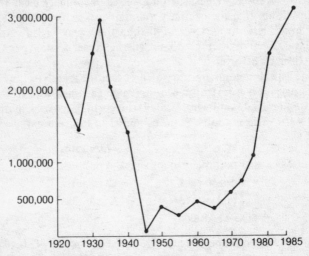

Figure 2.1 Unemployment 1921–1985

How, then, are income and wealth shared among the population? Let us begin with two relatively simple statistics. In Britain now the richest 5 per cent still own 41 per cent of all marketable wealth. Income is less unequally distributed, but here again the richest 1 per cent take home about the same amount as the poorest 20 per cent. They each have, in other words, more than twenty times as much income. These are quite spectacular inequalities.

The distribution of market income

From the First World War to the 1970s there was slow and unsteady progress towards a more equal distribution of personal income. By the early 1970s the top 10 per cent of income receivers were taking about one-quarter of total income, and this one-quarter share was also the amount being taken by the bottom half of income receivers. Comparing manual and non-manual earnings a trend towards decreasing inequality can be traced at least as far back as the 1920s. In 1978 the ratio of non-manual to manual earnings was 1.25.

The trends in distribution of income from 1959 were carefully explored by the Royal Commission on the Distribution of Income and Wealth.[15] The Commission summarized them as follows:

Over the whole of the period from 1959 to 1974/5, the share of the top 1 per cent has declined continuously; the share of the next 2–5 per cent has declined but not continuously; the share of the 6–10 per cent group has shown little change. The share of the top 10 per cent as a whole in the before tax distribution has fallen from 29.4 per cent of total income in 1959 to 28.0 r·r cent in 1967 and to 26.6 per cent in 1974–5. Over the same period (1959 to 1974–5) the share of the top 1 per cent has fallen from 8.4 to 6.2 per cent of total income. The d· cline in the income share of the top 10 per cent as a whole is balanced by a corresponding increase in the overall share of the remaining 90 per cent, within which only one decile—61–70 per cent—did not increase. Approximately three-fifths of this increase accrued to the remaining 40 per cent of tax units in the top half of the distribution. Their share increased from 47.5 per cent to 49.2 per cent of total income between 1959 and 1974–5 while, over the same period, the share of bottom 50 per cent of tax units increased from 23.1 per cent to 24.2 per cent of total income.

These equalizing tendencies in the market fortunes of occupational classes came to a halt with the passing of the post-war period. Between 1976 and 1982 the distribution of market incomes became more unequal. The top one-fifth of households increased their share from 44 to 47 per cent, while the bottom one-fifth sank from a share of 0.8 per cent to one of 0.4 per cent.[16]

Redistribution by the state

The impact of taxes and transfers is a complicated one and much debated. It operates, as R. M. Titmuss pointed out,[17] through three loosely related systems of state intervention—fiscal policy, the social services, and occupational welfare. Essentially these political interventions can only be understood as collective action to change the unacceptable outcome of market exchanges: and that means the outcome of class. Historically, the development of these elements of social policy starts from the liberal governments before the First War. Their complexity mirrors the increasing complexity of the division of labour. They give Britain now a social division of welfare which is not by any means simply a political antidote to class distribution of what is produced by collective labour. On the contrary, social policy itself has been powerfully shaped by class. For example, the fiscal system has been no simple extension of progressive taxation from its introduction in 1907. We have noticed that the richest one-fifth of households in 1982 took 47 per cent of the nation's income. After taxes and benefits that share was reduced to 39.4 per cent. The poorest one-fifth of households had taken 0.4 per cent of market income. Taxation and benefits raised that share to 6.9 per cent. These figures can scarcely be interpreted as evidence of a hugely redistributive 'welfare' state. Welfare, it would appear, is largely self-financed for the bulk of the population. The activity of the state makes for no dramatic reduction of market inequalities.

Similarly, the social services are not to be thought of as a steady development of 'class abatement' through politics. In education, for example, throughout the twentieth century, a policy of expansion has been frequently justified as a means to equality of opportunity. But in spite of a slight tendency to more equal investment in the school education of children from different classes, the development of further education more than counterbalanced this equalizing effect because it was concentrated on middle-class children. If we compare boys born between 1913 and 1922 with those born between 1943 and 1952 (and standardize the figures by putting them into 1958 prices), it turns out that the average son of a professional or managerial family had seven times as much spent on him as the son of an agricultural labourer in the earlier period, and six times as much in the later period. A comparison of these First War and Second War children in absolute terms shows that the average professional son got an extra £566 a year for education after school, and the agricultural labourer's son an extra £103 a year as a result of the intervening expansion of educational opportunity.

Inequality of wealth

Again, the third system of occupational welfare is more of a complement than a counterweight to class inequality. Occupational pensions are earnings-related. Sick pay and pension arrangements are better for non-manual than for manual workers. And there has been a considerable growth of tax-deductable fringe benefits since the war with the effect of increasing inequality between highly paid executives and the rest.

Up to this point we have documented continuing, if slowly decreasing, income differences: and we have shown that they are related to class. But the more challenging task is to explain them. For orthodox Marxists the distribution of capital is crucial: it fundamentally defines the class structure. Professor Westergaard and Miss Resler, who have produced a voluminously and soberly argued empirical account from the Marxist standpoint, conclude that it was the exceptional circumstances of war which produced lasting effects on the contrasts in income and wealth. They insist, however, that the two Wars

formed no part of a continuous trend toward equalization, and that they entailed only modest redistribution . . . Disparities may indeed have widened since the 1950s. They certainly did not narrow significantly, from the early 1950s to the early 1970s under governments of either political shade.[18]

Moreover, these authors find the root cause of continuing inequality in the condition of property-less labour of most people: and this in turn they attribute primarily to the concentration of property ownership. 'It is for that reason above all', they argue, 'that capitalism can make no claim to a steadily more equal spread of wealth. Inequality is entrenched in its institutional structure.'[19]

Liberal theorists, for their part, do not deny the inequality of distribution of personal wealth. But they do not accept the importance that Marxists attach to it, and would contest the further Marxist theory that status and power in society are derived from it. Instead, they begin by arguing the significance of trends towards a more equal spread of both wealth and income. Argument about the exact measure of the distributions themselves is relatively unimportant. The various authorities would agree that the proportion of personal wealth held by the richest 1 per cent of the population before the First World War was about 70 per cent. By the mid-1930s it was reduced to 56 per cent, and by 1960 to 42 per cent. Subsequent official figures are on a slightly different basis. They show the percentage held by the top 1 per cent of people as moving down from 37 per cent in 1962 to 24 per cent in 1977. More detailed figures from 1960 are reproduced in Table 2.2 from the fifth report of the Royal Commission on the Distribution of Income and Wealth. At first glance, then, these figures would appear to contradict Westergaard and Resler, and to show a strong and steady trend towards equality. But essentially Westergaard is right because the redistribution has very largely been a spread of wealth to the richest 5 per cent instead of 1 per cent, and much of it reflects arrangements for gifts *inter vivos*—gifts between the living as distinct from those bequeathed at death. In this way rich families have passed on their wealth and legally avoided tax.

The Royal Commission, chaired by Lord Diamond, was abolished by the Conservatives when they came into office in 1979, and the official statistics on inequalities of wealth distribution have become less detailed. They do, however, tell a somewhat different story. Table 2.3, derived from the government publication *Social Trends*, shows the trends since 1971. Its figures for marketable wealth among UK adults tally with those of the Diamond Commission in the early 1970s. But the authors of *Social Trends* go on to point out:

Apart from housing and land, few forms of marketable wealth have kept pace in value with inflation in recent years, and for many adults their non-marketable rights in pension schemes, whether occupational schemes or the state pension scheme, have represented an increasingly important component of personal wealth over and above holdings of marketable wealth. In 1982, the richest 5 per cent of the adult population owned 41 per cent of marketable wealth, but only 24 per cent of all wealth including all pension rights; thus inequality in the distribution of wealth is reduced by pension rights.

There were substantial reductions in the percentage of marketable wealth owned by the richest groups in the early 1970s, largely because of the fall in the prices of stocks and shares which form a significant part of the wealth of the wealthiest. The late 1970s and early 1980s brought very little change to the pattern of ownership of marketable wealth. The distribution of wealth including occupational pension rights broadly follows the same trend. For marketable wealth plus occupational and state pension rights there was also a movement toward less inequality in the early and mid-1970s, but since 1977 there has been little change.[20]

Table 2.2   Trends in the distribution of personal wealth 1960–1975

Percentage shares of estimated personal wealth of given quantile groups both of the population covered by the Inland Revenue estimates and of the total population aged 18 and over, with Gini coefficients; at specified dates between 1960 and 1975. The figures from 1960 to 1974 are for Great Britain, and those in the last two columns refer to the UK.

Quantile group	1960	1962	1964	1966	1968	1970	1972	1973	1974	1974	1975
Population covered by Inland Revenue estimates (Series A)											
Top 1 per cent	28.4	27.2	25.9	23.6	24.2	20.7	22.1	21.8	18.4	18.3	17.2
Top 5 per cent	50.9	48.8	48.5	43.7	45.2	40.9	41.8	38.8	36.7	36.7	35.0
Top 10 per cent	63.1	60.7	60.5	56.0	57.1	51.9	53.9	50.9	49.0	49.1	47.3
Top 20 per cent	76.2	73.9	74.1	70.8	71.2	66.4	68.5	66.6	64.9	65.0	63.3
Bottom 80 per cent	23.8	26.1	25.9	29.2	28.8	33.6	31.5	33.4	35.1	35.0	36.7
Gini coefficient	73	72	72	67	68	65	66	65	63	63	62
Total population aged 18 and over (Series B)[1]											
Top 1 per cent	38.2	36.0	34.4	31.8	32.7	29.0	29.9	27.6	25.3	25.2	23.2
Top 5 per cent	64.3	60.7	59.3	56.7	59.0	56.3	56.3	51.3	49.9	49.9	46.5
Top 10 per cent	76.7	74.0	73.5	71.8	73.8	70.1	71.9	67.2	66.0	66.1	62.4
Top 20 per cent	89.8	88.4	88.4	87.8	89.4	89.0	89.2	86.4	85.5	85.6	81.8
Bottom 80 per cent	10.2	11.6	11.6	12.2	10.6	11.0	10.8	13.6	14.5	14.4	18.2
Gini coefficient	89	87	87	86	87	86	86	84	83	83	81

[1] Assuming that persons not covered by the Inland Revenue estimates have no wealth.

Sources: Inland Revenue and the Royal Commission on the Distribution of Income and Wealth, Report, No. 5, Cmnd. 6999, 1977, Table 33.

Table 2.3 Distribution of wealth 1971–1982

Percentage shares of estimated UK personal wealth held by given quantile groups of the total population aged 18 or over.

Quantile group	1971	1976	1978	1979	1980	1981	1982
Marketable wealth							
Top 1 per cent	31	24	23	22	21	21	21
Top 2 per cent	39	32	30	28	28	28	28
Top 5 per cent	52	45	43	40	38	40	41
Top 10 per cent	65	60	57	54	51	53	56
Top 25 per cent	86	84	83	77	76	79	81
Top 50 per cent	97	95	95	95	95	96	96
Total (£ billion)	**140**	**263**	**369**	**453**	**529**	**565**	**602**
Marketable wealth plus occupational pension rights							
Top 1 per cent	27	21	19	19	17	17	17
Top 2 per cent	34	27	26	24	22	22	23
Top 5 per cent	46	40	39	34	33	33	34
Top 10 per cent	59	53	52	45	45	46	47
Top 25[1] per cent	78–83	75–81	70–74	70–74	68–72	68–73	71–75
Top 50[1] per cent	90–96	89–93	89–93	88–92	90–94	90–94	91–95
Marketable wealth plus occupational and state pension rights							
Top 1 per cent	21	14	13	13	12	12	11
Top 2 per cent	27	18	17	17	16	16	16
Top 5 per cent	37	27	25	25	24	24	24
Top 10 per cent	49	37	36	35	33	33	34
Top 25[1] per cent	69–72	58–61	57–60	56–59	55–58	56–59	56–59
Top 50[1] per cent	85–89	80–85	79–83	79–83	78–82	78–82	78–82

[1]Estimates vary with assumptions. See *Social Trends*, No. 15, Appendix, Part 5: Personal wealth.

Source: Social Trends, No. 15, 1985, p. 90.

The technicalities leave room for further argument about the exact degree of concentration of private wealth and its long-run trends. But if, following R. H. Tawney, we distinguish between property for power, by which I mean property that carries with it control over the lives of other people, and property for use, possessions that free a man from other people's control, then we can reasonably say that, throughout the period we can collectively remember, three-quarters of the British have been virtually property-less in that area which covers the central part of life and occupations—how men and women earn a living and how they relate themselves most fully and creatively to their fellows. A minority has monopolized wealth, and an even tinier minority of that minority has monopolized property for power.

At the same time, of course, harking back to the fact of rising affluence, we should not ignore the social significance of the spread of property for use. Most of the under-40s take a wide range of amenities and consumer durables for granted. Only the over-40s remember those primitive instruments of washing day—the poss-stick and the dolly-tub.

To sum up a formidable ledger of evidence, we can say that distributions through the capital and labour markets were dramatically unequal at the opening of the century. Wealth, part of which is property for power, was always more unequally spread than income. And both distributions have remained unequal around a rising average level. Over and above such wealth for use as housing and personal possessions, property for power still has a most impressively unequal distribution. But the trend to a relatively more equal sharing of income has increasingly dominated the structure of inequality as a whole because the labour market distributes much more income than does the capital market. In 1976 income from employment accounted for well over two-thirds of all income. The self-employed accounted for less than one-tenth, and so did unearned income from rent, dividends, and interest payments. On the evidence so far, then, the problem is to decide whether to attach more importance to the remaining inequality, or to the expanded material freedom which has attended the rising norm. The judgement will turn on whether one is impressed by absolute or by relative riches.

Inequality and limited horizons

In either case, we have still not fully explained the inequality of a rich society. The question of how it has survived can again be put in class terms by quoting what J. B. Priestley had to say on his journey through England in 1933, when he came to Jarrow—a wholly working-class town.

Wherever we went there were men hanging about, not scores of them but hundreds and thousands of them. The whole town looked as if it had entered a perpetual penniless bleak Sabbath. The men wore the masks of prisoners of war. A stranger from a distant civilization, observing the condition of the place and its people, would have arrived at once at the conclusion that Jarrow had deeply offended some celestial emperor of the island and was now being punished. He would never believe us if we told him that in theory this town was as good as any other and that its inhabitants were not criminals, but citizens with votes.[21]

Jarrow provides one example of the remarkable absence of resentment against class inequality. In an attempt to explain this feature of British society, W. G. Runciman has put forward the theory of relative deprivation.[22] On this theory, satisfaction or resentment is not a function of inequality as documented by economists, but of a man's assessment of his positive relative to other people with whom he compares himself. In Runciman's view the period from the end of the First World War up to 1962, against a background of trends towards the equalization of class, status, and power in Britain, working-class status resentment increased, and class resentment fluctuated, but at a remarkably low level. Working men compared their lot with other people in the working class and not with non-manual groups, who, incidentally, were just as likely to feel deprived despite their objective advantages. In the decades before 1962 there was seldom a close correlation between class inequality and resentment of it. Both World Wars raised expectations and lifted the horizons of working-class people. But the egalitarian hopes thus engendered receded in both post-war periods. The economic depression of the 1930s inhibited comparisons between manual wages and white-collar salaries. After the Second World War there was widespread belief that a programme of class redistribution was taking place when in fact it was not. Runciman's 1962 survey showed that resentment was still low among working men and their wives because they compared themselves, in the traditional way, with those near to them in the factory and the neighbour-hood. They did not compare themselves with barristers, or the residents of Mayfair. Relative deprivation was in fact more likely to be felt by middle-class than by working-class people.

Repeating the survey thirteen years later in 1975, W. W. Daniel found that the same patterns of restricted social horizons of com-parison were still present.[23] Several years of serious inflation and still more years of high publicity to pay claims and incomes policy had not significantly altered them. Most importantly, the more recent survey showed that people cared not so much about how other people were getting on as about how they saw their own financial position this year compared with last year. It seems that government policy for 'gentling the masses' is more likely to be successful if it looks to economic growth for all, rather than to redistribution between unequally placed groups.

From this point of view the period from 1979 has been grimly paradoxical. Government strategy was diverted avowedly towards economic growth for all but by means which have pro-duced mass unemployment and a reversal of the slow long-run movement towards less inequality. Many occupational groups have continued to prosper alongside the three or four million unemployed and the seven million on Supplementary Benefit. By 1985 the Trades Union Council was arguing before the National Economic Development Council that those groups which had suffered the sharpest cut in wages had also endured the highest unemployment rates. On TUC calculations the real wages of unskilled workers (after allowing for inflation) had fallen 9.9 per cent between 1979 and 1984. By contrast there had been a rise in real wages of 16 per cent for white-collar workers.[24] Unless this reversal towards inequality is halted, relative deprivation and class antagonism must surely increase.

Conclusion

For the twentieth century as a whole, though with an at least temporary and significant reversal in the 1980s, we have explained the continuing inequality of a rich society mainly in terms of the slow growth of prosperity and the limited social horizons of the relatively poor. This explanation, however, still leaves open the question of whether we can properly call the inequalities we have found class inequalities. If we follow post-Marxist and liberal theorists and define class in terms of occupational structure rather than capital ownership and if, further, we treat the family rather than the individual as the unit of the class system, we shall have to recognize that many inequalities are of status rather than of class—those between men and women, or between older and younger people, or between ethnic groups. For example, if we take the average earnings of all white males to be 100, the comparable figure for coloured men is 88. Nor is this inequality of earnings between ethnic groups to be explained in class terms. Within classes the differentials are still to be found except among the lower-paid groups of semi-skilled and unskilled workers and personal service workers.[25]

Class, we may conclude, remains fundamental to stratification in Britain but it does not tell us the whole story.

3

The reconstitution of status

Class is a necessary but not a sufficient explanation of the continuity of inequality in British society. Status must be added in a country where the tiniest detail of manner or style was once a symbol sufficient to place a person immediately in a national and unitary hierarchy of prestige. Such was the Victorian order on which the sun set for Lord David Cecil with the death of his prime-ministerial grandfather in 1903. It is now widely agreed from several different ideological standpoints that British twentieth-century history is the history of the decay of the values and status system of the Victorian period. My aim in this chapter is to trace the historical stages of the relation between status and class. The intended result is to dispose of both the Marxist theory that status is simply a by-product of class and the liberal assumption that status is an independent aspect of society. In reality they are mutually interacting forces: and, so understood, they throw light on the persistence of inequality, the social sources of belief in 'the decline of Britain', the emergence of a new division of social labour (Chapter 5), and the prospect of intensified class conflict in response to the new Conservatism of the post-1979 period (Chapter 8).

These are, to be sure, large promises; but they stem from the combination of powerful theories. And they lead finally to an understanding of the emerging status of citizenship—a status quite different from the old status order. In the twentieth century citizenship has been pitted against the forces of class and, in the 1980s, has faced a reactive challenge from the resurgence of economic liberalism.

Status and class theory

To understand these present and future issues we must return to the past and to the theory of class and status. My description of present disarray already implies that I will argue an important role for status, and later party, in understanding inequality—its continuities and its changes, and its relations to liberty and fraternity. There are two main arguments for the significance I accord to status. One is that some socially recognized distinctions which are highly salient to issues of equality are nevertheless not a basis for class formation. Thus, once it is accepted that the family, and not the individual, is the unit of class systems, it follows that neither age-groups nor sexes can constitute classes. Yet equally clearly there are social conflicts which turn on the claims to equality of women and young people. Both groups have status disadvantages; but their *class* interests in the allocation of resources are predominantly dependent on their families, first of origin, and later of affinity.

The second main argument is that a new form of status has been advanced in the twentieth century to claim a second distribution or redistribution of goods and services through the state and based on criteria of need as distinct from purchasing power. This has been explicitly aimed against the class distributions of capital ownership, labour market earnings, and work conditions, and against the traditional status inequalities of generation, sex, and race. We shall see, in other words, that a reconstitution of status has accompanied the dissolution of the old order.

But neither of these arguments is intended to deny the stubborn capacity of class to survive, nor, still less, to argue inequality out of our way. Class systems and their inequalities are intrinsically prone to persist. They resist change in two ways. Those who do well out of them do not usually volunteer to surrender their advantages, and they also use their powers to pass on superior opportunities to their own children. And the more this happens, the more are classes formed. A fully developed class system is both a structure of market inequality and also a hereditary system of recruitment, in practice if not in theory.

All this is obvious. What is not so clear is how class and status can either support or oppose each other. Here the first thing to notice is that class power can be translated into status power and vice versa. The encroachment of the one upon the other is a central thread in British social history. Medieval Britain was an estate society: power and advantage were primarily distributed to people on the basis of their rights and duties in relation to landholding, in a hierarchy extending upwards from the peasants, through the gentry and aristocracy, to the monarch. A class system was cradled in this pre-industrial order through the establishment of liberties and privileges for particular craft and merchant guilds. The origins of individualistic freedom, so basic to British ideological tradition, are to be found in this order of status inequality.

Class supersedes status

The outstanding feature of social development in Victorian Britain was the usurpation of status by class. Liberal nineteenth-century capitalism distributed the goods and services of an industralized earth through the social mechanisms of the market. Distributions were therefore the outcome of interests. They arose from a division of labour which treated labour as a commodity and removed responsibility from the rich and powerful for the lives of the poor and dependent. The enlightened spokesmen of English liberal capitalism, Adam Smith, Ricardo, Bentham, and James Mill and John Stuart Mill, elaborated impressive theories of personal freedom and material plenty, which, for a brief period, formed a consensus of sound opinion among all classes. But the actual outcomes of the market were impossible to justify. The dogma of *laissez-faire* was no defence against the evidence of the horrors of women's work underground, the exploitation of child labour in the mills, and the squalor of the new industrial cities. To the men and women caught up in, exhausted, and demoralized by this system, the 'free market' seemed to be a canting phrase for organized plunder. Class polarization and class antagonism emerged from the very conditions of free and equal access that established the market system in the first place. The legitimacy of such a class-based social order could hardly be expected to escape challenge from revolutionary or reformist movements. In fact both types of movement appeared. Both based themselves on a principle of legitimation opposed to individualism. So socialism emerged into British politics. And a principal reason for the dominance of reformism and revolution was the role of status in supporting the legitimacy of a modified class system.

The integration of class and status

In the mid-Victorian period 'the upper class' meant gentlemen and gentlewomen, and was still basically a hereditary caste of titled persons and their families. However, this landed aristocracy and gentry had always absorbed new men, and in the last century the new rich of trade and industry were gradually drawn into it until in the end they overwhelmed it. A new upper class was welded together. By 1900 the House of Commons, previously an assembly of gentlemen, contained 250 bankers, merchants, tradesmen, stockbrokers, company directors, and the like, alongside and overlapping with 70 Lords, Baronets, and Honourables.[1]

The rise to high status of many British families in the nineteenth and early twentieth centuries, initially through class mobility, is both a myth and a reality. The stereotype is the factory owner accumulating capital in a Northern or Welsh industrial town in the first generation; the firm expands in the second generation; and in the third is a large public corporation, vertically integrated and with metropolitan headquarters. The status translation of family members runs from the original artisan—provincial, respectable, chapel-attending; the sons are educated in local grammar schools and perhaps Armstrong College in Newcastle, or Josiah Mason in Birmingham, and the grandsons in a major public school and an Oxford college. The family journey also runs from chapel to church, from Liberal to Conservative voting, from business to the major professions and management, and from the Commons to the Lords. The Heralds' Office attends to the details.

This caricature indicates that, though classless societies have existed, and more are conceivable without classes, status depends in the long run on access to material resources, and such access in this case was primarily afforded through the capital and labour markets.

Edwardian Britain had a secure alliance of class with status. The bourgeoisie had adopted modified versions of the tastes and style of life of the aristocracy and the gentry. The old barriers between Church and Dissent had been widely breached, and trade had married title as Sybil had wedded Egremont in Disraeli's novel. This formidable combination dominated the manners and consciousness not only of its cadets in what Orwell called the 'lower-upper-middle class' of home and imperial administration, and not only of the slowly growing but still inferior ranks of the professions and the salariat, but also of its remote dependants beyond the great divide—the men, and particularly the women, of the manual working class.

I say remote, and the sense in which the word remote describes the relations of the upper to the lower classes is plain enough. But for some if already a declining number of working-class families, relations were intimate through generations of domestic service. Thus, while it was true of the status order that 'an Englishman had only to open his mouth to make another Englishman despise him', the language of U and non-U was not a simple binary division barring the middle from the upper classes, but also a language linking the 'governing class' to their 'lower-class' servants along a different dimension of symbolic subordination. This direct association was already declining, but its function of binding unequals together was still of some importance then. Along with the vocabulary and the routines of domestic management, larger conceptions of hierarchy and place were deferentially absorbed. An integrated inequality was the central principle of social life in Britain before the First World War. A status hierarchy lent legitimacy to class inequality.

Status control over time and social distance is one of the themes running through Robert Roberts's account of the working-class district of Salford in which he grew up in the first quarter of this century.[2] 'By 1900', he tells us, 'those cherished principles about class, order, work, thrift, and self-help, epitomized by Samuel Smiles and long taught and practised by the Victorian bourgeoisie, had moulded the minds of even the humblest.'[3]

The boys of Roberts's community avidly read the *Magnet* and the *Gem*—comic papers exalting the life and manners of public schoolboys. While they went daily to a seedy elementary school, they vicariously adopted Greyfriars as their Alma Mater. 'The "mouldering pile", one came to believe, had real existence: of that boys assured one another.' They placed it vaguely in the Southern counties—somewhere between Winchester and Harrow. It came as a 'curious shock' to Roberts, who revered 'the Old School', when it dawned upon him that he himself was a typical example of the 'low cads' so despised by all at Greyfriars. 'Over the years', he claims, 'these simple tales conditioned the thought of a whole generation of boys. The public school ethos, distorted into myth and sold among us weekly in penny numbers,

for good or ill, set ideals and standards.' In Roberts's opinion,
'Frank Richards [the author of these fictions] during the first
quarter of the twentieth century had more influence on the mind
and outlook of young working-class England than any other
single person, not excluding Baden Powell.'[4] Nor did these
ideologies disappear with the new generation after the war. In the
1930s and 1940s too, working-class boys identified no less enthu-
siastically with the public school heroes of 'Red Circle', the
mythical public school of the *Hotspur*, and with the imperial
ethic in its purest form—The Wolf of Kabul'. The adult, and
more subtle, version of Harry Wharton, I might add, is Jeeves,
created by P. G. Wodehouse, and widely enjoyed by a mass
readership. Jeeves is essentially the servant, clearly more able
than his feckless master, who none the less devotes a lifetime of
service to the preservation of traditional privilege.

The Salford proletariat was arranged in an elaborate status
hierarchy, rooted, of course, in the different market and work
situations of workers with different levels of skill, but extending
to cover all men, women, and children in a closed urban village of
crowded streets, sharing a common culture of bare subsistence
and survival. The arbiters of status in the community were
women, centred on 'a powerful inner ring of grandmothers'. The
poverty-stricken analogue of landed possessions was not even so
much what one owned by way of domestic equipment, but what
one pawned. To hock clean clothes gave higher status than dirty
hearth rugs, or the pots off the table. When neighbours quar-
relled the symbols of status were hurled back and forth

to prove to the world that the other party and its kindred were 'low class'
or no class at all. One waved, for instance, a 'clean' rent book (that great
status symbol of the times) in the air, knowing the indicted had fallen in
arrears. Now manners and morals were arraigned before a massed public
tribunal . . . Purse lipped and censorious, the matriarchs surveyed the
scene, soaking it all in, shocked by the vulgarity of it all, unless, of
course, their own family was engaged. Then later, heads together, and
from evidence submitted, they made grim readjustments on the social
ladder.[5]

Nor were the growth and grip of these virtues left to chance or the
comic book. Similar legitimations were incorporated into the
public agencies of child-rearing throughout the nation. With a
confidence now unimaginable, the Elementary School Code of

1904 delineated in exact terms the morality to be inculcated by schoolteachers. They were to 'implant' in the children 'habits of industry, self control, and courageous perservance in the face of difficulties'. The Catechism of the Anglican Prayer Book, repeated millions of times by the ancestors of these urban proletarians, was not wholly forgotten in the new unnatural world of the factory town.

My duty towards my Neighbour, is to love him as myself, and to do to all men, as I would they should do unto me: To love, honour, and succour my father and mother: To honour and obey the King, and all that are put in authority under him: To submit myself to all my governors, teachers, spiritual pastors and masters: To order myself lowly and reverently to all my betters: To hurt no body by word nor deed: To be true and just in all my dealing: To bear no malice nor hatred in my heart: To keep my hands from picking and stealing, and my tongue from evil-speaking, lying, and slandering: To keep my body in temperance, soberness, and chastity: Not to covet nor desire other men's goods; but to learn and labour truly to get mine own living, and to do my duty in that state of life, unto which it shall please God to call me.

The decline of the Victorian status system

The reinforcement of class inequality by status continues to this day, but it has lost much of its Victorian and Edwardian efficacy. One cause is to be found in the transformation of the class structure itself. Although, as we have seen, inequalities persist between classes, the internal composition and hence the status assumptions and outlook of the classes have drastically changed. At one end, the old upper class of the landed aristocracy has virtually disappeared, to be replaced by a more varied collection of employers, trade unionists, politicians, administrators, and professional people, between whom social connections have loosened, to whom recruitment from white-collar and manual origins has greatly increased, and among whom there is less agreement and confidence as to the symbols of social superiority.

Status distinctions within the working classes have often been ignored or simplified. I have used Robert Roberts's description of Salford to illustrate the internal status structure of the urban working class in the earlier decades of the twentieth century. But in so doing, I have avoided his title, *The Classic Slum*, and this is deliberate. While it is true that Engels (in his *Condition of the*

English Working Class in 1844) had used this phrase to describe the Salford through which he passed daily in the early nineteenth century, it is dangerously misleading to suggest that there was an identity between working-class communities and slums in the early part of the twentieth century. The slum existed in the Edwardian industrial town, but was typically a sharply segregated and distinctive quarter within a working-class district, within which domestic violence, child neglect, drunkenness, and the low brothel were concentrated. These quarters were in no way representative of working-class life, and the working class is wrongly and romantically depicted if it is thought of as having been rescued from the slum. Working-class districts, including those where incomes were very low, and housing and amenities poorly provided, were also areas of domestic peace and neighbourly trust of a standard which we do not know today. People never thought of locking their houses if they went out during the day, and theft would have been cause for amazement. The traditional problems of the slum have since been more widely spread through the town and cities, with the result that old working-class areas have lost their capacity to police the activities of strangers with the almost total efficiency of the period before the First World War. These districts and neighbourhoods have also lost the capacity, even if not the cultural aim, of 'keeping up standards', such as they were, of 'workman', 'workmate', 'neighbour', 'mother', 'housewife', etc. These standards were neither noble nor 'cultured', and indeed may be argued to have been pathetically misguided expressions of status conformity. Nevertheless, what Roberts calls 'the cherished principles' were not the values of the 'classic slum'.

Journalism and quasi social science continue to find the myth that identifies 'the working class' with the slum fatally attractive. But historical accuracy gives us a quite different picture. The point may be illustrated by recalling how Beatrice Webb made her 'romantic' discovery that there was a wage-earning family among her kith and kin whom she visited in Bacup, whence she wrote to her father in 1883:

> You would have laughed, father, to see me sitting amongst four or five mill-hands . . . I was surprised at their fair-mindedness, and at the kindliness of their view of men and things . . . This class of respectable working man . . . The old man and his daughter with whom we are

staying, are a veritable study of Puritan life on its more kindly side . . .

I can't help thinking that it would be well if politicians would live among the various classes they legislate for, and find out what are their wishes and ideas . . . Of course, it would be absurd to generalize from such a narrow basis: but . . . Mere philanthropists are apt to overlook the existence of an independent working class, and when they talk sentimentally of the 'people' they really mean the 'ne'er-do-wells'.[6]

This less dramatic description of the working class was no less (and probably more) typical of the first half of the twentieth century than of the 1880s when Mrs Webb was writing. Richard Hoggart's description in *The Uses of Literacy*[7] of Hunslet in the 1920s and the 1930s is a similarly accurate account of working-class life in this period.

Over the past generation, since the Second World War, and of perhaps greater import, there has developed a more homogeneous and indeed more hereditary working class in Britain. This is not, by any means, the expanded and impoverished or 'immiserated' proletariat of classical Marxist prediction. Quite the opposite. It is contracted, better off, and more collectively powerful. But it is largely recruited from second- and third-generation people of working-class antecedents. This development is not yet widely appreciated even by sociologists, but emerged clearly from the studies of the English and Welsh population in the 1970s and 1980s which have been carried out at Oxford,[8] and from a parallel enquiry in Scotland. An older study led by David Glass at the London School of Economics, looking back from 1949, depicted relatively caste-like conditions at the top of British society.[9] In the post-war period, however, it is the working class which has to be thought of as closed and stable in its membership, and the middle classes as relatively open to a wider range of new recruits from different class origins. Two out of every three middle-class men today were not born into a middle-class family.

In consequence, the status claims of those with class advantages have become less clear and less confidently uttered. Appeals to blood or family connections are now seldom heard; and in any case are discordant with the meritocratic values which offer them ideological challenge in a modern industrial society. Ascription is not in practice, however, debarred from presenting itself as achievement in a competitive labour market. The older upper and upper-middle classes recruited on both criteria, but the resulting fusion of a class weakened its status pretensions: and meritocracy by definition continually invites further recruitment from below.

The development of a more homogeneous working class, with reduced differentials and therefore less sharp status distinctions between skilled, semi-skilled, and unskilled workers, had complementary effects. The skilled man's rate of wages was twice that of the labourer in 1867. By 1914 the skilled rate was about 50 per cent more than the unskilled, and by 1952 the difference had narrowed to 16 per cent.[10] The material basis for status differences within the working class was, thus, eroded. It is not until the 1980s with the return of mass unemployment that these trends towards narrower economic differentials have been reversed.

In part, of course, the unheavenly host of ennobled or honoured leaders of the British proletariat served to maintain a modified form of the older status hierarchy. There was, it is true, debate within the socially conscious elements of the Labour movement as to whether Ramsay MacDonald should wear ceremonial dress (in fact he loved it), or Walter Citrine accept a knighthood. When, earlier, Ben Tillett was criticized for dining too often at the Ritz, he had to defend himself with the rejoinder that 'only the best is good enough for the working class'. But few advocated direct rejection of upper- and middle-class styles of life. It was a Rugby, Balliol, Church of England, middle-class socialist, R. H. Tawney, who refused a peerage in a letter to MacDonald saying that 'no cat ties a tin can to its own tail'. Nevertheless, in the process, the symbols lost some of their lustre.

In any case, the slowly growing affluence and mobility of the working class supplied the material base for new and less dependent status positions. Between the Wars these came in fantasy form from Hollywood through the screens of the local picture palaces. After the Second World War international 'pop stars' were carried into every house and flat by what we now call the media. A history of football heroes would sharply illustrate the point: it would run from Eddie Hapgood of Arsenal and England in the 1930s, with short back and sides, deferential to the manager, Mr Chapman, proud to play for his country, paid the wages of a skilled manual worker, and leaving Wembley or Highbury to return home by bus and train. By the 1970s the archetypal hero had become George Best of Manchester United, idolized by teenagers, forever flouting the authority of referees and trainers,

frequenting boutiques and nightclubs, practising widely publicized sexual promiscuity, driving a Jaguar, and catching planes
to Los Angeles.

Geographical mobility, quickened by the two Wars, broke the
grip of the working-class matriarchs. The patterns of social
mobility over the past generation have had still more far-reaching
effects. Men and women, moving and marrying between different occupational levels, both over the generations and also within
their own working lives or careers, have become an increasingly
common feature of British social life in the past half century.

The patterns are complicated. They have occurred over both
long and short occupational distances; they have often involved
geographical migration; they are different for men and women.
Pathways through education have broadened. The net result has
been an upward movement through the generations. Mobility in
the course of working life has not, as some Marxists have argued,
developed a counterbalancing narrowness.[11]

All this might appear, incidentally, to overturn the picture of
persistent inequality that I previously drew. But this is not so. It is
perfectly possible that a high degree of inequality of relative
chances of mobility for people of different social origins should
exist alongside high and rising absolute rates of movement
between classes. Where there is an inverse correlation between
class and fertility, as well as an expansion of professional and
managerial jobs, this coincidence of unequal relative chances and
high absolute chances of upward mobility can easily result.

I will return to a more detailed consideration of class mobility
in Chapter 6. The point here is that people carry images of social
worth from their older to their newer class positions, and this
weakens any pre-existing accord on a hierarchy of life-styles.
This is what has happened in Britain. It has added to the problems of social control, whether by employers, managers, policemen, tax gatherers, parents, or teachers. It goes, in other words,
beyond class to the social order as a totality. The stabilizing force
of the status order we inherited from the nineteenth century has
been comprehensively dismantled. Moreover, and what is perhaps more important, attitudes of resentment to the remaining
status distinctions have moved in the opposite direction; they
have been strengthened. This is argued cogently by Runciman in
his study of attitudes to social inequality in twentieth-century

England. As he puts it, 'the magnitude and frequency of relative deprivation of status in the manual stratum has, on the whole, risen as inequality of status has declined'.[12]

If, as sociologists now agree, such a supportive status system had been dissolving in Britain, then class must also have been losing its legitimacy; and its persistent inequalities are less and less protected from challenge. This is in fact what has been happening, especially since the Second World War (which, incidentally, was itself a period of accelerated decay of traditional status assumptions).[13] In the later 1970s and in the 1980s most Britons have had the sense that the social contract is being renegotiated; that all the methods which distribute and redistribute burdens and benefits—the collective bargain, the statute, the judge's ruling, the executive decision, the routine of administration in central and local government, the customary expectations of work places and bus queues, and even the give-and-take of family life—that is the arrangements for the social division of duty, wealth, and welfare are in debate, their principles and procedures in question.

The rise of citizenship

Social status, then, has a peculiar history. Yet we have still to explore its most significant feature, namely the rise of citizenship as a special form of status. At this point we reach a crucial step in the discussion of class and status. What I am essentially arguing is that the Marxist emphasis on class interest trivializes status by relegating it to a subsidiary role as a more or less complicated apparatus of control over subordinate classes. At the same time, I am also arguing that the liberal emphasis on status, which comes in one form or another of a pluralistic theory of stratification, constitutes the reciprocal error—it trivializes class by denying its role in undermining the freedoms promised by a liberal society.[14] In the Butskell period from 1945 to 1979, the Marxist error was increasingly obvious. In the 1980s the liberal error has been revealed. But both theories lead to false doctrines of historical progress, and neither deals adequately with the problem of social order.

There is, however, an open channel between this Scylla and Charybdis of sociological mis-explanation. It was charted by T. H. Marshall as long ago as the 1940s.[15] Marshall avoids both traps, and accurately pictures the history of conflict in Britain over the distribution of work and reward, by postulating a developing battle between the two great dramatis personae of our social history—*class* operating through the labour and capital markets, and *status* operating through the political and legal systems to define the rights of citizens.

The double thrust of Marshall's theory goes to the heart of social change in twentieth-century Britain, and places contemporary struggles in the wider context of the slow and contested development of citizenship through civil rights during the period from the middle of the seventeenth century and the revolution of 1688 to the First Reform Act of 1832—including Habeas Corpus in 1679, the abolition of Press censorship, and Catholic emancipation. Quoting G. M. Trevelyan,[16] Marshall points out that by the early nineteenth century 'civil rights had come to man's estate and bore (except for the right to strike) in most essentials, the appearance they have today'. The Hanoverian epoch had established the rule of law, 'and that law, with all its grave faults, was at least a law of freedom'.[17]

Subsequently, in the nineteenth century, citizenship began slowly to acquire the dimension of political enfranchisement. Class and traditional status began a long retreat from direct control over organized politics. This conquest of politics by the principle of citizenship remained incomplete down to our own period: the enfranchisement of women was not completed until the 1918 and 1928 reforms, and the dual voting for businessmen and university graduates was not ended finally until 1948. Indeed, it can be argued that political rights were not entirely freed from their attachment as privileges to a restricted economic class to become attributes of citizenship until full manhood suffrage was adopted in 1918. In the early years of the century the registered electorate was only 60 per cent of all British men, and those left out were mostly working-class.

The development of the *social*, as distinct from the civil and political, rights of citizenship belongs pre-eminently to the twentieth century. The 1834 Poor Law had been the last monument to the sharp separation of social rights from the status of citizenship. The break-up of the Poor Law is the central element in the even now unfinished story of the struggle of this new status against class in our lifetime. Its first milestone is to be found in the legislation of the Liberal landslide government of 1906. No wonder that Robert Roberts, from the vantage point of a corner shop in a working-class street, tell us how the new old-age pensioners—new, that is, since 1909—when spending their allowances of 7s. 6d. per week for a married couple, 'would bless the name of Lloyd George as if he were a saint from heaven'.

Citizenship won further victories in the field of social rights as the century advanced, especially after the Second World War with the establishment of Beveridge's social security programme based on insurance, and the National Health Service based on direct taxation. By 1977 the 'social wage' distributed by the Welfare State had become a sizeable sum: it was nearly £1,500 a year for each member of the working population of the United Kingdom.[18] But the story remains unfinished because the two principles of distribution—class and citizenship—remain in contention. Indeed the struggle has intensified since 1979 in battles over the level of public expenditure, welfare rights, and the National Health Service. A class society uses the market as its distributive instrument. It had evolved historically under powerful impulses toward economic freedom, as Marx, as well as the liberal theorists, well appreciated. Citizenship, on the other hand, is a special form of status which looks to the state and seeks a different type of distribution which turns on the political process and on the secondary form of industrial citizenship which has developed in its wake. Citizenship is also different from class in that it is intrinsically levelling. But it is not simply an assertion of equality against freedom. As Marshall was at pains to point out, it permits sanctioned inequality, for example in advanced education, or specialized medical need.

Citizenship, we should note in this context, has been defined nationally. This point is fundamental. It has been fateful for Britain in this century that the nation state was seen as the political unit appropriate to its purpose. The emerging political organization of the working classes aimed, from the start, to conquer national politics. In so doing, it necessarily took on the immense challenge of forming a national community: for citizenship status depends for its support on fraternity. Looking at the Labour party in this way—as a movement aspiring to transform a hierarchical social order into a national community—its handicaps become plain.

The Labour movement at the beginning of the century was based on the solidarity of local class communities. Labour markets and kinship networks were bounded by walking distances. For the vast majority of ordinary people national concerns were remote from daily life. Only war made Britons out of people whose social horizons were normally enclosed by the street, the village, or the neighbourhood. The bid for men's minds, which was made by appeals for a broader national or even international class solidarity before the First World War, was in any case weak. In peace, class solidarity was dissipated in day-to-day preoccupations with survival in the close social networks of the industrial town and the agricultural village. In war, it retreated before the siege-solidarity of response to external threat. Both phenomena, of course, parochialism and nationalism, may be interpreted as expressions of social control by the governing class. But this, too, further emphasizes the barrier to national community which stood in the way of the Labour movement. A political organization committed to universal and democratic freedom had also to face the dilemma of either persuading the powerful minority to join a new national community by giving up its privileges, or forcing them to do so by reducing the economic freedoms they had previously won for themselves in the establishing of free capitalism. Moreover, the very process of economic growth, on which state welfare depended for its development, also involved changes in the occupational structure which steadily diminished the size of the working class and enlarged the lower-middle- and middle-class groups of white-collar, technical, and professional people.

Class and status have, then, been in complex contention in our time, and that contention has largely determined the application of the social principles of liberty, equality, and fraternity.

The theory of citizenship

The theory of citizenship which I accept can be challenged. It can be misinterpreted as a benign, even complacent assumption that history is the evolution or progress of civilization towards a welfare society. It can be so-called Whig history—a self-congratulatory account of the gradual ascent of liberal values. T. H. Marshall can be misread in this way, particularly with respect to what he termed the secondary system of industrial citizenship.

Marshall treated industrial citizenship or economic rights more briefly than either political or social rights. His history in this respect is all the more likely to be misinterpreted as Whig—that is the gradual unfolding of liberal principles through enlightened institutions of bargaining and conciliation, parallel or assimilated to the steady evolution of the institutions of parliamentary democracy. On this view, as Alan Fox describes it, 'the growth of strong trade unions and systematic collective bargaining [was] an evolutionary triumph of liberal principles and civilized restraints, with workers coming gradually to "learn" what was required of them in this best of all liberal worlds'. Fox's alternative view is that 'groups of workers fumbled their way towards [collective bargaining] as the most promising way of reducing the uncertainties of their immediate work experience; employers reacted in the light of their particular interests and exigencies'.[19] Marshall would agree, but remains less easily read as one concerned to stress the contingencies as well as the continuities of history.

Anthony Giddens, however, takes this criticism further and remarks on an 'odd similarity here between [Marshall's] interpretation of the development of contemporary capitalism and that of some Marxist authors who in other respects have very different views from those of Marshall'.[20] These authors interpret citizenship rights (what Marx himself had dismissed as 'bourgeois freedoms') as a form of concessionary social control by the ruling class. In a wider context Frank Parkin takes a similar view when he emphasizes 'how readily an "equality of opportunity" version of socialism can be accommodated to the institutions and values of modern capitalism' and that 'the allocation of benefits to the less privileged serves to damp down radical or revolutionary movements'.[21]

Giddens's point is that such accounts, Marshall's or Marxist, put too little emphasis on *struggle*. He is empirically justified in insisting that all three elements of Marshall's citizenship rights had to be fought for over a long period by those classes and organizations which were excluded from power and advantage by the development of capitalism. And the recent resurgence of market liberalism in Europe and America demonstrates that none of the three elements is either secure or irreversible.

Yet Giddens's criticism cannot be fully sustained when, as he himself notices, Marshall describes class and citizenship as principles or social forces which have been 'at war in the twentieth century'[22] and this conflict of principles 'springs from the very roots of our social order'.[23] Unlike Durkheim and unlike some of his own interpreters, Marshall saw conflict (though he would not have used the Marxist term 'struggle') as a permanent and indeed desirable feature of a dynamic society.

'The affluent societies of the mid-20th century', he believed, 'contain within themselves elements producing a discord that has not yet been resolved and which . . . could remain unresolved for a long time without disrupting the social order.'[24] In his very last essay he concludes with respect to 'democratic-welfare-capitalism':

The system survives in . . . a precarious and somewhat battered condition . . . It is obvious that an acute incompatibility of values prevalent in different sectors may cause intolerable friction or possibly the destruction of one value system by another. But it would be absurd to assume that the coexistence of different value systems in different contexts must necessarily be on balance 'disfunctional', since this kind of ethical relativity has been a feature of very nearly every society since civilisation began. The question is whether potential conflict can be managed . . . Each case must be judged on its merits.[25]

In the same essay Marshall returns to a personal affirmation of both his liberalism and his belief in the chronic conflict embedded in what Richard Crossman had called 'civilised capitalism':

I am one of those who believes that it is hardly possible to maintain democratic freedoms in a society which does not contain a large area of economic freedom and that the incentives provided by and expressed in competitive markets make a contribution to efficiency, and to progress in the production and distribution of wealth which cannot, in a large and complex society, be derived from any other source. But I also believe that the capitalist market economy can be, and generally has been a cause of much social injustice. The vital question whether this is an inevitable outcome of its ethos or a malady which could be treated . . . without destroying all that is of value in the system, has yet to be answered.[26]

Marshall was, on balance, optimistic about the future of the Welfare State. Though insisting on open possibilities rather than any inevitable trend, he believed in the probability of a favourable balance of collective welfare against private acquisitiveness.[27]

Of course it is no less rational to put a more pessimistic value on these probabilities. Recent experience, particularly in Britain and the USA, strongly suggests a stable possibility *in a parliamentary democracy* of majority support for 'the spirit of acquisitiveness' and its associated market inequalities buttressed by social and political control of dispossessed and deprived minorities minimally maintained by state charity. Even so Marshall's non-historicist view of history, his weaving together of ideological with institutional factors in a theory of change, and his scepticism about structural solutions to the problem of inequality still stand as firm contributions to our understanding of the genesis and contemporary state of capitalist society.

Moreover, Giddens's picture of the importance of struggle— 'the outcome of the active endeavours of concrete groups of people'[28]—can itself easily be overdrawn. The clash between the interests of capital and labour in the development of the industrial relations system in Britain, though real enough, is no simple story. For example, as Alan Fox reminds us: 'Even within the socialist element [of the working-class movement] there was a strong tradition which gave only qualified support to the international Marxist appeal—a strand of indigenous as against exotic socialism, characterized by such names as Morris, Blatchford, Tawney, and later Orwell and Edward Thompson, which remained strongly libertarian and shared the old radical love of country.'[29] And the political ruling class was never a mechanically reliable 'executive committee' of the capitalist class. It maintained a commitment to constitutionalism, law, and a not-too-heavy hand on the lower orders, partly no doubt, as Fox points out, because it was not wholly dependent on the domestic economy, but in such a way as to make the struggle for civil, political, and social rights into a process far more complicated than one of crude class conflict. In short, the system of industrial citizenship, and still more the development of political and welfare rights, was neither a predictable process of liberal enlightenment nor a new set of controls invented out of the cunning of a Fabian ruling class.

None the less Giddens is able, I think successfully, to find a weakness in Marshall's account of the sequence of the establishment of civil, political, and social rights as they developed from the status hierarchy of feudalism in the capitalist era. Marshall

gives the impression that civil rights were fully and finally established before the long march of political enfranchisement and the
subsequent expansion of social rights in the nineteenth and twentieth centuries. Giddens argues that civil rights, or we might say
legal citizenship, established in the courts, always remained at
issue. Especially in what Marshall treated as their extension into
industrial citizenship, these civil rights were at least as much a
battle-ground of class conflict as the basis for class abatement or
amelioration. Present struggles serve Giddens's view that the
separation of the economy from the polity as arenas of conflict
between class interests and citizenship principles, which was so
characteristic a feature of the history of capitalist society, throws
doubt on the classification of economic citizenship as an extension of civil rights. Such struggles have also to be seen as a challenge to the separation of the 'economic' from the 'political' by
labour movements. Working-class entry into parliament was a
necessary step towards reforming anti-working-class law. In
Marshall's own terms, political rights have been used to gain
extended civil rights just as much as civil rights were used as a
basis for demanding the extension of the political franchise. The
'political' strike is notoriously contentiously defined. More generally in the analysis of contemporary capitalism we are well
advised to think of the three citizenships as in mutual or inter-
active fragility, always threatened by class conflict, just as we
must think of the civil rights of individuals under state socialism
as always diminished by monopolized party political power.
Thus the Marshallian analysis, rid of its residual evolutionism,
can be turned powerfully against both the tendency of liberal
theory towards envisaging a 'post-industrial' society in which
citizenship has replaced capitalist class conflict and against the
shortcomings of Marxist theories of the state in both capitalist
and socialist societies.[30]

Citizenship and ethnicity

Perhaps the most difficult test of the strength of the citizenship
principle has been its application to the immigrant population of
ethnic groups with origins in the so-called 'New Commonwealth'
—mainly from Africa, the West Indies, India, Bangladesh, and
Pakistan. These are the Black and Brown British, small ethnic
minorities in a dominantly white society. The most recent

estimate of their numbers, including those born in Britain, was 2,309,000, forming 4.4 per cent of the total population of Great Britain in 1983.[31] Their contribution to births in 1977 was 7.2 per cent.[32] Taking into account the age structure of these minority groups and assuming that current law and policy do not change, their total numbers in Great Britain will represent 5 per cent of the population by 1991, compared with 3 per cent in 1976. They will account for less than 1 per cent of people over 65, but 6 to 8 per cent of those under 15.[33]

The coloured ethnic groups in Britain therefore constitute a small, but significant, minority. They suffer both class and status disadvantages and discriminations. Their citizenship is assured in law, but fragile in practice. Their history in Britain is a short one, dating from 1948 when the former German pleasure cruiser, the *Empire Windrush*, brought 492 West Indians to work in Britain. Policy towards them was timidly pragmatic. There was a restricted preoccupation with the facts of immigration. Thus, in the 1950s, the 'stranger hypothesis' in sociological theory[34] was the academic equivalent of a policy of assimilation. Academic theory and official policy were mirrors of each other. The problem was seen as that of a small number of newcomers who would be either willing and able to learn a learnable British culture, or would accommodate temporarily and return whence they came. The process of assimilation assumed capacities on both sides—on the part of the host 'to be kind to the foreigner, the poor chap can't help it', and on the part of the immigrant to understand the reluctance of his host to expose himself hastily or to commit himself unduly by identification with a stranger whose behaviour, by definition, was imperfectly controlled by the tacit understandings of a complex, historically evolved, and slowly learned code of morals and manners. The conceived scale of the problem is well illustrated by the story of Leary Constantine's arrival between the Wars to settle in a mining town as a professional in Lancashire league cricket. On the Sunday morning after his arrival he went for a walk and, true to his nature, joined in with a group of boys kicking a football in a side street. The first boy's greeting was, 'Hasta been downt' pit, then?'

But both theorists and policy-makers were forced in the 1960s to recognize that the assimilationist policy was no longer possible in the face of the rapidly increased rate of immigration, especially from India and Pakistan, at the end of the 1950s. Hence restrictions on entry were brought in by the 1962 Commonwealth Immigration Act. The paradoxical consequences were a temporary reversal of the intentions of the Act, which brought a sharply increased flow of Indian and Pakistani families to settle permanently in place of the groups of male temporary workers intending to return.

These developments undermined the assumption of the older assimilative policy that the coloured population was a homogeneous collection of individuals. This was never a fact. Distinctions have to be drawn not only between different nationalities and ethnic groups, but also within these between castes, classes, and occupations, and between individuals, families, and types of community group. E. J. B. Rose showed at the end of the 1960s that the pattern of group formations among the British coloureds was changing rapidly and in different directions among West Indians, Pakistanis, and Cypriots, as well as between the first and second generation of immigrants.[35] In particular, an unassimilated group of depressed status within the working class was being formed. More generally, the developing size and heterogeneity of the coloured population demanded not assimilation but integration where the process had to be seen as a highly differentiated one of absorption, incorporation, and accommodation to the multiple relationships of locality, occupation, politics, religion, and indeed the whole network of society.

Similarly, effective race relations policies had to take account of the facts of change in the host society. The terms of assimilation have been transformed. British society is no longer as assimilative as it was when the earlier wave of Jewish immigrants arrived at the end of the nineteenth century. There has been an 'Americanization' of British society with decreasingly certain use of informal sanctions through tacit understandings, and with growing impersonality, mobility, and aspirations towards privatized affluence. Moreover, the quiet and polite xenophobia of the average Briton has been overlaid with explicit racism ranging from the ugly militancy of the National Front to the intellectualized prejudice of Enoch Powell. In the mid-1970s the National Front had gained in its minority support and attracted much publicity. In a by-election at Stechford in 1977, its candidate had 8.1 per cent of the votes cast (2,955 out of 36,240), beating the Liberal into fourth place.

In the autumn of 1976 the *Guardian* newspaper printed extracts from the Central Policy Review Staff Report on race relations, which was presented to the Labour government in 1974 but never published. The Report stated:

There are uncomfortable parallels between the situation of Britain's coloured population and that of the Catholics in Northern Ireland. For fifty years British governments condoned discrimination and deprivation in Ulster, and in the end Ulster blew up in their face. We believe that not only for reasons of social justice but also to preserve social stability and order in the longer term more should be done to deal with the problems of race relations in this country.

What was needed, it said, was an attack on three fronts—against urban poverty, racial discrimination, and language disabilities. Such an approach would require extra money directed specifically at improving the situation of coloured minorities, particularly in the areas of housing, education, and employment. It also demanded a clear government policy on race relations rather than mere declarations of principle. Meantime, ugly confrontations with the police, as in Bristol, or with the National Front, as in Wolverhampton, continued to rend the social fabric of Britain in the 1980s. For, although successive governments had declared their support for policies of positive discrimination, they gave no lead themselves in treating Black and Brown people as equivalent to whites.[36]

There were serious riots in Brixton and Toxteth in 1981. A crisis of relations between citizen and the law was recognized in the inquiry subsequently led by Lord Scarman. The crisis receded in subsequent years in the sense that no further riots took place (up to 1985). But the underlying conditions of citizenship denial scarcely changed. Here are my impressions of Liverpool in 1982 and 1984.

I was going to Toxteth, or to be more precise, to Lodge Lane and the Granby Ward on the inner south-west side of the city, the centre of the 1981 riots. The proportion of Black citizens is at its highest here. This was the battlefield, and Lodge Lane still bears the ugly marks of riot—broken windows patched with old cardboard or boarded up; graffiti; empty shops and grey dirt—amid which people live normal lives, gossiping on the pavements, carrying vegetables, wheeling infants in pushchairs, and generally pursuing business as usual. Here, in the Granby triangle, is where the ethnic mixing-bowl of Liverpool has concentrated a fantastic variety of human faces, crowded together in economic decline, bad housing, poor amenities, low morale, and high crime.

At its worst, Toxteth is the jostling proximity of the rawest community at the lowest common denominator of individuals thrown together with no common social inheritance. The best dream of what it could be is the hope of multi-cultural harmony in a civic stability of Merseyside cosmopolitans.

What in fact is its fate? I talked first to a man dedicated to realizing the dream—an active, thoughtful, and committed Church of England priest. The measure of his commitment is not so much that his redbrick church itself seems less important than the play group which it houses, nor so much the spartan austerity of the Victorian vicarage next door, as the fact that two of the children in his own family are adopted Blacks. I would not wish to embarrass him and his family with a public parade of their personal virtue. They seem to me to *live*, in private, the belief to which we as a nation have so far paid little more than lip-service.

Put in public and constitutional terms, the question is whether Toxteth belongs to Britain, whether the blacks are British citizens—or whether these territories are to be seen as under the alien occupation of foreigners (more politely described as 'immigrants' or 'New Commonwealth')? If they are citizens, then they have equal rights and duties with the white majority. They have a claim to equality, not only before the law, but also before the teacher, the employer, the doctor, and the social worker. If they are not citizens, the white majority should explicitly renounce the promises which brought them, or in most cases their ancestors, to these islands, and the state should be obliged to negotiate real citizenship for them elsewhere.

I have no doubt myself that the first is the more honourable and, indeed, the only practical answer. We are talking here about 40,000 people, and the majority of this Liverpool minority is strictly Black British: they were born here, brought up here and know no other home.

Talking to a young girl of mixed African, Chinese, and white British ancestry, I asked whether she would like to take a job in another country. She replied with an expressive shrug of the shoulders, and in the purest Liverpool dialect said: 'Where would I go? I'm a Liverpool girl.' It is *her* voice that should command attention; and it's a special British voice that the British have created. Whether by the ancient and cruel accidents of slave-trading, the propaganda of colonialism, the labour demand of a once buoyant British economy, or the plain fact of birth in the United Kingdom, the 4 per cent minority have just as much right to a place on the island as any descendant of a Saxon or Norman invader.

I was to spend the morning at the local Caribbean Club with the older generation of those who had immigrated during the forties and fifties from the West Indies. One of them came to fetch me from the vicarage. A dapper, relaxed, and articulate brown man with an elegant trilby hat, he sat for a while with the priest and me in the sitting-room.

His story was a typical one. I noticed, incidentally, that in telling it he used a markedly more biblical vocabulary than that deployed by the vicar. During the Second World War, he had enlisted in the Royal Navy as a cook and eventually found his way to Liverpool, via Canada and the United States. He is now one of the very few Black employees of the Liverpool City Council. His children are Liverpudlian Black British and unequivocally your compatriots and mine.

The club was as austere as the vicarage, but single-storey and modern. The members sat in an alert and lively circle on hard, straight-backed, institutional chairs, and the story was repeated over and over. One of them expressed the common mood: 'We are a special breed of British raised in the Caribbean. We learned to sing "God Save the King" in infancy; Barbados was always known as Little England; we joined the Royal Navy out of patriotism. We are British by origin, by upbringing, by experience, by inclination, and by invitation. And now they want us to pay £150 to be recognized as British.'

They had more than a trace of that peculiar form of English snobbery in which respectability is heavily identified with literacy and hygiene. They recalled with horror the shock of learning that native British ratings of the Second World War were not infrequently functional illiterates needing help to write home. From the point of view of these Caribbean volunteers, many of the native Britons were unsatisfactory shipmates because they had not acquired the standards of hygiene taught so assiduously in the colonial West Indian schools. All the sharper, then, was the bitterness of learning to live for the first time with racial prejudice in the imperial homeland. A well-known sugar company, ambassadors, diplomats, and English aristocrats came in for a good deal of stick as 'villains, rogues, and murderers', and upper-class British diplomacy was equated with deceitfulness.

Their resentful sophistication with respect to race prejudice was elaborately illustrated by anecdotes of their experiences in pubs and on public transport. The bartender who somehow fails to notice that a Black man is waiting to buy a drink, the ticket collector who examines their money with suspicion. Bank managers and bureaucrats, personnel officers and policemen are seen by them as the purveyors of hypocritical rejection.

The overdraft is impossible. The job vacancy exists on the telephone but has unfortunately just been filled in face-to-face interview. And their bitterness is further accentuated by recognizing that on the whole, race relations in schools are so much better than in the world of work and adult social life.

Their demands were simple. They wanted equality of opportunity, not merely in the polling-booth, but in the work place and in the offices of the public authorities. They were denied it, sometimes crudely, but more often by evasive fobbing off. They saw themselves as having patiently endured injustice.

They claimed no hatred in their hearts for individual white people. Instead, they attributed moral blame to a corrupt system. And, above all, they vociferously warned that the rising generation would not be prepared to put up with the treatment that they themselves had suffered.

In the afternoon, I walked a mile from the vicarage to talk to that rising generation. The two cathedrals rose above a chaotic urban horizon—Anglican solid Gothic, Roman Catholic futuristic contemporary, both reaching towards heaven, incongruously and unconvincingly, out of the jumble of Liverpool streets. Between the remaining Victorian terraces and the flat rubble of a demolished working-class district, I walked through streets of post-war co-operative housing, but with Dickensian names—Pecksniff, Copperfield, Micawber, Nickleby—and my spirits lifted. After all, Dickens had described horrifying urban squalor and was haunted by terror of the mob. Victorian and

Edwardian Britain survived its problems—worse problems— with fewer resources. Surely we could do the same.

I had an appointment with a young man in one of these trim new houses. His was a younger version of the morning voice, and the edge of bitterness was sharper still. With his frizzy hair tumbling round an intense white face, he described the torment of being brought up to talk, think, and feel scouse by a white mum and a Black dad and a Liverpool school, only to learn as he tried to enter the job market that he was Black and therefore unlikely to be employed.

He and a group of other young Blacks were temporarily employed in the hazardous and unrewarding job of trying to find jobs for local Black school-leavers. They operate from an old board school, standing gaunt and lonely in the wasteland between the opulent district on the right side of the Anglican cathedral, and the ethnic working-class quarter on the wrong side. Many of the employers, including the city council itself and the large department stores, had made declarations of intent to be colour-blind in taking on new recruits. But not only do statistics show a highly unequal pattern of racial recruitment but, in case after case, choice seemed clearly to have been made, all other things being equal, on colour of skin.

These young people in the job-seeking centre, like their fathers, insisted that they had no prejudice against whites. Instead, they had begun to learn the contemporary analytical phrases and talked about institutional racism. They mean, for example, that Blacks are tacitly defined in school as academically unpromising and in work as unreliable. Their bitterness was more violently expressed than that of their parents. Their experience has made them both more Liverpudlian and more alienated. And they, in almost every case, are cynically dismissive of the police. A few of them, some of their kin and more of their friends have been in one kind or another of trouble with the police, starting, as they see it, in harassment, and ending in arrest and sentencing, mostly for real, often for trivial and sometimes for non-existent crimes. The restoration of confident community-police relations with Toxteth has a long period of miserable failure behind it too, and if that does not change, those who come after the young people to whom I spoke will be yet more disposed to mutiny.[37]

All in all, then, the changing circumstances point to the need to develop a complex policy of integration.

Social inequality, conceived as differences in power and advantage, is the basic condition of the Black British. There is overwhelming evidence that the coloured population suffers discrimination on grounds of colour in employment, housing, leisure activities, and over the whole range of social relationships. Differences in power and advantage, whether based on colour or any other socially evaluated attribute, tend to be generalized and to be transmitted between generations. The social outlook for the ethnic minorities is accordingly bleak. Whether admitted directly to citizenship through the immigration officer, or indirectly through an upbringing in Britain and through the school system, they typically have all the disadvantages of the lower levels of the native working class, as well as those of colour prejudice.

The effectiveness of the deliberate pursuit of equality through governmental action in the twentieth century has been severely limited in respect of the relative chances of the working class. In so far as the integration of Africans and Asians is thought of as a recapitulation of the gradual admission of the working class to full citizenship, the task calls for much more politically forceful action than is embodied in the Race Relations Act of 1968 or 1976, or the mild gestures towards 'positive discrimination' which have been incorporated into the government's Urban Programme. Without such action, the position of the second and third generations of coloured people is likely to worsen. For example immigrant children generally have poorer educational performance (with all that this implies for later life-chances) than natives. Children of West Indian antecedents, even with a full British schooling, have distributions which are 'negatively skewed' (that is, relatively large numbers with low scores) on all the measures of school attainment and, what is of the greatest significance, they do worse the more they are concentrated (as housing and employment policies force them to be) in predominantly working-class districts. The Black share of youth unemployment is accordingly disastrous.

Obvious and persistent inequality, quite apart from its moral effectiveness, is a threatening source of conflict. In the context of class relations, John Goldthorpe has analysed the paradox of the coexistence of gross inequality with a high degree of political consensus.[38] He divides the current explanations into two main types, 'social psychological' and 'culturalist'. I have discussed

W. G. Runciman's contribution to the first type. What determines behaviour is not actual but *felt* deprivation. Limited imagination has served to integrate an unequal society. Goldthorpe's second type of analysis complements Runciman's. The British political culture is characterized by a balance 'that holds, even across lines of class and party, between participant, activist attitudes on the one hand, and acquiescent, passive attitudes on the other, between emotional commitment to political principle and cool pragmatism; between consensus on matters of procedure and conflict over particular issues'.[39] Socialization into the culture makes for apolitical and unfanatical citizens. In the past it has offered little basis for politically extremist egalitarian movements. Thus, as Runciman put it, 'there has been woven a social fabric in which traditional privilege blends with egalitarian socialism and class-consciousness with a veneration of existing institutions'.

Will race relations in Britain tear this fabric apart? Continuing conflict leaves open such a possibility. Race relations legislation is explicitly egalitarian. But the question remains of what responses are likely from those who are legally declared equal in an unequal society of conflicting interest groups, what economic and social costs will have to be paid for the absence of moral consensus, and what external controls will be required by those who prefer to maintain the status quo. The answers are far from comforting.

Conclusion

In this chapter we have traced the complex interplay of class with status. The decline of the Victorian status order which so powerfully legitimated a class society was a feature of British social stratification at least until the end of the post-war period. The reconstruction of status on the basis of the principle of citizenship also emerged as a fundamental conflict in British society. The war of citizenship against class won some battles for social equality against class inequality in a polity of parliamentary democracy and a mixed economy. But the war continues, and the position of the ethnic minorities shows grimly that an equal commonwealth of citizens remains an unattained objective of social reform.

4

The rise of party

Class and status, it has emerged, are social structures which both constrain the lives of men and women and offer them opportunities. We have described the continuities and changes in this enveloping framework of life-chances. Yet still the picture of social inequality is incomplete. A full view of the stratification system, following Max Weber's analysis, must include those movements through which individuals band together to seek collectively for power and advantage. A dynamic theory of stratification is a three-sided analysis of class, status, and party. The next task therefore is to examine how people have used deliberate organization in pursuit of their ends. By studying organized movements we can begin to answer the question of 'structure' and 'agency', that is, how far have or could people alter the framework of constraint and opportunity by deliberate social action? How far can power and advantage, which we have seen in Britain as a structure of class and status inequality, be changed by political and industrial interest groups? In short, what, in Max Weber's terminology, is the power of party?

An answer for Britain at the end of the twentieth century involves five elements: first the rise of working-class organization geared to the market and the state, second the containment of these movements by a resourceful and adaptive Conservative party, third the incorporation of Labour leaders, fourth what sociologists call the institutional segregation of industrial conflict, and fifth a resurgent economic liberalism which captured the Conservative party at the end of the 1970s. This movement, together with disintegrative conflict within the Labour party, finally raises the question of whether the whole balance of British politics has been transformed with momentous implications for the future shape of British society.

At the beginning of the twentieth century the trade unions and the Labour party were the practical means of those whose weak market position could only be transcended by mobilizing their

superior numbers both industrially and politically. Consideration of these popular movements of class, status, and party will
lead to the conclusion that they had eventually to face the problem of 'alienation of the organizational apparatus from the membership'.[1] This fate befalls all large organizations. They tend to
become remote from the interests they are created to serve, the
more so the more successfully they recruit members. Thus Marx's
remarks that 'history is made behind men's backs' applies to
those who consciously seek to change that history as much as to
those who do not.

The age of organization

There is no more commonplace description of the twentieth century than the phrase 'an age of organization'. If we pursue that
phrase we find as its corollaries the age of alienation and the age
of anomy (or normlessness). I shall not cover the whole sweep of
advancing organization, nor shall I more than refer to what Professor Finer has termed the *Anonymous Empire*[2] of pressure
groups which lobby Westminster and Whitehall, and fill the gap
between government and electorate between elections. There are
many such interest groups. Some obscure and some ephemeral,
some of long standing and widely known, they cover the whole
gamut of social, economic, and political life. Confining examples
to the first letter of the alphabet there is the Automobile Association, Aims of Industry, Amnesty, Alcoholics Anonymous,
Action on Smoking and Health, and Associations of almost anyone anywhere ascertainable. My main concern, however, is with
the central phenomenon of party in twentieth-century Britain—
the rise, and in the 1980s the possible demise, of an organized
working class.

The more general background of the age of organization can
be summarized as one in which more people are more involved in
social relations beyond kinship at every stage of their lives. One
indicator of the general trend is the number of enquiries received
by the advice network of Citizens' Advice Bureaux (CAB). In the
year ending 31 March 1984 this was almost six million, which was
nearly a fourfold increase from 1971. Another indicator is the
likelihood of being employed in a local firm. People now typically work for an organization which is unlikely to be confined to
their town or even their country. It is more and more likely to be a

multinational company. Concurrently, within the contracting private sector of employment, there has been increasing concentration into a smaller number of larger firms. The invention of the limited company in the nineteenth century had paved the legal way for this development,[3] and sounded the knell of classical political economy as a valid theory applicable to the real world. Though at the beginning of the twentieth century the hundred largest companies still produced only 15 per cent of manufacturing output, today the hundred juggernauts of industry account for half the output, and the 90,000 firms with ten or fewer employees which were operating 70 years ago have been reduced to about 35,000.

In short, the organizations of production have expanded their range, reduced their numbers, and enlarged their scale. Married women have moved into paid employment, and what the Registrar-General is pleased to call 'the economically active population' has therefore expanded, despite the fall-off in economic activity rates among older men and the parallel increase in the number of old and retired people. Leisure experiences, too, as well as work and education, are supplied by large-scale organizations, or take place in premises or with apparatus controlled by them. Even to watch television in the home is in fact to participate as a consumer in the final result of an enormous organizational effort. Similarly, in the case of children's play, the humble *Dandy* is replaced by the video game, and juvenile prestige has come to depend less on skill with four old pram wheels and a few bits of wood and more on the ability to buy the most sophisticated and fashionable products of technology.

The largest organization is, of course, the state itself. The state supplies cash, personnel, buildings, and other resources for a vast network of financial, personal, educational, and social services. The Welfare State is a vast employing agency. Of the 24 million in the United Kingdom employed labour force in 1984, 7 million were in the public sector of industry, and over 5 million in central and local government. Half of those were in the National Health Service or education.

The growth of trade unions

At the beginning of the century economic organizations were dominated by a private owning and controlling class, and political

The rise of party

organizations by the Conservative and Liberal wings of the middle and upper classes. The Labour party did not exist, and the trade union movement, though it had deep roots, especially among skilled workers, in the earlier stages of industrialism, was struggling to extend its organizational sway among semi-skilled and unskilled workers. There were 2 million union members at the beginning of this century, out of a total potential membership of nearly 16 million. In other words, only one-eighth of all possible recruits had in fact been recruited. Put more technically, the density of membership was 13 per cent in 1900. This figure rose rapidly to reach 45 per cent by 1920. Since that date unionization has had fluctuating fortunes, but did not attain a higher density than it had in 1920 until the 1970s. By 1979, it had reached 55.4 per cent.

At this point, which we now see as the end of the post-war period and the re-emergence of economic liberalism, it now appears that traditional unionism reached its zenith (Figure 4.1). Economic recession and political opposition combined to reverse the tide of union strength. Union density was down to 48 per cent by 1982, a level more like that of the 1960s. During the first half of the 1980s union membership declined from the high point of 13.3 million in the UK in 1979 (compared with less than 10 million in 1961). In the first three Thatcher years membership fell by 13 per cent, the highest losses occurring among unions recruiting in manufacturing industry, where unemployment rose most rapidly. Figures for unions affiliated to the TUC show membership falling by 17 per cent between the end of 1979 and the end of 1983.

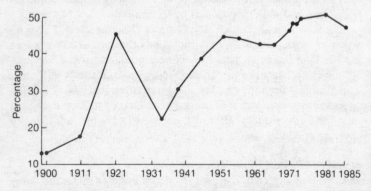

Figure 4.1 Density of union membership 1901–1985

Were it not for the relative buoyancy of unionism among women, professionals, and public-sector employees, the picture of a traditional male working-class union movement in retreat before Thatcherism would be still more dramatic, especially perhaps with the miners' strike of 1984, which ended in 1985 with the miners returning to work without any satisfaction of their demands for greater protection from pit closures.

Unionization of women has always lagged behind that of men: so, too, has that of white-collar employees compared with manual workers. But after the Second World War, unionization of white-collar workers increased very quickly. Thus while union membership among manual workers increased by only 0.9 per cent between 1948 and 1970, the increase among white-collar workers was 79.8 per cent. The densities in 1979 were 63 per cent for manual workers and 44 per cent for white-collar workers.[4] Unionism remains an organized force or 'party', but the pace of its march has slowed and its male working-class character is drastically modified.

The class struggle in economics and politics

The end of the nineteenth century had brought the period of peaceful bourgeois domination to its late autumn of economic progress, imperial expansion, and national security. Political conflict divided contestants by religion more than class. But class politics were soon to sweep away the old divisions. The class struggles previously fought in an autonomous economic sphere were to enter into the political sphere, forcing governments to move from a passive 'keeping of the ring' into economic intervention and management. These movements towards a kind of 'Britain incorporated' were essentially the consequences of developments in class structure, but the form they took, and particularly the part played in them by an organized working class, was conditioned by those developments in the status of citizenship which T. H. Marshall has analysed[5] —the civil right to free association, out of which the trade unions were built, and political enfranchisement, which gave the Labour party its opportunity.

Class conflict and political consensus

These interconnected industrial and political movements were, to be sure, class and collectivist organizations. But, much more so

The rise of party

than their counterparts in the continental countries, their character was outstandingly individualistic and social democratic in their commitment to the idea that opposition and dissent were not merely tolerable but essential to a progressive society. Part of the explanation lies in the strong historical link between the period of religious cleavage and that of class cleavage in British politics. In its secular effect, organized religion is usually and properly seen as primarily an apparatus of social control. The 'heart of a heartless world' as Marx acknowledged, but also, then a striking phrase if now a cliché, 'the opiate of the people'.[6] In industrial Britain, the nonconformist chapels were the bearers not only of religiosity but also of a radicalism which schooled more than one generation of activists. Even the Church of England nurtured its socialists—men like R. H. Tawney, or Archbishop Temple, whose conception of the social order began with the morality of the New Testament, and who saw capitalism not simply as unchristian, but antichristian in that it converted economic means into overriding ends and thus introduced the worship of false gods. I remember as a child in the 1930s intoning the Magnificat at evensong in a Northamptonshire church—'He hath put down the mighty from their seat and hath exalted the humble and meek.' And I vaguely assumed that the archaic language of my elders had led them to essential truth but with wrong tenses, just as they appeared also to be confused as to the geographical location of Jerusalem.[7]

At all events, the religiously moulded inheritance of native radicalism of the early years of this century was responsible and respectable. It was a radicalism that accepted many traditional and middle-class values, not a radicalism of class warfare. It was therefore less terrifying to the dominant classes, making their resistance to the spread of political suffrage weaker and encouraging the political wing of the ruling class to stay as far as possible out of the battle between capital and labour in the work place—a policy in any case enjoined by nineteenth-century liberal theories of economics and politics. It gave working-class leaders to the twentieth century who, though tenaciously defensive of union interests in dealing with owners and managers, were anti-Marxist, non-revolutionary, pragmatic, and piecemeal in their reformist intentions.

At least until the 1960s there was a marked asymmetry in the class relations of economics and politics in Britain—the one characterized by low and the other by high relations of trust. This asymmetry was formed out of a long history. Relations in the work place in industrial Britain reflected liberal doctrines of the market, defining labour as a commodity. The 'laws of market economics' provided an external 'scientific' substitute for ethical principles in the division of the fruits and declared that private charity rather than the employer was responsible for the mitigation of hardship, with the state as the ultimate but minimal provider when neither charity nor self-help prevented destitution. In the work place itself, the working class accepted the definitions imposed upon it by its economic masters. Collective bargaining resulted between employers enforcing a commodity conception of labour and a largely alienated work-force conditioned by the system into a zero-sum game conception of management/worker relations. As Alan Fox puts it: 'So far as work relations were concerned, the classes existed alongside each other, self-contained and independent; mutually alienated; the one seeking to protect itself against the superior power of the other by means of a process of low-trust bargaining.'[8]

Fox chooses his words carefully. He uses the phrase 'existed alongside', rather than 'confronted', because working-class independence ran only along certain dimensions of class relations. It was not an independence grounded in any generalized conception of class war in the Marxist sense.

Indeed it could be argued that the working-class independence that expressed itself through Trade Unionism, collective bargaining, and the sub-culture which celebrated solidarity and collectivism, was only conceded legal status and . . . social acceptance by the more powerful groups in society because working-class independence showed clear signs of limiting itself to relatively marginal challenges of a bread-and-butter kind at the work place.[9]

Political relations were able to rest more directly on social bonds outside the work place that were strongly antithetical to doctrines of class struggle. That is why it can be reasonably argued that the norms of political attitudes were ones of high trust by contrast with the established and enduring low-trust industrial relations.

Paradoxically, the General Strike of 1926, which may reasonably be described as a moment of tense confrontation between

the two main classes, also provided unmistakable evidence of a
consensual political culture. The stories of good humour and fair
play between strikers and soldiers have since taken their place
in national mythology. I am not thinking of those, but rather of
the exchanges in the House of Commons and in Downing Street
before and after the event between the Conservative Prime Minister, Stanley Baldwin, and the Labour members. The year before
the strike, two Tories (one a Conservative trade unionist) put
down a Private Members' Bill to end the political contribution to
the Labour party from trade union dues. The Bill would probably
have succeeded, but Baldwin opposed it. After discoursing on the
growing power of the organized employers and organized workers, and on the tradition of letting Englishmen develop their own
associations in their own way, he went on as follows:

We find ourselves, after these two years in power, in possession of the
greatest majority our party ever had . . . because, rightly, or wrongly,
we succeeded in creating the impression that we stood for stable Government and for peace in the country between all classes of the community
. . . I want my party today to make a gesture to the country . . . and to
say to them: We have our majority; we believe in the justice of this Bill
. . . but we are going to withdraw our hand; we are not going to push our
political advantage home. Although I know that there are those who
work for different ends from most of us in this House, yet there are many
in all ranks and in all parties who will re-echo my prayer: 'Give Peace in
our time, O Lord.'[10]

Fourteen years later David Kirkwood, described by G. M. Young
as 'once the firebrand of Clydeside', wrote a letter to Baldwin
remarking on the change in attitudes between 1914 and 1938. In it
he said 'it seemed to me . . . that in your speech you made flesh
the feelings of us all, that the antagonism, the bitterness, the class
rivalry, were unworthy, and that understanding and amity were
possible'.[11]

We are listening here to two characteristic voices of British
politics even after the organized working class had become the
major opposition party. Disraeli's one-nation Toryism and
social-democratic Labour were those two voices. The hard heads
of right and left poured scorn on them then, and still do today. It

is easy to dismiss them as rhetorical sentimentalists. It is wiser perhaps to recognize that the creation of universal suffrage, and all the apparatus of industrial bargaining and conciliation, also entailed the creation of vested interests in them for both classes.

The deferential British worker?

Alternatively, these British political peculiarities have been explained by the thesis of a deferential working class. On this there is a large literature.[12] The point of departure of the thesis is that, extension of the suffrage notwithstanding, a country with a hugely preponderant proletarian electorate has returned more Conservative than Labour governments. Even if we start from ·1918, so as to ignore the early period of Labour party formation and the still restricted male franchise, the party of the working class has held office for only twenty of the subsequent sixty-eight years to 1986.

This comparative electoral failure cannot be explained away by denying the proposition that Labour has been the working-class party. The Communist party has never attracted more than a fraction of 1 per cent of votes,[13] and the decline of the Liberals after their split in 1916 took more Liberal voters into the Conservative than into the Labour camp. Between the Wars the class base of the Labour party took a long time to establish. Consolidation came only with the Second World War when there was a profound national shift of political outlook which led to the Labour landslide of 1945. The share of the vote at general elections taken by Labour is shown in Figure 4.2. Even so, the capture of the working class as a potentially overwhelming political force was never complete. Labour electoral support levelled off after the Second World War to leave the two main parties in fine balance.

Between the Wars, the Labour party increasingly attracted the loyalties of working men and their wives, partly at the expense of the Liberals and the Conservatives, but most of all among those families with no history of party allegiance. Nevertheless, a large residue of cross-voting, that is, voting for the party of the other class, remained, and it is at this point that interest in the Tory-voting worker becomes salient. As Butler and Stokes put it, there was

The rise of party

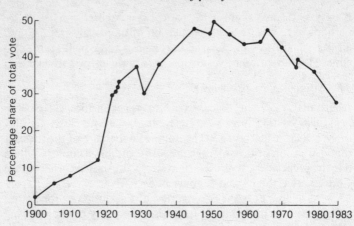

Figure 4.2 Labour's share of the vote 1900–1983

one grand historical paradox: the first major nation of the world to become industrialized, a nation in which 70 per cent of the people regard themselves as working-class, has regularly returned Conservative Governments to power. Between 1886 and 1964 the Conservative Party was defeated by decisive majorities only twice—in 1906 and 1945. Such a record could only have been achieved through heavy 'defection' to the Conservatives among the industrial working class . . . the working-class elector was likelier than the middle-class elector to support the party of the opposite class.[14]

This is true, at least on a generous definition of the working class—and incidentally crucial for the survival of the Conservative party in the period we are discussing. In 1970, the Conservatives took 45 per cent of their votes from manual workers. Nevertheless, it is also true, and no less important, that in that same year the manual-worker vote was split between Labour and Conservative 64 per cent to 36 per cent. At first glance, these figures appear to contradict one another—the one showing Conservative success in attracting nearly half of its votes from manual workers, and the other showing that nearly two-thirds of manual workers voted for their natural party. They are, in fact, the same figures put in two different ways as answers to two different questions. If we ask where parties *got* their votes, we find that the Tories got 45 per cent of them from the working class. But if we ask where the classes *sent* their votes, we find that only 36 per cent of the working class sent them to the Tories. The difference is due simply to the fact that the working class was still, at that time, larger than the middle class.

The slow growth and limited success of the Labour party as the political organization of the working class was therefore to be explained partly by its relatively late start, partly by the inevitably slow process of building up loyalty as parents passed on their party commitment to their children, and partly from the brilliant ingenuity of the Conservative party in rebutting the twentieth-century assumption that political parties should be seen solely in terms of class interest. It is the success of the Conservatives in combating this one-dimensional view of politics, and the corresponding failure of Labour to maximize its appeal to class that accounts for British electoral history, not the deferential working-class Tory voter. Such voters are, of course, to be found: and those manual workers who vote Conservative are more likely to be strong supporters of the monarchy than are their workmates who vote Labour. But before the inference is accepted that the working-class Tory vote is deferential, we must also notice that more than half of the working-class *Labour* voters are royalists, and that monarchist sentiment is more common among the Labour-voting working class than among the Labour-voting middle class.

We are dealing here, to be sure, with only one indicator of what writers have in mind in defining deferential voting: but weighing all the evidence we are forced back to Walter Bagehot's judgement that the English *as a nation* are deferential. We have no need to ascribe these attributes exclusively to the Tory working class.

Why did Labour lose?

The incomplete but steady consolidation of class loyalties to a two-party division of society continued for half a century. But this description fits only half of the graph of Labour's share of the vote (Figure 4.2). The complete graph is an inverted U-curve. Labour dropped its share of the vote in the 1979 election, and Mrs Thatcher's Conservatives turned a defeat into a disaster for Labour in 1983 when a further dramatic decline of Labour support reduced its share of the vote to 27.6 per cent, with 42.4 per cent going to the Conservatives and 25.4 per cent to the new SDP/Liberal Alliance. The question therefore arises as to whether the old political mould is broken or, in terms of our concerns in this book, whether the class base of British politics has come to an end involving the collapse of the political organization of the working class.

The answer is no. The analysis of the 1983 election by Dr Anthony Heath and his associates[15] rebuts the theory that politics has become detached from the traditional stratification of British society. Admittedly class loyalties have been attenuated: middle-class Conservative voters plus working-class Labour voters fell as a proportion of all voters from 67 per cent in the 1951 election to 47 per cent in 1983. But within this framework of attenuating class loyalty the differences between occupational classes in their alignment with the parties have remained stable. The odds of middle-class electors voting Tory compared with the odds of a manual worker voting Labour (i.e. the odds ratio) have changed little. The odds ratio was 4.8 in 1945, 6.1 in 1959, 4.5 in 1970, 3.7 in 1979, and 3.9 in 1983. There has been, in short, trendless fluctuation and certainly not a de-alignment of politics from class.

The really significant change therefore has been not so much the political propensity of the classes as a change in the class structure itself. As Dr Heath puts it 'in focussing on class de-alignment, political scientists have concentrated on a minor re-arrangement of the furniture while failing to notice a major change in the structure of the house'.[16] In the 1960s, 1970s, and 1980s, Britain has been moving strongly from a blue-collar to a white-collar society. I drew attention to this transformation in Chapter 2. On Heath's class schema, whereas in 1964 the working class was nearly three times the size of what he terms the dominant class (our middle-class professional and managerial groups, and Dahrendorf's or Goldthorpe's 'service class') and constituted nearly half the electorate, in 1983 these two classes were of almost equal size. The dominant class had grown from 18 per cent of the electorate in 1964 to 29 per cent in 1983 while the working-class proportion had dropped from 47 to 31 per cent. Heath also distinguishes three intermediate classes—routine non-manual (22 per cent in 1983), petty bourgeois (8 per cent), and foremen and technicians (10 per cent).

Incidentally, the advantage of this five-class model over the Marxist two-class model, which I criticized in earlier chapters, become crucial in this question of interpreting the emerging relation of class to politics. The two-class model (paradoxically in the light of its historical and ideological origins) yields an impression of a much looser relation between class position and party preference than is warranted in reality. Using the five-class schema, Heath is able to show much more precisely the middle-class character of the Conservative and the Alliance parties (the former most solidly based in the petty bourgeoisie), and the working-class base of the Labour party. The organization of British politics along class lines is actually obscured by the historically outmoded two-class model.

To be sure, the declining electoral fortunes of the Labour party are not wholly attributable to changes in (a more elaborately conceived) class structure. There have been short- and long-run changes in the organization of the parties, their ideological outlook, and the subjective values of the nation as a whole. For example, while left-wing militancy has captured some constituency parties and trade unions, popular views on nationalization and privatization have moved significantly to the right in all classes, and hostility to the bureaucratic apparatus of the state has grown in post-war experience. The Falklands episode of 1982 demonstrated a deeply entrenched nationalism (which supports Mrs Thatcher) and possibly reflected a resentment of lost imperial glory which is felt in different ways among widely different class and status groups. And the defection of prominent middle-class Labour leaders and supporters to the SDP was a serious blow to the electoral effectiveness of the Labour party. Nevertheless the class basis of politics remains central to the understanding of the parties. The Conservative party as well as the Labour party has become a less successful class party in the sense of retaining as high a proportion of the voters of its natural class supporters. The Conservative heartland has, however, waxed while the Labour heartland of industrial manual workers has waned.

Prosperity

In any case, political action is responsive to the quality as well as the quantities of class relations. From this point of view the periods before and after 1979 may now be seen as involving opposite tendencies. Discussing the earlier period in Chapter 2, I was at pains to juxtapose two contradictory features of British economic development—the persistence of inequality, and the growth of affluence. Affluence has unquestionably made the stronger impact on popular political perceptions. Post-war prosperity, continuing into the 1970s, gradually established expectations of annual increments of income and welfare, with the political parties increasingly seen less as class organizations than as competing instrumentalities—a competition, incidentally, in which Macmillan was at least as adept as Gaitskell in the eyes of ordinary voters. And intellectual fashion supported popular opinion. There was, in the 1950s, a confirmed confidence in Keynesian economic management. Full employment seemed to be assured by it, and bitter memories of the slump years could be dismissed as irrelevant relics of a banished society.

Indeed in the pink glow of 'Butskellism', and the politics of the centre ground, inequality was difficult to discern. The traditional call to uneasy conscience from the survey traditions of Booth and Rowntree seemed to have ended with the last short book published by Rowntree in 1951.[17] This told us that the percentage of the working class who were in poverty, which had been nearly one-third in 1936, was now reduced in 1950 to less than 3 per cent. And the triumph was attributable to Keynesian full employment. Poverty was no longer a class phenomenon. Indeed it was widely regarded as no phenomenon at all, and had to be rediscovered in the 1960s.

Ironically, in those years Labour party intellectuals, even at a time when the class alignment of voting had gone as far as it ever did, became more than half convinced that the social base of their party support was being eroded by embourgeoisment—the assimilation of the working class into the life and manners of the middle class. The famous study of Luton workers by a group of Cambridge dons[18] dealt severely with this doctrine and called instead for a new and determined political leadership of the Labour party. The Cambridge dons got no response from the Labour leaders, but meanwhile the 1964 election left no one prepared to argue further the crude form of the embourgeoisment thesis with them. In retrospect, what was most telling in Goldthorpe and Lockwood's study was the identification of *privatization* among the relatively prosperous new working class, and of *instrumentalism* in the work place among employees of all classes. Affluent workers were becoming more privatized in that they sought the good life more at home with their wives and families than at work or in the traditional male organizations of the pub and club. And all employees were becoming instrumental in that they increasingly regarded unions, politics, and work not as ends in themselves but as means to private ends. The Royal College of Nursing increased its membership by 38 per cent between 1979 and 1982. The unionization of white-collar employees is the story of a principle treasured by the working class—collectivism—disseminated to other classes, but at the same time made instrumental. In the process the trade unions began to lose their class character, if not their class rhetoric. Even the Association of First Division Civil Servants is now affiliated to the TUC.

Incorporation of working-class leaders

Where embourgeoisment *had* taken place was not in the rank and file, but among the political leaders of the organized working class. The social composition of the Labour benches and cabinets had undergone a striking transformation. Between the Wars 72 per cent of Labour MPs came from rank-and-file employment, and 15 per cent were university graduates. By 1945 only half came from the working class, and by 1970 only one-quarter, by which time the proportion of graduates had risen to more than half. Among cabinet ministers the trend was even more striking. In MacDonald's 1924 cabinet, 30 per cent were graduates. In 1969, under Wilson, the graduates made up 83 per cent.

These changes in the social antecedents of Labour leaders do not, of course, demonstrate subversion of working-class interest. It is what people do, not where they come from, on which that question has to be settled. What the statistics do indicate, however, is a gradual change in the image presented to the electorate. In the case of Labour politicians, that image never was and never became exclusively proletarian, whether revolutionary or gradualist. In a more literal sense, the television image further emphasizes the common social personalities of Labour and Conservative party leaders. They both have their extremist wings—a hard Marxist left and a hard racist right—each playing off the other, amplified by the media. The SDP and the Liberal party complicate the stage with further claims to recognition as the moderate political solution. Television is *par excellence* the centre ground over which the parties squabble, and they do so decorously, reinforcing an indistinguishable impression of alternative teams of natural governors.

In parallel with these developments, participation in local Labour parties has become pathetically weak. Since 1952 the individual membership of the Labour party has fallen continuously. It had risen to a peak of over one million in 1950. But by 1976 it had declined, even on official returns, to two-thirds of that figure, and on other estimates was as low as a quarter of a million.[19] On the basis of individual party membership per hundred party voters, Labour is now numerically among the smallest socialist parties in Western Europe.[20] In short, the increasing incorporation of the Labour party at the national centre of power has been accompanied by a spectacular decline of participation by members in local organizations.

On the other hand, the rise of locally based direct-action groups is also a marked feature of the 1960s and 1970s. They were, at least in part, a response to the alienation of leaders from members in organizations of massive scale. In the work place, these forces contributed to the increasing power of shop stewards. In consequence, the capacity of the TUC to maintain agreements with Labour or Conservative Chancellors was undermined. Control over the membership by the union leaders, who represented them in the corporatist negotiations with government, was just as uncertain as is that of the CBI over its 12,000 member companies and 200 trade and employer associations. Wages and even local plant management were more and more determined on the local shop-floor, and not by conversations in Westminster. This is one powerful reason why observers like Alan Fox refused to accept fashionable warnings of the imminent coming of a British corporate state. The continuance of low-trust relations in the direct dealings of shop stewards and plant managers is the principal manifestation of the class struggle. What Fox describes as 'arms-length contractual bargaining' is deeply ingrained: on the one hand, it is a defence against corporatism; on the other hand, it holds little prospect for industrial democracy because such a development requires managers and employees to pursue efficiency together in something other than a zero-sum game.

Thatcherism and opposition

In its first six years Thatcherism has not fundamentally changed the pattern of organizations or 'party', though it has given renewed emphasis to their class character. The 1978 'winter of discontent' excited widespread popular antipathy towards the power of the unions, exposed the weakness of the Labour party in relation to them, and provided electoral support for Mrs Thatcher's new Conservatives as well as for the subsequent anti-union legislation. The rolling back of the organizational frontier of the state has also failed to show dramatic results. But the effort has again reinforced class antagonisms. The policies of monetary control to combat inflation and 'non-interference' to promote market efficiency have led to declining national standards of living, mass unemployment, impoverished public services and civic amenities, and increasing inequality. While dole queues lengthened and bankruptcies were commonplace, it was announced in 1985 that the chairmen of Imperial Chemical Industries and British Petroleum had had their salaries increased to £287,261 and £241,547 p.a. respectively. Thus does the market distribute its rewards.

Such news together with the experience of an extended and, in the end, bitterly futile miners' strike had begun by 1985 to affect popular opinion. The polls of March 1985 gave Labour a six-point lead over the Conservatives (38 per cent against 32 per cent), with the Alliance in third place and commanding one-quarter of the intended vote. Nevertheless organization in Westminster and Whitehall, as distinct from opinion, still heavily favours the new Conservatism, and opposition, at least up to 1985, came as effectively, or ineffectively, from traditional Tories (the 'Wets') and from the Church of England bishops as from Her Majesty's Opposition in the House of Commons. We shall return to these issues in Chapter 8.

Conclusion

Meanwhile, to sum up three-quarters of a century of organizational development: we have witnessed the massive development of working-class political and industrial combination, and a parallel response by the dominant classes through the Conservative party and the employers' associations. In this sense, we have seen the rise of party; and between them they have created a vast proliferation of the organs of state. We have also seen the rise of a host of sectional interest groups about which I have said little. As a whole, these developments amount to an organizational revolution. But it has been no revolution in the Marxist sense. Certainly the working class became consciously organized, industrially and politically, in the first two decades of the century, and certainly some of its members envisaged social ends inspired by the Russian Revolution. After the First World War, many poor families who had voted Tory when first admitted to the franchise, were drawn not to Liberal but to Labour allegiance. Older men might grumble that before the War there was, as one put it, 'very little o' that clap-trap about profit an' t' bosses an' Socialism an' there being no God . . . Now everyon's at it.'[21] Fellow-travelling was fashionable in small intellectual circles,[22] and the Webbs thought of Russia as a new civilization.[23] But no serious Leninist vanguard movement ever emerged. Class struggle was muted and fragmented.

The main consequence of the rise of the working-class party was national incorporation of its leaders—a development as unanticipated by its pioneers as it was intended by the liberal-minded elements of the upper and middle classes. Over the following half century, a new Establishment was welded together and supported by the vested interests not only of the traditionally powerful, but also of the new men of power who now also stood to lose by any departure into radical adventures from the established framework of industrial bargaining and parliamentary procedure. And these convergent interests always had popular support. Class was never the sole dimension of life as subjectively experienced by ordinary people. It had its place in politics and the Labour party came to occupy that place: but it was limited by rising affluence and mobility, and by localism as well as nationalism—both entrenched sentiments which enabled Conservatives to hang on to a vital segment of votes across the class divide. 'My country Right or Left' was not only Orwell's instinct in the early days of the Second World War: it was also a national disposition.

Yet organizational decay was eventually the price that had to be paid for incorporation. The Labour leaders who set out to conquer national politics could not have anticipated either their metropolitan success, or their later provincial failure. Local Labour parties now are even more deserted than the chapels to which they owed so much of their early education. The mass membership is alienated and inert.

After the Second World War there was a gradual consolidation of trade union strength under conditions of full employment. The market continued to be the regulator of both political and industrial relations until the mid-sixties. Since then, economic stagnation and inflation have together created a new situation which we can describe as the spread of politics into the economy. Even the revival of liberal doctrines by a Conservative government pursuing monetarist policies in the 1980s has to be seen in the same terms. Unions have become more militant and extended their organization far beyond the industrial proletariat. The state has become less parliamentary and more the centre of attempts to incorporate and pacify competing economic interests—all of whom are recalcitrant corporatists. And localized conflict is rife. The old struggles have shifted back to the work place and the locality where they began, and where horizons are narrowest and objectives most limited and sectional.

Since 1979, the shop-steward movement has been weakened by economic recession and unemployment, and the national union leadership has been excluded from political decision-making. Thatcherism has supported these movements with explicit ideology and through monetary and fiscal policies which have sharpened conflict between classes, created new inequalities between regions, and divided the employed against the unemployed. The balance of power between organized capital and organized labour has re-emerged at the centre of political dispute after a long period of compromise and consensus between class interests.

5

Between the generations

Whether or not a society changes its structure, the ineluctable fact of mortality dictates that it must change its members. So in this and the next chapter we are concerned with social reproduction, with people rather than institutions, incumbents rather than roles, agent rather than structures. How do individuals come to be fitted into institutions? How does a society reproduce itself? To answer these questions, I shall deal in this chapter with kinship and in Chapter 6 with mobility and education.

Again, however, the discussion is based on the analysis in earlier chapters of the changing structure of class, status, and party. We may begin with a maxim from the liberal school of sociology.

'What the few have today the many will demand tomorrow.' That is Professor Daniel Bell's summary of the social history of industrial society.[1] Michael (now Lord) Young and Peter Willmott have called it the principle of stratified diffusion and turned it into a metaphor. They picture successive ranks of families in Britain drawn up in a column of social class, but a column on the march. 'The last rank keeps its distance from the first and the distance between them does not lessen. But as the column advances, the last rank does eventually reach and pass the point which the first rank passed some time before.'[2]

With this metaphor in mind, let us look back for a moment to the beginning of the century. Here is G. M. Young remembering the coronation year of 1902,[3] when he was an Oxford undergraduate:

We looked forward to living, with some improvements, the sort of life our fathers had lived. By *we* I do not mean the wealthy classes but the sort of people who filled the public schools and the two ancient universities, not rich, but comfortably off, who took games, books, and hospitality for granted: sons of lawyers, civil servants, MPs: young men who might succeed to their father's share in some old family business, or seek an outlet for their energies in India, or the Sudan, with Cromer for their ideal, and Milner for their example. It was an attractive life, I think we might say the most attractive that European civilization had ever fashioned for itself, and the prospect of living that life and transmitting it to our sons and daughters was an incentive, I should judge, more powerful than any quest for wealth or power. In a word, and it was a word often spoken in those days, England was a very good country for gentlemen. And it all rested on two things—an income tax so moderate that it was hardly felt: and an unlimited supply of cheap and efficient domestic service. Pull those pillars down, and that social hierarchy topples. That also we could not foresee.

That was the England of G. M. Young's youth. But at the same time, some two hundred miles further north in the same country, Robert Roberts was growing up in industrial working-class England, and tells of how his elders told him

of a man with a large family struggling to keep his sick father with them. At last the old man insisted he should be taken to the workhouse. They set off, the wife picking up his few belongings, and the father on his son's back. *En route* they stopped to rest a while on a stone seat. 'It was here', said the old man, 'I rested, too, carrying my father to the workhouse.' The son rose, took the burden on his back again and turned with his wife for home. 'We'll manage somehow', he said.[4]

Here, then, are the vanguard and rearguard of the extended column of class in Edwardian Britain. There was much for future generations to demand.

Significance of the family

My theme in this chapter is the relation between the generations: and my focus is on the primordial link between them—the family. The nuclear family of parents and dependent children is the basic ascriptive unit of society. But it is much more. It is the reproductive social cell of class, of status, and of culture. If, therefore, we examine its history, we should see from another angle the continuities and changes of social structure in Britain in the period covered by our collective memory. We can map the journey of the advancing column. That we shall find significant differences in the substance and meaning of family life between now and three generations ago is already implicit in my account of the transformations of class, status, and party. The question now is how the pressures of these macroscopic social forces have modified the shape and process of the microcosm of their reproduction.

But before setting out to follow the trail of biological, social, and cultural reproduction, let us recognize the strange character of intellectual discussion of a subject so thoroughly known, so commonplace, so deeply and comprehensively learnt by everyone. The very word 'familiar' is used to denote what everybody knows. Can there then possibly be anything to add? I think so: and this is because we can have recourse to macroscopic information and to history—both necessary additions to the idiosyncratic experience on which personal knowledge is based.

I should also remark on the passion that lies between personal knowledge and scholarship on the family—a vast literature of ideology. The family is both eulogized and vilified down the ages. Its immense power over the shaping of minds is constantly rediscovered. Confucius of the Analects tell us that: 'Those who in private life behave well towards their parents and elder brothers, in public life seldom show disposition to resist the authority of their superiors. And as for such men starting a revolution, no instance of it has ever occurred.'[5] Resentment of that power was vehemently expressed by Sir Edmund Leach in his Reith Lectures: 'Far from being the basis of the good society, the family with its narrow privacy and tawdry secrets, is the source of all discontents.'[6] There is no lack either of celebration of its beneficence. Here is Eleanor Rathbone in 1924:

Yet when we are considering society from any other point of view than the economic, we can all see well enough that, of all its institutions, the family is after all the institution that matters most. It is at once indispensable as a means to all the rest and, in a sense, an end in itself . . . the strongest emotions, the most enduring motives, the most universally accessible sources of happiness are concerned with this business of the family.[9]

Demographic transition in Europe

So if we retreat awhile to the calmer and more arid regions of demography, it is to gain the light of factual perspective rather than to escape the heat of fierce engagement. Demographers have evolved the quaint custom of comparing fertility rates with the even quainter customs of the Hutterites—a flourishing community of agrarian fundamentalists in North Dakota. Demographers have chosen these people because they have the highest known levels of what is termed 'natural fertility', that is that fertility which is not affected by fertility-reducing social practices which are themselves dependent on the number of children already born. They have no deliberate birth control within marriage. On average, their families have over ten children. Against the Hutterite yardstick, Britain and Europe have low reproductivity. Even in the 1870s, before the onset of widespread fertility control, Britain recorded little more than one-third of the Hutterite rate. By 1931 fertility had plunged still further, by more than half of the 1871 level in England and Wales, and slightly less than half in Scotland.[8]

But we must not rely on the Hutterite yardstick (which in any case has shown signs of instability since mid-century). A more general measure is the *total fertility rate* (TFR), i.e. the number of live-born children a woman would have if she survived to the end of her child-bearing period and had children at the rate specific to her age-group and period. In other words, TFR measures what completed family size would be if current patterns of fertility continued from a particular point of time. In the 1870s the TFR for all women was 4.8, and for married women only was about 6. By 1931–5 the TFR was at its lowest point in history (until the 1980s) at 1.78 for England and Wales.

This remarkable demographic transition is not peculiar to Britain. British reproductive history is not specially remarkable by comparison with other European countries, except that it might have been expected that the first industrial country would have been the first to experience it, whereas in fact the transition came nearly a century later than in France. It is also worth noting that, within Great Britain, there has been more similarity of experience between regions, apart from Scotland, compared with the variability within countries like Germany, Belgium, or Spain. Over the centuries British fertility and mortality have both been relatively moderate by comparison with countries on the European continent.

Consequences of demographic change

The demographic transition in Europe had three stages. In the pre-industrial stage a slowly growing population was maintained by a balance of high death-rates and high birth-rates. In the second stage of early industrialism extending well into the nineteenth century, fertility habits remained from the first stage, while a growing array of life-preserving practices reduced mortality. Then in Stage III, fertility declined at a rate which overtook the still-falling mortality rate until a new population equilibrium was reached by a balance of low birth-rates and low death-rates.

This simplified description, leaving out migrations and variations, though it roughly fits the facts and places our period in Stage III, is useful more for the questions it raises than for those it answers. Above all, it invites attention to changes in the place of the family in society, both causal and consequential. It has become clear from modern demographic research that the population history of England up to 1800 was pretty much as Malthus described it. Population growth was held back largely through the 'preventive check' of delayed marriage which was in turn a response to movements in prices and wages.[9] Rates of growth fluctuated more through fertility than mortality. Accordingly it would be difficult to overemphasize the importance of the West European pattern of relatively late and avoidable marriage which was particularly strongly developed in England. This pattern, which still to some extent persists, created a uniquely low-pressure demographic regime in Western Europe.[10] There is, however, at least one modification to the simple description which must be added in order to bring experience since the Second World War into view. There was a fertility upturn after the War, followed by a downturn in the 1950s, and a longer birth-rate bulge in the 1960s. Stage III does, nevertheless, seem to be real. Births in England and Wales in 1983 totalled 530,000, giving a TFR of 1.76—the lowest of the century except for 1977.

Fertility in the twentieth century has shown unprecedented volatility. Fluctuations have occurred not only because of the traditional variations in rates of marriage but also because of the advent of virtually complete contraception within marriage. The volatility in question is primarily due to changes in the timing and spacing of births rather than to changes in intended sizes of family. Yet they have had dramatic effects on the size of successive birth cohorts—the variation in the birth-rate has been as much as 20 or 30 per cent in less than a decade. The difficulties of planning the number of school places, for example, have been consequentially increased in Western Europe.[11] Demographically Britain belongs closely to this group of countries which in the second half of the twentieth century have converged in their levels of fertility, marriage, divorce, mortality, and even in their demographic fluctuations.

The consequence of the Victorian population explosion are an important part of the social heritage of twentieth-century Britain. They include the growth of industrial cities at home,[12] and the global sweep of what might aptly be termed 'white peril' abroad, colonizing continents. Together foreign domination and domestic urbanization created an unprecedented empire within which the reminiscences of G. M. Young in Oxford and of the working man in Manchester combine to illustrate the comment that, if it was an empire on which the sun never set, there were parts of its heartland on which the sun never rose.

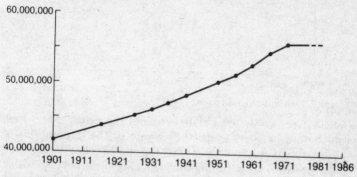

Figure 5.1 United Kingdom population 1901–1986

The birth-rate, when our period opens, was still very high by today's European, if not by Hutterite, standards. In 1900 one-quarter of the married women were in childbirth every year. Yet thirty years later that proportion was down by one-half to one in eight. The earlier history of Stage III of the industrial demographic cycle need not concern us, though it continues to attract careful scholarship to its still unsolved problems.[13] One thing, however, is clear. For whatever reasons, the head of our metaphorical column had long since taken a decisive turn towards the ideal of the small family. And among the whys and hows of this movement towards what Young and Willmott describe as the symmetrical family, there was a fall in infant mortality after 1905 (Figure 5.2), especially among professional and middle-class families, which set conditions for subsequent generations that have enabled us to think of the twentieth century as 'the century of the child'.

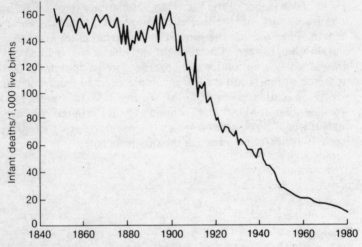

Figure 5.2 Infant mortality 1846–1981

It may be, as Sir John Habakkuk has suggested, that it took time before people became fully aware of the implications of lower levels of child mortality, that the middle classes did so first, and responded by planning and reducing their fertility within marriage. Working-class men and women followed more slowly. When child mortality had been high, it was both more difficult for married couples to predict the size of their surviving family, and less urgent for them to do so. But it must be acknowledged that the problem of explaining fertility decline in the modern period is an extremely complex one. It is certainly no single conse-quence of reduced mortality. A full explanation has to take into account the vast transformation of relations between men, women, and children which has accompanied the development of industrial society. These changes include those in the economics of reproduction—for example the declining market for child labour, the Factory Acts, and the gradual introduction of com-pulsory and extended schooling—and the rise of professions and administrative careers recruited by public examination. All these forces weighed in the balance of the decision to have children among couples of different class and status positions. Moreover, the quality of gender relations was itself changed with the increasingly secular definition of means and ends and the decline of religious observance.

Falling fertility during the first three decades of the century may be thought of, then, first as an adaptation to these changes of circumstances and attitudes including a continuing fall of child mortality: people wanted, and were increasingly able, to control procreation according to their notion of a desirable style of life. But second, following the principle of stratified diffusion, we must notice that the course of reproduction in the twentieth century has arrested the inverse relation of social class and fertility which had been inherited by Edwardian Britain as a feature of the demographic transition we have discussed. At that time, social distribution of the reproductive burden operated on the exact, if lunatic, principle of largest load on weakest back. In the following thirty years, the working class moved towards the earlier middle-class fertility norms. Those at the rear (or at any rate, towards the rear) of the historically marching column of social ranks aspired to catch up with those ahead of them; and this they were able to do at roughly a ten-year distance. Class differences in fertility began slowly to be reduced: so that, in this sense, the stratified diffusion metaphor has to be modified—the tail was closing up on the head of the queue, the queue was beginning to re-form into an advancing line abreast.

Could this very different principle of progress be fully realized? Perhaps not, for there was yet another change of direction among the social leaders in the 1940s and 1950s. They changed course towards larger families, while manual workers and their wives continued along the old path.[14] Thus we find Habakkuk in 1968 asking 'May it not be that the middle classes who in the 1870s led the country into the fashion of small families, are now leading us back to big families?'[15] He doubted whether the steps would be retraced very far, and the evidence of later years has justified his doubt, and there has been an important consequence. The fertility of those who have married since 1965, when projected to estimate completed family size, comes to 2.06 children for the average wife which is just below the so-called 'replacement' figure of 2.1, and just above the completed family size of the lowest point of fertility reached by those who married around 1930. The demographic transition to an equilibrium of low fertility and low mortality may at last be complete.

Nevertheless, there remain two unresolved questions for demographers. One is whether there is any naturally stable level of fertility appropriate to an industrial society like Britain where children have negative economic value. Since 1973 all Western European countries (except Ireland and Iceland) have dropped and stayed below replacement fertility. Their total fertility rates are 1.7 or 1.8, not the replacement level of 2.1. The renegotiation of sexual relations which is so central a feature of contemporary society has the possibility of long-run population decline as one of its outcomes.

The other question is that of the future relation of class or family income to fertility. There is now the prospect of the elimination or even the reversal of the inverse relation between class and fertility which began in the middle of the nineteenth century. There is, in other words, a possible future in which births are distributed between families in roughly the same way as income. One view insists that the natural relation between income and fertility is a positive one and that the U-shaped pattern of class and fertility which was shown to exist in the 1971 Census is caused by incompetent family planning among the poorer and less well educated—a feature of reproduction which may be expected to diminish. Trends in fertility by class or income in both Britain and the United States tend to support this view. Some evidence for Britain in the decade up to 1983 is given in Table 5.1.

Table 5.1   Fertility (legitimate) and social class in England and Wales

Year	Total births (000)	Social class					
		I&II	IIIN	IIIM	IV&V	I&II total (%)	I&II total (%) for women aged 30 +
1973	618	148	65	247	131	24	33
1977	514	142	53	193	106	28	41
1980	579	164	62	212	120	28	43
1982	536	159	58	190	109	30	44
1983	530	156	57	188	108	29	45

Source: Birth Statistics 1983, HMSO, 1985.

Table 5.1 (*cont.*)

Expected births to women born	Non-manual	Manual
1950–4	2.03	2.18
1955–9	2.24	2.12
1960–4	2.39	2.32

Source: *General Household Survey*, HMSO, 1982, Table 4.21.

Between 1973 and 1983, the overall number of legitimate births in England and Wales declined from 618,000 to 530,000, while births to the professional and managerial classes (Classes I and II) actually increased, and those to semi-skilled and unskilled workers' families decreased. The relative fertility of middle-class married women over 30 was especially high, and more markedly in the early 1980s.

Table 5.1 also contains evidence on expected legitimate fertility which lends further support to the hypothesis of a trend towards positively correlated class and fertility. The evidence must, of course, be interpreted against a background of marked retreat from marriage, a rise in pre-marital cohabitation, and a growing contribution of illegitimate to total births (16 per cent in 1983).

A summary of the transformation of family structure accompanying Stage III of the demographic transition is shown in Table 5.2.[16] The basic demographic development of the twentieth century is that the social classes have all adapted to a small family pattern. More people have gained greater freedom. Virtually all can now choose the timing of their parenthood. This is as important a feature of social change as any I could mention. And it has three further correlates, if not implications: the emancipation of women, the domestication of men, and the enrichment of childhood.

Gender relationships

The place of women in society has been transformed. In his essay on *The Origin of the Family, Private Property, and the State*, Engels confuses class with status analysis, but arrests our attention by declaring that 'the first class antagonism which appears in history coincides with the antagonism between men and women

Table 5.2   Some demographic changes over a century

Estimates of the average ages at certain vital events in England and Wales, classified according to the year of birth of the persons to whom those events occurred.

	Year of birth					
	1850	1870	1890	1910	1930	1950
First marriage						
Men	27	27	28	27	26	24
Women	26	26	26	25	24	22
Birth of first child						
Men	29	29	30	29	28	26
Women	28	28	28	27	26	24
Birth of last child						
Men	37	36	35	32	30	28
Women	36	35	33	30	28	26
Spouse's death						
Men	56	60	62	64	66	63
Women	55	58	61	63	65	67
Own death as widow or widower						
Men	75	77	79	80	81	82
Women	75	79	81	81	82	83

Source: See note 14.

in monogamous marriage, and the first class oppression with that of the female sex by the male'.[17] No one can read the history of marriage in our own time without being struck both by the material inequalities suffered by earlier generations of wives, and also by their reduction in more recent decades.

The burden of childbirth is central to the story. At the midpoint of the century, R. M. Titmuss summed it up by pointing out that, at the beginning of this century, a British woman aged 20 could expect to live 46 years longer. But approximately one-third of this life expectancy was to be devoted to child-bearing and maternal care of infants. Today a woman aged 20 can expect a further 55 years of life. Of this longer expectation only about 7 per cent of the years to be lived will be concerned with child-bearing and maternal care.[18]

But no less important than the virtual slavery of Edwardian working-class women on the wheel of child-bearing was the relation of women to the economy and the state. In the earlier decades the great majority of families depended entirely for their material support on male employment. The establishment of a new position for the mother, independent of her link to the economy through her husband, was therefore a prominent theme of feminist reform. Eleanor Rathbone is again an outstanding voice. Child-rearing, she argued, should be seen as a public service as well as a private pleasure, and the costs spread accordingly. The only practicable agent was the state, and Miss Rathbone was, in effect, arguing for an extension of the social rights of citizenship for women. The main working-class demand in her day was for a 'living wage' for men. This she attacked as a continuation of ancient male tyranny. Even if achieved, the 'living wage' was intrinsically unrelated to family size. Women should not be regarded as dependants of the male in the labour market.

A wife and children and the wherewithall to keep them, are conceded to the wage earner as though they were part of the 'comforts and decencies promotive of better habits' for which he may reasonably ask . . . But if he prefers to use the margin thus allowed him for breeding pigeons or racing dogs, or for some other form of personal gratification, instead of for keeping a family, that is assumed to be his affair, not the State's or his employer's.[19]

In the event, the state response was less than fulsome and the political descendants of Eleanor Rathbone, like Margaret Wynn,[20] or Frank Field,[21] still vigorously point out that both social security and taxation policies continue to treat families less favourably than bachelors, spinsters, and childless couples.

The state has contributed indirectly towards the liberation of women, especially through the expansion of health services and education. But the loneliness of mothers with young children is still well attested and the absence of communal provision for such women remains an unsatisfied need. Meanwhile, more direct emancipating influences have come from developed methods of birth control and, most important, the gradual movement of women, including married women, into employment. In the first two decades of this century less than 10 per cent of married women in Britain went out to work: in 1951 the percentage was 21.74: by 1966 it had risen to 38.08.[22] According to the *General Household Survey* of 1982, 58 per cent of married women aged

16–59 were employed in 1976, 25 per cent full-time and 32 per cent part-time. These upward trends continued to 1980 and then halted or partly retreated from a high point of 60 per cent (33 per cent part-time) to 57 per cent (32 per cent part-time) in 1982. The slow spread of affluence has also played its part in combination with the invention of power appliances to relieve some of the drudgery of housework. Suburbanization and geographical mobility have provided escape for some from the matrilocal matriarchies of the traditional urban working-class communities—a point which reminds us that partial women's liberation has discriminated so far in favour of younger as against older women. So we could go on through a catalogue of economic and technical changes, and their consequences, which have made possible the trend towards *The Symmetrical Family* of Young and Willmott.

The correlative history, which is rather less noticed, is that of husbands and fathers. This too is a social transformation deserving its own detailed history. It would begin with young men of the Victorian upper-middle classes moving into marriage with prejudices mitigated at least to the point of co-operating in planned parenthood. Stratified diffusion would again emerge. Later, working men returning from the First World War had to accommodate, in many cases, to wives who had acquired a more independent outlook from having worked in the munitions factories, and from having run their homes unaided. Literacy and the wireless pushed back horizons between the Wars. Unlike previous wars, the Second World War did not tip the demographic balance so sharply in favour of men: the number of men and women remained roughly in balance, the reserve army of women disappeared.

Still more important, seventy years ago, working men typically lived in local occupationally homogeneous communities, of which mining and dock work were the classic examples.[23] Such communities evolved essentially male public organizations—the pub, the betting-shop, the football club; organizations which loosened marriage bonds and took resources away from women and children. But the newer patterns of inter-war industry around London and Birmingham, in the Home Counties and the Midlands, took their toll of the older male domination—

reducing class solidarity perhaps and inviting more romantic love certainly. Particularly after the Second World War, hours of work were reduced, holidays lengthened, home ownership became more common, children were less ever-present, and men were drawn into a more intimate and longer spousehood than their predecessors had ever known. We noted in Chapter 4 that privatization was a key description of the affluent worker in Luton by the 1960s.[24] It involved a closer, more co-operative, domesticity for millions of men. Perhaps the growth of the pornographic industry and the verbal obscenities which are hurled across football stands are each in their way further correlates of the pressure on men to adopt the new familial civilities.

Quite apart from the well-documented inequalities of pay, status, and promotion opportunities for women in the labour market, the sexual division of labour in households seems to be stubbornly traditional. A national survey by the Harris Research Centre in 1984 reported that half the adult population agreed that 'the man of the house should be the main breadwinner and the woman should be mainly responsible for looking after the home and the children, even if she works'.[25] Moroever, when asked about the sharing of household chores, men thought of themselves, and women thought of their husbands, as doing considerably less than the average man, especially with respect to cooking, looking after the children, and the menial tasks of household cleaning and washing. Thus British couples have an inflated notion of the norms of sharing and/or low expectations in their own households of what domestic labour should be contributed by men. The symmetrical family, whether as an ideal or as an idea, is yet to be realized.

Nor is it the only possible end to the journey. Looking back we can say that the social column has advanced and that the working class is much less conspicuously relegated to its rearguard. Yet the new freedom is by no means costless. Divorce and separation have largely replaced death as disruptors of the early and middle years of marriage. In 1980 there were over a million people in Great Britain who had been divorced and had not remarried. We cannot, of course, weigh the cost or gauge the misery caused by marital breakdown now or at any point in the past. We can estimate roughly that one-third of contemporary marriages will

founder before reaching their twenty-fifth anniversary. We can
also agree with Young and Willmott that their symmetrical
family, since it asks more of its partners, exposes them also to
greater strain and higher risk of failure. Moreover, as Juliet
Cheetham has put it:

the possibility of controlling fertility, although usually accepted as an
unqualified blessing, brings its own problems. It challenges women to
contemplate social roles other than full-time motherhood. Acceptance
of this challenge threatens prevailing assumptions about family life and
about equality. Efforts to maintain the status quo frustrate women's
aspirations and achievements. Discontent and conflict may be necessary
preliminaries to human advancement but they are not comfortable to
live with.[26]

There are now three-quarters of a million one-parent families
with dependent children. The woman left to raise children alone
is among the most pathetic casualties of an affluent society.[27] One
child in eleven now lives with a step-parent, and one child in five
will experience the divorce of its parent by age 16. Nor has the
pattern stabilized. Even though remarriage rates are constant or
even falling, the proportion of failed marriages is such that
remarried couples will become an increasing proportion of all
marriages in the future. Step-parenting has accordingly a larger
future place in the upbringing of children.

Enrichment of childhood

None the less, the third estate of the nuclear family—the child—
has been the chief beneficiary of the developments I have
sketched. If I have to choose a single word to identify the changes
in social reproduction in this century it would be 'individualism'.
this is the motif that has increasingly informed every aspect of
child-rearing, whether in the family or in the public sphere of play
groups, clubs, schools, holiday camps, juvenile courts, or Bor-
stals. The essential background, of course, is the decline of infant
mortality and the spread of the small family. Yet this move to
smaller families, though important in itself, has to be seen as the
base and not the whole edifice of a more general trend towards
higher standards of upbringing. For example, of those children
born in the decade around the First World War only one-fifth
grew up in owner-occupied houses, though in families with, on

average, 3.4 children. Those born in the decade after the Second World War belonged to families with on average 2.1 children, and well over one-third of them were owner-occupiers.[28] Most children in the early years of the century grew up in the streets of industrial cities, while there has been a more recent move to the suburbs in council estates and private dwellings. A working-class area is not now, so much as it once was, a kind of dormitory annexe to the work place. The working-class family has become less closely geared to the factory hooter. This, combined with shorter hours of work, may well have increased the amount of attention men give to their children. On the other hand, the gradual growth of women's employment outside the home may have had an opposite effect on mother–child relations.

Children now are more likely to come from middle-class families. The working class has fallen and the middle classes have risen as suppliers of children. Before the First World War more than two-thirds were of working-class origin. Moreover, even within the working class, the chances of being born into the home of a skilled rather than an unskilled worker, and into a smaller rather than a larger family, with rather higher income and rather better housing, gradually improved for those born later in the century. The norm shifted, in other words, from the description given by Richard Hoggart[29] of his childhood in Hunslet in the 1920s to the modest prosperity enjoyed by Britain since the 1950s.

With these changes in material conditions, there has been a transformation of relations with parents, especially mothers. There has been, so to say, a Freudian revolution. For those born, like me, in the 1920s, it was as if their mothers had read and inwardly digested James Thurber's book *Let Your Mind Alone*. Those born after the War had mothers who, through women's magazines and the mass media, have absorbed some version or other of the psychoanalytic approach to children, heavily slanted in the direction of hedonism.[30]

But though the standards and expectations of childhood have undoubtedly risen in the lifetime of the oldest Britons now alive, we must not forget that throughout our period the probability of membership of a large family, and of low income, poor housing, illness, and early death, had continued to mark off the social classes from each other. Some children have continued to grow up in traditional working-class communities in the industrial cities, and a deprived minority among the working class is variously estimated at about half a million, even today. In December 1978 there were 535,000 families with children who were normally on supplementary benefit. The number of children involved was 1,082,000. Poverty in large families remains a hazard of childhood.[31] For example, though the average size of completed family among manual workers has fallen, a description of the childhood circumstances of those living in the Birmingham educational priority area in 1969 showed that no less than 91 per cent came from families of three or more children.[32]

Changing relations between generations

What, then, are we to say about relations between the generations? From one point of view, the changes I have traced in the twentieth century seem to have created a children's paradise. No age has ever been more child-centred, or gone so far towards making death socially invisible. Yet parental anxiety, exacerbated by marital uncertainty, is endemic. Fathers, and more especially mothers, inhabit a world which takes away their control over, and simultaneously insists on the responsibility for, the fate of their children. Most parents have lived through a dramatic shift in the standards expected of them. It is not enough, as it once was, to look after bodily health and physical security. Parents must also answer for the mental and moral character of their sons and daughters, despite influences from the street, the so-called peer group, the mass media and youth culture which children cannot escape, and with which parents cannot contend. They are increasingly made to feel amateurs in a difficult professional world. The old 'Us and Them' of the working-class mother is now a more generalized division between the inner life of families of all classes, and the external public forces. Such circumstances, together with the appreciation of schooling as a matter largely beyond family control, which determines the future jobs and incomes of their children, may add up to intense frustration. Relations between the generations in all classes are prone to anxiety and conflict, and the family is hard-pressed.

This is strange when we consider how much the twentieth century deserves its description as the 'century of the child'. So much of modern politics has been about children. Not only increasing educational expenditure but also infant and maternity services, population policies, family allowances, adoption and fostering, treatment of young offenders, and so on. Even the principal objective all over the world of economic growth is essentially justified as 'for the children'. The old are relatively political outcasts. The future is all. 'Trailing clouds of glory do they come.' We have lived through a revolution, demographic, economic, and social, as a result of which the child has become the quality product of industrial society. The recalcitrant Andy Capp who says, 'What have my grandchildren done for me that I should care for them?' is at best a pre-freudian anachronism.

We should start by recognizing the frustration of the modern parent—whether a West Indian mother in Brixton who is baffled by the apparent failure of the school to teach her boy either good letters or good manners, or the anxious suburban father calculating the costs and benefits of buying a place for his boy in the private sector now that the comprehensive school is the only alternative.

Despite the increasing central *dirigisme* of the Department of Education and Science since 1979 it can be argued that Her Majesty's Inspectors have lost confidence as to what schools ought to be doing and therefore the authority to guide those they inspect. They deserve sympathy, for the loss of confidence is not only theirs. We *all* live in confusion as to what is the good life. Rereading Richard Hoggart's account of working-class life before the 1950s, I am struck by the integration of ordinary families in those days with the moral traditions of the old class and Christian society which he so accurately and lovingly described. That moral structure has ebbed away fast under the assault of the classless inequalities and the secular materialism of the post-war world and, in the process, the familial controls over upbringing have steadily attenuated.

A traditional culture weakened by multiple forces of change falters in its transmission to the next generation and the lonely crowd of adolescent age-mates look to each other for guidance. They too, like their parents, are essentially powerless, even those who enjoy relative material prosperity. Their powerlessness is reflected in their collective amnesia, their unknowingness of the history of their conditions, and even more in their uncertainty as to their future. No wonder that fashionability, hedonism, and a desperate individualism serve as substitutes for a securely held

morality. Hoggart's working-class family is romantically remote
in the 1980s.

Of course, they were never church or chapel attenders in substantial proportions but, as Hoggart put it:

They believe, first, in the purposiveness of life. Life has a meaning, must
have a meaning. One does not bother much about defining it, or pursue
abstract questions as to its nature or the implications which follow from
such a conclusion: 'We're 'ere for a purpose', they say, or 'There must
be some purpose or we wouldn't be 'ere.' And that there is a purpose
presupposes that there must be a God. They hold to what G. K.
Chesterton called 'the dumb certainties of existence', and Reinhold
Niebuhr, 'primary religion'. Equally simply, they hold to what George
Orwell called 'those things (like free-will and the existence of the individual) which we know to be so, though all the arguments are against
them'.[33]

Since Hoggart wrote not only the further decline of church and
chapel, but also the changes in the typical position of married
women—their reduced fertility and their sharply increased rate
of paid employment—have been of greater moment in changing
the character of the learning process among children than all the
expansion and reorganization of schools which has gone on since
the Education Act of 1944, including its development of schooling, its provision of secondary education for all, and its raising of
the school-leaving age.

Institutional child-rearing

In short, a weakening of the bond between parent and child, and
exacerbation of conflict between them, are a fundamental and
paradoxical part of the so-called century of the child. From one
point of view this may be seen in the growing power of public
authorities to override the traditional rights of parents over children, albeit justified in the name of ever-rising standards of child
care. Standards belong to experts. From another point of view,
weakening bonds and sharpened conflicts are seen in child-
avoidance by adults. This was, of course, always the way of the
rich down the ages through such bodies as house-slaves, tutors,
and (in this context aptly named) public schools. Characteristically, it now takes the form, in middle-class districts, of an
endless round of parties and play activities which in effect share
out the stint of child-minding on an informal rota system,

releasing the other mothers. In the working class, the child-minding industry has become an essential adjunct of recognized women's employment, punitively contained by a public administration in the vain hope that it will somehow go away. From another point of view, the parent and the teacher tacitly conspire to retreat from the harsh realities of their own lack of confidence to leave the children corralled before the television set. Later, adolescents are given up to their peer-group activities in segregated territories which they increasingly monopolize, such as the disco, the football terrace, the student union, and the pop music festival. These age-segregated phenomena are surely among those which the Martian anthropologist would pick out as significant features of a modern urban upbringing.

Class reproduction through the family

Meanwhile, the impact of class on upbringing may have been changing with respect to the nature of transmitted capital. In a pure class society it is, or was, material capital which differentiated the classes, and education basically served to put a stamp of class culture on fates already decided by class origin. The social reproduction of generations was primarily a transmission of material capital and therefore of its attendant inequality of income and opportunity.

But as the economy slowly developed its technology, and gradually complicated its division of labour, the fate of a family's children began to turn more on the successful transmission of cultural rather than material capital. Both still exist, of course, and are partially interchangeable—for example, conspicuously in a private or marketed system of schools. But cultural capital is of increasing importance. It is affirmed and publicly recognized in degrees, certificates, and credentials. And it is acquired first and foremost through familial transmission—for example, through knowledge of how to use the public properties of libraries and museums, through elaborated language codes which are indispensable to success at school, through appropriate levels of academic aspiration reinforced in the home, through information about learning or job opportunities.

The result is (just as much in Communist Russia or Capitalist America as in Britain) that the social reproduction of generations is a reproduction of a hierarchy of cultural capital. This permits considerable mobility for a minority upwards and downwards in the hierarchy, but its main feature remains the continuity of familial status between generations.

Conclusion: a renegotiated division of labour

Social scientists, working in apparently unrelated fields, seem to be converging on to a more adequate conception of social change, showing that the traditional division of labour in classical industrial society is being radically renegotiated—the division of labour, that is, between the sexes, between the classes, between childhood, adulthood, and old age, between the family and the economy, and between the economy and the state.

The old conception of industrial society posited an essential triangle; the family, the economy, and the state. The conception of the life cycle was congruent. Families raised children; men worked; women ran households. The economy produced, the state redistributed, and the family consumed. The state collected taxes from the exchanges between the family and the economy and used the proceeds to redistribute resources for the education of the child, the relief of men temporarily out of work, the maintenance of women without men to connect them to the economy, the sustenance of the old, and the protection of the health and safety of the population as a whole. In the new conception, however, all of these relationships are revised. The family produces as well as consumes. Women are incorporated into the formal economy and men into the household and the informal economy. It is recognized that people live as well as work in factories and work as well as live in houses. Adults learn as well as children. Leisure becomes do-it-yourself work. It is also recognized that part of the growing informal economy lies outside the apparatus of tax collection and is therefore independent of the redistributive activity of the state. This leads us not only to revise conventional economic calculations of national income, but also to reappraise the politics of welfare (and taxpayers' revolts are not the only manifestation of that reappraisal). So childhood, education, work, and leisure are all words acquiring new meanings.

In the short run the division of labour, despite rising unemployment, divorce, and DIY, changes slowly from its traditional forms. But technological change, in interaction with the increasingly vigorous claims of disadvantaged class, ethnic groups, women, and regions, holds out the ultimate possibility of radical social transformation.

Action for or against these possibilities is the business of citizens. Meanwhile, for the student, a new sociology is beginning to put together a usable analysis of modern society—its economics, its structure of class, status, and power, its politics, and its administration. Out of that analysis I see the possibility of new social movements seeking to work out a viable politics of devolved democracy, and a freer and more equitable pattern of education, work, and leisure.

6
Mobility and education

Vilfredo Pareto pointed out that 'history is the graveyard of aristocracies'.[1] Marx recognized that 'the more a ruling class is able to assimilate the foremost minds of a ruled class the more stable and dangerous becomes its rule'.[2] Mobility stabilizes social structures by moving individuals within and between generations. So to draw a complete picture of social and cultural reproduction we must take account not only of the family but of all the institutions which pass on skills, knowledge, and belief through channels other than those of genetic transmission. The development of education as an active agent of cultural evolution and social selection is one of the more obvious features of change in British society in the twentieth century.

I want, in this chapter, to ask about educational change and social reproduction by putting one version of a central question about any society: is it an open one? And I choose this approach because 'the open society' has been the traditional aim of liberal policy, with education in the forefront as one of its principal means.

The question can, of course, have many meanings. For the liberal it may turn on whether there is access to knowledge and freedom to use it. The interest of the egalitarian is different. He is typically concerned to question unequal distributions of skill and knowledge and to assume that, unless there is proof to the contrary, inequality of outcome in the social distribution of knowledge is a measure of *de facto* inequality of access. The ensuing debate has provided the stuff of educational politics in Britain, as in other countries in this century. Behind it lies the more general question of what distributions between the members of each new generation are possible and desirable.

Is Britain, as a capitalist society in the late twentieth century, moving towards greater openness? Do boys or girls in the 1980s have more or less equal chances of becoming rich or professional or unskilled or unemployed compared with their fathers or mothers or each other? Are we to believe, with Marxist labour process theorists,[3] that the work-force is becoming more and more proletarianized as work itself is necessarily degraded or deskilled under capitalism? Or are we to prefer the more optimistic liberal theory of upward march to greater opportunities for everyone in a post-industrial society[4] and a service economy offering more and more professional and technical careers?

These contrasting theories of the 1970s can now be appraised in the light of empirical evidence from studies of social mobility. The idea of mobility implies movement from somewhere to somewhere else and the 'somewhere' in question may in principle be any social or geographical position. In the sociological literature it usually means some kind of class, status, prestige, or socio-economic position.

The chances of poverty

Has post-war reform equalized opportunity? What happens to those who are born into different circumstances of power and advantage? We can begin with a historically important and particular version of the question, 'Who falls into and who escapes poverty?' Professor Atkinson and his colleagues have recently offered new evidence.[5] In 1950 a tired but triumphant Attlee government had launched the Welfare State. Its supporters were comforted after their 1951 defeat by good news from social researchers in York.[6] Poverty had been virtually abolished under the impact of full employment and Beveridge's social security. Earlier Rowntree and Booth had exposed both late Victorian and inter-war Britain as a society in which one-third of its people had incomes too small to support a minimal subsistence, defined by the Victorians as the wherewithal to maintain physical health, and by the Georgians less savagely but still severely. Such mass misery was now to recede into unhappy historical memory. We were entering an age of secure abundance. Though biblical sociology warned us that the poor would remain with us till the crack of doom, we were now assured that they henceforth would be largely banished to afflict backward countries, leaving only a tiny proportion of our unfortunate or feckless compatriots to be looked after by social workers and the functionaries of the National Assistance Board.

What, then, happened to these first children of the Welfare

State? Did they stay poor if born poor, or move up in the world to be replaced by the children of the better off: and, whatever the case, what explains their financial fortunes? Atkinson and his colleagues provide an answer as well as a lucid lesson on how social science can formulate the complex varieties of such apparently simple questions. The authors adopted a heroic research design. They decided to find, to describe, and even to explain the fate of the children of the families surveyed by Rowntree and Lavers in York in 1950. This earlier study of a sample of the working class was chosen because it included both income data and the names and addresses of the sample members. Other extant studies did not satisfy both criteria and official records proscribe access. It would, of course, have been possible to begin a longitudinal study. Such studies lend themselves to the testing of hypotheses about life cycles if one has the patience to wait a generation for results: and the sample can be both national and directed towards particular social groups—the very poor, the unemployed, or, for that matter, the very rich. Alternatively a sample of the nation can be taken from which it is possible to reconstruct history by asking retrospective questions and arranging the answers into successive birth cohorts. But this always involves unreliable data—not least in the case of incomes—and hazardous inferences. To follow the Rowntree children was to avoid impatience and some inaccuracies. But this method too has hazards enough and Atkinson not only does not hide them but points to others and their implications which might easily have escaped the notice of an incautious reader. So much so that the book is just as valuable as a guide to method as it is a substantive answer to the question of how and how far poverty is inherited.

Of these children of the 1950s, two-thirds were still in York in 1975–8, and a further one-fifth in Yorkshire and Humberside. Were they better off than their parents? To arrive at a precise answer we must follow Atkinson's lead and be sophisticated about the words, such as income and earnings, which ordinary people use and about words like life cycle or measurement error or perfect mobility which sociologists use. Here is an answer from the numbers set out in Table 6.1.

'Low-income' is defined as below 140 per cent of the National

Table 6.1   The fate of the Rowntree children

Parents 1950	Children 1975–8 (percentages by row)			
	Low-income	Intermediate-income	Comfortably-off	All
Low-income	224 (48.2)	155 (33.3)	86 (18.5)	465
Intermediate-income	95 (25.8)	129 (35.1)	144 (39.1)	368
Comfortably-off	158 (26.5)	174 (29.1)	265 (44.4)	597
Total	477 (33.4)	458 (32.0)	495 (34.6)	1,430

Assistance scale in 1950, or below 140 per cent of the Supplementary Benefits scale in 1975–8. 'Intermediate-income' is defined as 140–199 per cent of the NA/SB scale. 'Comfortably-off' is defined as 200 per cent or more above the NA/SB scale. These three categories divide the 1,430 descendants into approximate thirds. The top row shows what happened to the 465 who were born into low-income families: 224 stayed in the low-income group, 155 moved up to the intermediate range of income and 86 became comfortably off. The raw numbers in each row show the passage from income origins to income destinations of all the Rowntree children. Putting the same story into percentages ('transition proportions'), we see that 48.2 per cent of those who were born poor stayed poor, 33.3 per cent became ordinary and 18.5 per cent became comfortable. All this is 'outflow' analysis, i.e. how the children are spread along the rows from their origins to their destinations.

A second version of the question can be answered by turning the table sideways and looking at 'inflow', i.e. where the children who ended up in an income category were recruited from. The first column, for example, tells us that of the 477 who ended up in the low-income group, 224 had been born into low-income families and 158 had been born comfortably off. So, looking at it either way, there was both continuity and discontinuity between the generations.

Taking a third version of the question we can ask what were the chances of 'income mobility'. For example, for those who were born poor the chances of staying poor were 2.6 times better than of becoming comfortably off (48.2 ÷ 18.5).

A fourth approach is to compare the actual pattern with the pattern which would have obtained if there were no connection between income origin and income destination. This is the notion of a perfectly open or perfectly mobile society, i.e. one in which there is a random relation between the incomes of parents and their children. Under those hypothetical circumstances the transition proportions would be the same for all rows. The table shows that post-war Britain was not completely open in this sense. But neither was it a caste society. It was in an intermediary position, which can also be given a precise measure—an index of association between the incomes of parents and their children. Atkinson patiently shifts the angle of vision of the raw table of numbers (and the proportions calculated from them) from one statistical viewpoint to another, so as to enable the reader to see just how complex was the original question.

Among the many results to emerge is that Rowntree's famous life cycle of traditional working-class poverty, which typically pulled people above the poverty line only in the brief periods of adolescence and of middle age between the departure of children and the advent of old age, is still with us. Nevertheless the fate of individuals can only be described in terms of chances not continuities, probabilities not predestinations. The poor were not mechanically doomed to transmit their poverty. For the most reluctantly numerate student perhaps it will suffice to say that the Rowntree children were scattered from their parents more in income than they were in height.

Sir Keith Joseph suggested in speeches in 1972 that a cycle of deprivation rolls on down the generations and accounts for a significant burden on the social services. Joseph's hypothesis never captured much substance either in his relatively humane formulation or in the harsher Victorian original version of Social Darwinism. Some of the poor are descended from the poor but others escape and the causes of poverty are to be found much more in the circumstances of people than in their personal traits. And in any case the implications for politicians in general and current Conservative members in particular are that poverty can be increased or reduced by *their* actions.

Mobility between classes: the 1972 evidence

From this focus on a particular social division—the poverty line—we can now turn to the more general phenomenon of social fluidity on which there is a long history of British 'political arithmetic'. In 1949 Professor Glass and his colleagues at the London School of Economics pioneered a study of mobility in that tradition.[7] Twenty years later, my colleagues and I at Nuffield College, Oxford, judged that, after an intervening generation of social-democratic reform, it was time to look again. And a study of the 1983 general election has yielded still more recent evidence.[8]

Political arithmetic is by no means the only approach to the complicated question of social mobility. Another pursues an interest in the process of class formation.[9] A third, which we glimpsed in Chapter 4, examines the correlates and consequences of mobility in electoral choice.[10] But whatever the approach we do well to appreciate the complexity of movements between social positions to which I pointed in Chapter 3. The intricacy of the structure of class, status, and party in Britain has already emerged in previous chapters. None of these dimensions, separately or together, yield a unitary hierarchy. Nor is the passage of individuals through the social structure a simple repetition of the experiences of one generation by the next. As we have seen, there have been fluctuations and trends in births and deaths, and in the occupational and other social positions to be filled. Moreover, mobility can be thought of as either group or individual, and either between or within generations.

With these various meanings and methodological cautions in mind we can begin to analyse the fluidity of the society experienced by recent generations in Britain. We can again use the simplification of three social strata of social classes, ignoring or evading the many sociologically created conceptual traps which are found in the study of social stratification, for example the vulgar Marxist theology of two classes at war in capitalist society, or the vulgar liberal conception of a continuous hierarchy of prestige or status which would make every individual a class.

The first of our three strata can be taken, as before, to mean the *middle class*: professional, managerial, and administrative occupational groups and higher technicians and their wives and children. Taken by their *origin* (that is, classified by their fathers' occupation when they were 14 years old) these formed 13.3 per cent of men in England and Wales in 1972. The second stratum is a heterogeneous *lower-middle class* of non-manual employees, small proprietors, self-employed artisans, but also lower-grade technicians and supervisors of manual workers. They made up 30.8 per cent of the 1972 men by origin. The third stratum is the *working class*—industrial manual workers and agricultural workers whether skilled, semi-skilled, or unskilled. They made up the other 55.9 per cent by origin.

In this simple classification each individual has one of three classes as an origin, but also (judged by his own job ten years after entering the labour market) one of the same three as a destination.[11] Distributed by destination as distinct from where they had started as boys, they appear in the following array:

	Social class destinations (percentage)
Middle class	20.1
Lower-middle class	24.9
Working class	55.0

It is immediately apparent that the structure of origins is different from that of destinations for this generation of Britons. On balance there has been movement out of the working class and lower-middle class into the middle class. We will return to this question of trends. But for the time being let us stick to our snapshot survey and put the origins and destinations together to form a grid of intergenerational class mobility (Table 6.2).

Table 6.2   Intergenerational class mobility: adult males, England and Wales 1972 (percentages)

	Destinations (ten years after entry to work)		
Origins	Middle class	Lower-middle	Working class
Middle class	7.0	3.7	2.6
Lower-middle	7.0	9.9	13.9
Working class	6.1	11.3	38.5

100

We now see nine kinds of intergenerational experience, each one measured as a percentage of the total. The columns of the grid tell us about *inflow* between generations to the three *destination* classes. The rows show *outflow* from *origin* classes. The diagonal cells from top left to bottom right denote those who were found, ten years after starting their working lives, in the social class where they started. The cells below and to the left of the diagonal are occupied by those who would be correctly described as having had upward mobility if our three social classes were arranged in a strict hierarchy. The cells to the right and above the diagonal would be men who have been downwardly mobile.

We should again remind ourselves at this point that this is a simplified picture. It conflates the experience of successive cohorts of births and entry into the labour market, it ignores the heterogeneity of the three social classes, it tells us nothing about the mobility of women, and it obscures intragenerational movement. Thus, for example, of those who had been born into the middle classes, and were also found in them as adults in 1972, half did *not* start their working lives in this social class, but began in a lower non-manual or manual job and later moved to a middle-class job.[12] In other words, our patterns and proportions of intergenerational stability of the middle class disguise intragenerational instability, what the researchers who gave us this evidence call 'counter-mobility'.

Nevertheless, returning to the simpler intergenerational picture, we can say that the typical Englishman or Welshman was born into and stayed in the working class. This is the largest group, more than three times as big as the next largest, which is those who started in lower-middle-class families and became manual workers. The three smallest groups are all mobile ones— from working class to middle class (6.1 per cent), from middle class to lower-middle class (3.7 per cent), and from middle class to working class (2.6 per cent).

Is this an open society? Certainly it is not a caste society. If we add all three diagonal cells, it turns out that the proportion who stay as adults in the social class in which they spent their childhood is little more than half (55.4 per cent). A very substantial minority of Englishmen and Welshmen in the last generation have been socially mobile (44.6 per cent). If we look at the rows (outflow) it turns out that, while 7 per cent were born into the middle class and stayed there, 3.7 per cent went to the lower-middle class, and 2.6 per cent went to the working class, together accounting for the 13.3 per cent of middle-class origin. If we look at the columns (inflow) it further becomes clear that the idea, which is quite widespread among sociologists, that the élite have effective means of closing their ranks against the entry of other men's children is clearly a false one if by élite we mean what we have here defined as the middle class. The number of newcomers from other social classes is getting on for twice the number of those who are, so to speak, middle-class by birth. This is a similar picture to that presented by Geoff Payne for Scotland.[13] The number of middle-class sons who moved into the lower-middle or the working class is not very far short of those who stayed where they were born.

Thus if we look at our three social classes expecting to find closed hereditary groups then the middle class disappoints us. Indeed it is the working class which approximates more to this notion. The typical factory worker is at least a second-generation proletarian, while the middle-class man who looks at his fellow will find that nearly two out of every three of them have come from birth in another social class. The first industrial nation now combines a mature working class with an *arriviste* middle class.

So far we have examined outflow and inflow as they have occurred and in relation to each other. An alternative is to consider them in relation to an external criterion. Politically this may be conceived as the open society. Statistically, in the way which the London School of Economics 1949 study made standard for subsequent mobility research, the same notion may be represented as that of 'perfect mobility', that is what the numbers or percentages would have been if destinations were randomly related to origins. The point is to compare actual movement with a defined hypothetical pattern of movement. Essentially the same method is to compare the *relative* chances of moving from given origins to given destinations. For example, the chances of becoming middle-class are highest for middle-class sons, more than half of whom retained their position, while fewer than one in nine working-class sons moved into the middle class. Notice too that the chances of moving out from the working class were less than one in three, while the chances of moving out from a middle-class childhood were very nearly one to one. Another and summary way of answering the 'open society' question is to measure the strength of the bond between fathers and sons. In a fully open society the correlation between the social class of fathers and sons would be 0.0 and in a rigid caste society it would be 1.0. In fact, calculated on our 1972 data, the correlation between father's occupation and son's occupation in 1972 is about 0.36.[14]

Trends in mobility

Now, we may ask, what are the trends in mobility? In terms of our metaphor, this means turning a snapshot into a film. The method in one form or another is that of cohort analysis. But there are many dangers here. The birth cohorts of our sample are not strict random samples of birth cohorts in the history which they are made to represent, if only because while all sons have one and only one father, the converse is far from true. Moreover, it is difficult to know how far differences between birth cohorts are attributable to age or to the particular period of history in which a cohort reaches a given age. Given the background of change in the occupational structure which we have already discussed in Chapter 2, there is every reason to be cautious in interpreting trends from a survey of the kind on which we are relying here.

Nevertheless, bearing in mind all these qualifications, I cannot do better than to paraphrase the findings from the Oxford mobility study.[15] These authors show that the view one can take of the question as to whether Britain has become a more open society will depend crucially on the method of measurement. They use three methods. First, following the method we have used in Table 6.2, they gauge 'absolute mobility rates' by tabulating the percentage movement from origins to destinations (which may be transit points in the case of first jobs or jobs ten years after entry to the labour market, and in any case cannot be taken as a pure definition of 'occupational maturity') in defined classes or occupational groups. On this measure they conclude that there has been a trend towards greater openness in that the younger men in the sample had better chances than older men of similar origins, of being found in the higher-class positions, that is, in professional, higher-technical, administrative, or managerial jobs.

Then, second, these authors turn to a simple measure of

'relative mobility rates', using disparity ratios. Absolute rates are those which are more or less visible to the participants (social actors) themselves. Relative rates are sociologists' concepts and not necessarily part of the social consciousness of participants: they relate the chances of mobility of men in different classes to some statistically defined norm or model, such as that of random relation between fathers' and sons' class position to which I have referred as perfect mobility. Measurement of relative rates of mobility by disparity ratios is a method which allows for change in the structure of classes or occupations. It enables us to gauge changes in the chances of being found in given destinations among men of differing origins. The disparity ratios are ratios between outflow percentages. For example, in a society divided into two classes the proportion of sons of Class I who themselves held Class I jobs as a proportion of all Class I sons is expressed as a ratio of the proportion of Class II sons who gained Class I jobs from the total number of Class II sons. Put formally, the disparity ratios would be

$$\frac{f_{11}}{f_1} \bigg/ \frac{f_{21}}{f_2} \quad \text{and} \quad \frac{f_{22}}{f_2} \bigg/ \frac{f_{12}}{f_1}$$

On this measure, the authors conclude that stability rather than change is the outstanding feature of intergenerational class mobility in Britain in recent decades. Whereas absolute rates give an impression of trends towards greater openness in the sense of there being increasing rates of upward movement into the expanding higher levels of the class structure, the relative rates show that these expanding opportunities have been fairly equally shared out between men of different class origins so as to produce no change in their relative chances of access. In the recent period, moreover, while the working class has been shrinking, the relative as well as the absolute chances of men of middle-class origin being found in manual work have also declined. In short, relative class chances have been stable or increasingly unequal.

Then, third, the authors use a more complex measure of relative rates by the use of odds ratios defined formally in a 2×2 mobility table as:

$$\frac{f_{11}}{f_{12}} \bigg/ \frac{f_{21}}{f_{22}}$$

That is, measuring whether the relative chances of the son of a Class I father being himself found in Class I rather than Class II are changing over time at the same rate as the relative chances of the sons of a Class II father being found in Class I rather than Class II. On this approach the conclusion is again reached that there have been no systematic or general shifts in relative mobility. The relative chances of men from two different classes of origin being found in one rather than another of two different class destinations have not changed.

In short, in a period in which the occupational division of labour in Britain was transformed to offer more middle-class opportunities, there was continuity in the underlying processes of intergenerational class mobility. Moreover, though there may have been some specific trends in relative chances of movement between particular classes, the evidence is that increased fluidity is to be found only when the class positions of sons and their fathers are compared at a relatively early stage in the working life of the son. When intergenerational mobility is measured using class origin and the point of 'occupational maturity' (beyond which there is little likelihood of further major shifts in class position), such trends as are to be found are in the direction of reduced social fluidity. In general, however, a model of 'constant social fluidity' best fits the data.

Mobility in late twentieth-century Britain

The picture presented so far is one of rising absolute and constant relative rates of mobility in the long period of post-war prosperity which came to an end in the mid-1970s. Did mobility patterns change with the end of the long boom and the beginning of a new period of political economy in which growth was halted, unemployment rose, deindustrialization accelerated, and economic management became 'Thatcherism'? John Goldthorpe and Clive Payne have provided an answer[16] by analysis of mobility questions included in the study of the 1983 general election. Their conclusion is unequivocal: 'that the stability of relative rates or chances of inter-generational class mobility, which our analyses of the 1972 data suggested went back to the 1920s, has *not* been disturbed to any appreciable degree in the first decade after the ending of the post-war era.'

But what of absolute rates? Has recession resulted in a freezing of mobility and especially the upward mobility of working-class and lower-middle-class sons into the middle-class professions, salariat, or 'service class'? The evidence, on the contrary, is that absolute rates of upward and of total mobility have continued to rise. A comparison of the 1972 and 1983 samples using our three-fold class schema and the 1980 classification of occupations[17] is given in Table 6.3. In 1972, 16 per cent of the men of working-class origin had found their way into the middle class: by 1983 the percentage had risen to 23.6. Again in 1972 over 60 per cent of those of working-class parentage were themselves in working-class jobs: by 1983 the percentage had fallen to 52.6.

Table 6.3   Class distribution of respondents by class of father, 1972 and (1983) inquiries

| Father's class | Respondent's class (percentages by row) | | |
	Middle class	Lower-middle	Working class
Middle class	57.7 (62.0)	23.2 (22.2)	19.1 (15.8)
Lower-middle	31.2 (34.2)	31.9 (34.3)	37.0 (31.5)
Working class	16.0 (23.6)	23.7 (23.8)	61.2 (52.6)

This continuing evidence into the 1980s of *both* stable and relative class chances or 'constant social fluidity' *and* increasing absolute rates of net upward mobility is clearly damaging to the degradation of work hypothesis of the labour process theorists, and is supportive of the optimistic liberal theory of the technologically led expansion of middle-class opportunities. Yet we must pause and heavily qualify the award of this particular prize in theoretical debate. We must consider unemployment.

In 1972 unemployment was virtually negligible. In 1983 it was 'double digit': there was an unemployment rate of over 12 per cent, and more than a million people had been out of work for at least a year. The unemployed could reasonably be viewed as an additional stratum of the working class (thus modifying the picture of the shrinking of the latter) which should objectively be analysed as a 'destination status' in mobility tables. Moreover, the 1983 study confirms what was generally known, that unemployment is a characteristically working-class risk.

Thus, while the expansion of the professional and technical

middle class remains a feature of late twentieth-century Britain, as it was in the long boom from mid-century, unemployment has also emerged as a structure of negative opportunity which tends to *polarize* mobility chances, especially of those who begin in the working class. The Thatcherite period has not reversed the trends of widening access to the middle class, but it has seen a raising of the stakes in the selective process. The class prizes and the risk of prolonged social deprivation have both increased. We have, in short, reached a more polarized society.

Mobility and education

The search for an explanation of these patterns of mobility naturally leads us to schools and credentials. Table 6.4 summarizes the educational career of each of the nine groups we distinguished in the 1972 study. It amalgamates the experience of those who had passed, at various times, through the expanding system of schooling in England and Wales from before the First to after the Second World War.

Table 6.4   Education and mobility (percentages)

	Private primary schooling	Selective secondary schooling	School exams	Some FE qualifications	Univ. degree
Stable middle class	32.0	88.4	82.0	33.1	29.8
Middle to lower-middle	24.9	65.1	53.6	17.2	5.7
Middle to working	3.8	33.5	15.1	7.0	0.5
Lower-middle to middle	11.7	67.9	62.1	34.1	13.5
Stable lower-middle	7.5	44.3	27.1	5.6	1.0
Lower-middle to working	3.0	21.9	8.1	1.8	0.1
Working to middle	1.6	63.1	58.5	32.3	12.8
Working to lower-middle	2.0	32.2	20.2	3.9	1.1
Stable working	0.6	14.7	4.6	0.4	0.1
TOTAL	5.8	34.8	23.9	10.3	4.3

The educational profiles of our nine mobility categories, apart from yielding recognizable stereotypes of Britons, show a regular patterning of the relations between education and mobility. It can be seen from the underlined rows of Table 6.4 that the educational norms for each of the three social classes, as represented by those who have had stable membership, are positively related to social class both of origin and destination. Thus the stable middle-class men are composed of 88 per cent with selective secondary schooling, and 30 per cent with a university education, compared with 44 per cent and 1 per cent for the stable lower-middle class, and 15.0 per cent and 0.1 per cent for the stable working class. In other words, those who find jobs in the higher occupational categories have more education and more qualifications. This will surprise no one.

Looking at the other six categories of those who have moved from their birth position, it is equally clear that mobility involves realignment of social class membership according to educational qualifications. Thus, those who have moved upwards have, in the process, exceeded the educational norms of their origin group, and those who have moved downwards have had less educational advantage and attained fewer education qualifications. This pattern is absolutely regular. But there are some details worth remarking. If we look at the destination classes it appears that those who move up from below do not, on average, have as much educational qualification as those who have been stable in the destination class in question. Similarly, those who move down still have a rather higher educational profile than the stable members of the class they join and, which follows from our remarks on the upwardly mobile, a still higher one than those who have joined the same destination class from below.

Putting these two tendencies together, that is, the association of education with social origin and also its association with mobility, what we then find is that exchange between the social classes is also a partial exchange of the educationally qualified. For example, those who have moved from the middle class to the working class include only 1 per cent of graduates, while those who have moved from the working class to the middle class include 13 per cent of graduates. There is thus, in the process of mobility, exchange not only of individuals but of social investment of education and qualifications which maintains a differential distribution of social qualities between the social classes. I would lay particular emphasis on this aspect of the reproduction of the stratification system. Intergenerational mobility serves to reconstitute the general pattern of distribution of attributes of the different social classes.

At the same time this evidence on education and mobility in Britain shows that neither a division into social classes nor into mobility groups completely differentiates the population by their education. It is just as important to notice that the great majority of those born into the middle class did *not* go to private primary schools or to universities as it is to notice that those who were either born into, or made their way into, the middle class were more likely to have had these educational experiences than those who came from, or went to, either the lower-middle or the working class.

Education and inequality

If these are the mobility patterns and their educational correlates, how are we to explain them in relation to familial and educational development? My account of social reproduction in Chapter 5 was a description of the supply of children. But the supply of children in turn constitutes a demand for education which, though fashioned by the principle of stratified diffusion, and made to fluctuate quantitatively by changes in the birth-rate, has risen qualitatively throughout the century. The demand has been met by a state policy of educational expansion. And this policy, advocated originally by Victorian liberal optimists, has always been seen as the promise of new and higher levels of both material prosperity and elevated culture for the nation, happily accompanied by more equality, since to raise the supply of educated labour would result in a reduction of its relative price.

The Oxford mobility studies enable us to assess the extent to which the Victorian vision has been realized.[18] That assessment has to be less than the hopes of the reformers, though it also contains no support for those 'Black Paper' writers who would have us believe that educational standards have declined.[19] Expansion there has been, and with it a cumulation of cultural capital. The outstanding feature of the state selective secondary schools, which developed after the 1902 Education Act, was always that the majority of their pupils were 'first-generation' recruits to advanced education.

Nevertheless, we have been forced to the depressing conclusion that over the century so far, the unequal relative educational chances of boys from different class origins have been remarkably stable, and that the conventional picture of a steady trend towards equality has been an optimistic myth. The metaphor of the column with which we began in Chapter 5 does, apparently, work for education if not for fertility.

What, then, is the connection between school and work? Launching a 'great education debate' in 1976, the Prime Minister, James Callaghan, called for a closer link between education and the needs of industry. This is an old story, which is not to say it is untrue. Every single generation in the history of Britain as an industrial nation has been told that the schools are failing to provide the skills of workers, managers, and professionals needed by a modernizing economy. This was the case when Britain led the world in the rate of economic growth just as much as it is the case now when it is portrayed as the ailing Western country, the sick man of Europe, the ageing bankrupt, etc. That, of course, is another story, which could be quite differently, if debatably, presented as one of a country with a deep and lively tradition of democracy and one which is leading the world rather than trailing behind it in pursuing the application of democratic principles beyond the polling booth in the factory and work place, the home, and the school.

Mr Callaghan was entirely right if he meant that there is a rather tenuous connection between educational and occupational changes in modern Britain. At first glance it might appear otherwise. Both the output of qualified people from the educational system and the intake of professional, managerial, and white-collar manpower into the work-force have risen year by year, especially in recent decades.

But the expansion of the 1980s made the relationship clearer. While the expansion of the professional and technical occupations has continued, there has been *both* deliberate governmental restraint on university expansion *and* a proliferation of training of 16-year-old school-leavers under the auspices of the Manpower Services Commission. One policy is simply part of a strategy of reducing public expenditure, the other is a reaction to the dangers of youth unemployment. Put together, there has been no automatic supply/demand relation between education and the labour market. They have proceeded independently of each other and no simple conclusion can be drawn along the lines of praising or blaming the schools for the level of efficiency or national income or unemployment or any other aspect of the economy. Of course, for an individual, job choice and protection against unemployment are improved the longer he stays in school and the more he collects educational certificates. But the wealth of the nation, the range of occupational opportunities, and the level of employment for British society as a whole are determined by quite other forces, such as monetary policy, the international market, and the collective attitudes towards work and leisure which prevail at any given time. Education alone cannot create either wealth or welfare.

The Oxford mobility study enables us to trace the educational experience of boys in four successive decennial birth cohorts—1913–22, 1923–32, 1933–42, and 1943–52. From the beginning of the century until the 1960s the crucial point of educational selection was at eleven-plus. At this age all children took tests of intelligence and attainment. From this result the most fateful decision was whether children went to a grammar or technical school, or to an unselected elementary or (after 1944) secondary modern school. The proportion of children attending grammar schools increased in every decade. Even for those born between 1943 and 1952 the supply of grammar school places kept pace with the growth in total population, although not with the growth in the middle classes. The proportion of grammar school children from all classes went on increasing right up to the mid-point of the century, the relative rates being highest for the working class, but the absolute increases being highest for the middle class. Then for the first post-war generation, the working class managed to protect its gains, while the now expanded middle classes lost some of theirs, though without falling back to the position they held a generation earlier. Hence, with respect to the grammar school, there were increased chances in general throughout the period and some narrowing of class differentials, both relative to the average, and relative to each other. The technical school picture, however, is very different. After the 1944 Education Act these schools began to disappear. The expansion of the grammar schools in the post-war period and before the comprehensive movement got under way in the 1960s was largely at the expense of the technical schools. What the working class gained through the expansion of the grammar schools, they largely lost through the decline of the technical schools. Thus, comparing the 1913–22 with the 1943–52 birth cohort, one hundred working-class families sent an extra eight boys to grammar school, but they also sent eight fewer to technical schools.

Meanwhile, after the 1944 Act, the emphasis of expansion gradually shifted to the later stages of secondary schooling, and to post-secondary provision. Here the class-differentiating forces continued to operate. The rewards for success and survival were high, and the result was that the amount spent on the education of children of different origin, far from equalizing chances, helped to maintain class inequality. Over the period as a whole, those born into professional and managerial families had three times as much spent on them as those born into the families of agricultural labourers. Those who went to selective secondary schools, private schools, and on to post-secondary education, especially in universities, were also relatively more expensively raised. The upshot was, as I pointed out in Chapter 2, that although there was a slight tendency to greater equality of invest-ment in the school education of boys from different classes, the development of post-secondary education more than counter-balanced this equalizing effect because it was disproportionately used by boys from the middle class.

We can illustrate these processes in twentieth-century Britain by focusing on the university graduate. The rise of the graduate in the twentieth century has occasionally been compared with that of the gentry in an earlier age and is sometimes described as a new estate (Eric Ashby[20]), an educational class (Ralf Dahrendorf[21]), or as the central element in the techno-structure of modern society (J. K. Galbraith[22]). These conceptions may be put into perspective by looking at the numbers revealed in the national sample of men aged 20–64 in England and Wales in 1972. It is not, of course, the whole picture, nor one from the main angle of vision of the research which is intended to portray the degree of openness or fluidity in modern British occupational and social structure. We can ask four simple questions:

1. How many men had university compared with other possible kinds of education? This is Table 6.5.
2. How much has the graduate element increased over the course of the century? This is Table 6.6
3. Where, educationally speaking, has the graduate come from? This is Table 6.7.
4. Where, occupationally speaking, has the graduate gone to? This is Table 6.8 and Table 6.9.

Again, while noticing the obvious risk of over-simplification, nine types of education can be distinguished and these are shown in Table 6.5. Three types of schooling are combined with three types of experience after school to produce this ninefold classification. They ascend, in conventional British evaluations of the desirability of different educational experiences, from a non-selective schooling in an elementary, secondary modern, or comprehensive school with no education after school, to a private education in a direct-grant or 'public' school followed by full-time attendance at a university. The first category accounts for 25.3 per cent of men in 1972, and the last for 1.6 per cent. The typical Englishman or Welshman has had a non-selective education in a state school plus some further education, usually in the form of apprenticeship or training within a firm, or part-time attendance at a technical college or night-school, or some combination of these. In the population as a whole 41 per cent are typical in this sense. The next most important group are those with some sort of selective education in a technical, central, or grammar school. The smallest groups are those who started at a non-selective school, but found their way to a university, and those who had secondary schooling in the private sector (including direct-grant schools) without any education beyond

Table 6.5 Types of education (each category expressed as a percentage of the whole)

School	No further education	Further education	Full-time university	Total
Non-selective	25.3	41.0	0.7	67.0
Selective state	4.6	18.3	3.9	26.8
Private	0.7	3.9	1.6	6.2
				100.0

school. Both of these groups constitute less than 1 per cent of the whole.

University men from all three kinds of school background amounted to 5.2 per cent of the male population in 1972. The comparable figure for those who have had a selective secondary education within the state system is 26.8 per cent and for those who went to independent schools 6.2 per cent. The numerical history of these three groups appears in the columns of Table 6.6. Of those born between 1907 and 1912, 1.5 per cent were graduates and the proportion rose steadily with a spurt (the expansion associated with the Robbins Report of 1963) for those born after 1947 to bring it up to 10.4 per cent. Private secondary schooling increased from the early years of the century but not either fast or steadily, reaching a high point for those born just before the Second World War. Selective secondary education provided by the state followed a roughly similar course but involving proportionately four times as many people. Thus, though this is the century of educational expansion, university graduates remained in 1972 only a twentieth of the adult male population, and those with a selective education were barely a third.

Table 6.6   Types of education since 1907 (percentages)

Date of birth	State selective	Private	University
1907–12	17.2	5.2	1.5
1912–17	21.5	4.9	2.6
1917–22	26.9	5.3	2.5
1922–27	28.9	4.4	3.3
1927–32	31.4	5.9	4.3
1932–37	31.3	7.6	6.0
1937–42	28.4	7.2	7.1
1942–47	26.9	7.4	7.3
1947–52	27.8	7.1	10.4

How have the schools supplied the universities? (Table 6.7.) Over half of the university men have come through the selective state schools that are now being reorganized as comprehensives. Rather less than a third have come from the private sector and 16.5 per cent have managed to get into the universities from a non-selective schooling. The trends during the century have not been dramatic. Selective state schools were gradually eliminating non-selective schools as preparatory institutions for the universities, but this trend will now presumably cease. The competition, meanwhile, between the state and the private sector, has fluctuated, although indecisively.

Table 6.7   Educational origins of university men since 1907 (percentages)

Date of birth	Type of school		
	Non-selective	Selective	Private
1907–22	30	41	29
1922–27	20	56	24
1927–32	10	55	35
1932–37	16	55	29
1937–42	13	62	25
1942–47	7	52	41
1947–52	11	62	27
Total in 1972	16.5	53.1	30.4

That university graduation leads to occupational advantage is perfectly clear from the second column of Table 6.8. Nearly nine out of every ten of the university men have found their way into the professional and managerial classes. But this is not the most interesting view of the distribution if we are looking for a meritocratic social order or some universal process of 'certification', labelling people for appropriate employment. The third column of Table 6.8 tells us more. The graduate element is still strongest at the top but nearly three-quarters of the top class are not graduates.

Table 6.8   Occupational distribution of university men

Registrar-General's class	Percentage distribution of university graduates by class	Percentage of each class who are university graduates
I	39	27
II	48	10
III Non-manual	8	3
III Manual	3	Less than 1
IV	2	Less than 1
V	0	Less than 1

Perhaps the graduate criterion underemphasizes the bond between education and occupation. So we return finally to the nine educational categories of Table 6.5 and show them again in Table 6.9 for the top class of professionals (the number above the diagonal in each cell) and the bottom class of unskilled workers (the number below the diagonal in each cell). The bond is clear and strong. The typical professional is a grammar school boy with education beyond school, though not in the university. The typical unskilled worker went to an elementary or secondary modern school and no further. What presumably is happening is that the occupational hierarchy is gradually being regraded upwards in formal educational terms.

Table 6.9   Education and occupation

Registrar-General's Class I (top diagonal of cells)
Registrar-General's Class V (bottom diagonal of cells)
Percentage of the occupational class with defined educational background

School	No further education		Some further education		University	
Non-selective	1.3		18.8		3.8	
		61.0		30.4		0.0
State selective	1.2		41.5		14.6	
		5.2		2.5		0.5
Private	0.0		10.1		8.8	
		0.0		0.5		0.0

Meritocracy

What, then, in the light of this description of the developments in education and an analysis of their relation to political aims or moral ideals, are we to make of the liberal optimisms of the twentieth century? Expansion there has been. It remains unfinished today; and along with this has been the creation of much cultural capital. But the anticipated greater equality of access to the national heritage has not materialized. Thresholds have certainly been raised and the area of free secondary education has been expanded under the auspices of the state. But the further activity of the state in expanding educational opportunity beyond the statutory leaving age has provided additional opportunities which have been seized disproportionately by those born into advantageous class circumstances. The overall result, on the various measures we have brought to bear, is that inequalities of class opportunity changed their form but retained their substance despite, if not indeed because of, a heavy investment by the state in enlarged educational opportunities.

In defining equality of educational opportunity, however, we have so far accepted the assumption that the characteristics of the average member of different classes were similar with respect to their claim and capacity to profit from whatever educational opportunity society provides. We must now question this assumption and explicitly consider a modification of it. Merit is commonly held to constitute a claim on social rewards and opportunities over against the claims, for example, of citizenship or rank or market power. Expressions of the liberal tradition in advanced industrial countries have characteristically justified the granting of opportunities to merit on grounds of efficiency in industry, government, and administration. As governmental bureaucracies developed in the nineteenth century, selection of entrants on merit increasingly replaced patronage, nepotism, and purchase. In Britain this movement can be traced to colonial administration, especially in India. It had a metropolitan milestone in the Northcote–Trevelyan reforms of the Civil Service. Merit in this context was educationally defined and the examination emerged as an instrument for detecting potential capacity for the performance of an expanding range of occupational positions.

This is what is meant by the general sociological thesis of a transition from 'ascriptive' to 'achievement' criteria in occupational selection. The theory of meritocracy evolved from this liberal movement and the definition attached to it by Michael Young is summarized in the label or slogan 'IQ plus effort'. The Oxford mobility data do not yield measures of the complex amalgam of mind and character which would fully represent any of the possible definitions of merit. They are confined to a definition in terms of measured intelligence and even here the IQ distributions between classes are estimated. Moreover, simplification apart, the meaning of measured intelligence in the context of explaining and justifying educational selection procedures is highly contentious.[23] There is an unresolved debate as to how far measured intelligence is cause and how far effect of class membership. There is continuing disagreement as to how far, if at all, past social selection has, in association with assortive mating, produced *genetically* distinct classes.

The significance of class comparisons of IQ scores must accordingly be limited and tentative. Nevertheless both the method and the result of the Oxford study is of some interest. The method consists of three steps. First, the social class composition of types of school can be estimated from the 1972 survey. Second, the share of places in each type of school which would accrue to each social class if allocations were made strictly on IQ scores can also be calculated. For this second step an assumption has to be made as to the appropriate rank order of each type of school and the assumption chosen is that public schools take the highest band of IQ. Then third, the actual shares are compared with the hypothetical IQ or 'meritocratic' shares obtained by each class in each type of school. The result turns out to be that the real world and the hypothetical meritocratic world are pretty similar. Moreover, this closeness of fit has been characteristic of secondary schooling for the past half century.

However, a crucially different result emerges when the same kind of analysis is applied to education beyond the statutory school-leaving age. Here the queue is reconstituted to give the universities the first slice of measured intelligence, the colleges of education the second, and part-time further education the third. When the quota which would have been allocated to each class in each birth cohort on IQ measurement is set alongside the actual allocation, it emerges that there was class equality of opportunity on meritocratic assumptions for some form of post-secondary education. But in the case of the most sought-after form of education beyond school—the university—there was still class inequality between the middle class and the other two classes. Privileged, that is non-meritocratic, access to the universities rose to its highest point among those born between 1933 and 1942, and then fell back, but not quite to the point recorded for the first cohort of those born between 1913 and 1922. Lower-middle-class boys born after the Second World War were relatively disadvantaged compared with their predecessors after the First World War, while working-class boys stayed at much the same level of relative disadvantage in the 1960s as they had been after the First World War, and with even more disadvantage in the years between. Thus, paradoxically, if the university is regarded as the crowning edifice of the state's policy of educational expansion, it is ironic to notice that this is the development which accords least with the meritocratic principle.

Though the study on which I have relied cannot tell us what effect, if any, has ensued from the further development of comprehensive secondary schooling and polytechnics since 1972, there is no reason to suppose that any marked change in the social distribution of educational *achievement* has been taking place over the subsequent decade. The evidence is that comprehensive reform of the secondary schools has contributed heavily to the output of entrants to higher and further education but without changing the correlation between social origin and educational attainment.[24] It is true, of course, that comprehensive reorganization and abolition of the direct-grant schools brought the vast majority of secondary as well as primary schoolchildren under one educational roof, leaving a minority of 5 per cent of children, mostly from rich families, in an increasingly isolated private sector with privileges which are difficult to defend.[25] But the continuing association of class origin with education destination still defies the declared intent of governments to secure what a Conservative Minister of Education, Sir Edward (later Lord) Boyle, described as 'the essential point . . . that all children should have an equal opportunity of acquiring intelligence, and of developing their talents and abilities to the full'.[26] The professional and managerial classes made up 18 per cent of the population in 1971: but their children formed 51 per cent of university entrants in 1975 and 54 per cent in 1979.[27]

Conclusion

The long words of politics—capitalism, socialism, communism, and democracy—have many and ambiguous meanings. So, too, has the educational system appropriate to a modern society. Education prepares children for society, transforming biological organisms into social personalities. Its capacity is essentially not to create but to re-create society, not to form structures of social life but to maintain the people and the skills that inform these structures. Education as a means of social change is secondary. It is not impotent because, *pace* Marx/Engels, man's social consciousness to some degree determines his social existence. Yet that social existence must be the starting-point for reforming educational policies of the past which come out of a class society, evolving perhaps towards one of classless inequality, complicated by the peculiar British history of political independence, of cultural homogeneity, and of primacy in the development of an urban-industrial civilization.

Ideologically, the national histories of education seem also to have echoed the themes with which we are concerned in this book—liberty, equality, and fraternity—against the constraining forces of structure and culture in each country. In Britain, the constraints have been those of a class society which gave rise, in the nineteenth century, to a mass system of elementary education imposed from above. Liberty gave ideological justification to the privileges of the minority in the public schools and the Oxford colleges, and later to an enlarged minority through selective secondary schools and universities. For the mass it was essentially freedom for a selected few to escape—a policy of selective educational embourgeoisment. This, at the same time, was the liberal approach to equality, taking the form of policies of equality of opportunity. Liberty also increasingly penetrated the infant school in that brief period in the life of a child in which there is some protection from the exigencies of educational selection. Thus, the twentieth-century debate in education has been dominated by a liberal solution which links equality to liberty but, with the exception of the comprehensive school movement, neglects the link to fraternity.

7

Order and authority

It is always possible that the United Kingdom of England, Scotland, Wales, and Northern Ireland could disintegrate. If for a moment we look beyond native British pieties and take instead the wider perspective of contemporary world history, the prospect of an approaching insular disestablishment becomes conceivable. Integration between nations and ethnic disintegration within them is the common pattern of current economic and political development all over the world. The British find themselves drawn simultaneously into the European Economic Community and into Scottish and Welsh separatism. The very different political and economic circumstances of the Soviet Union, of China, and of Africa reveal on a larger scale in each case the same story. Enlarging economic organization, with modernity as its aim, combines with sharp internal conflicts between Russian and non-Russian within the USSR, Han and non-Han minorities in China, and tribal groups in Africa.[1] The British experience is not unique. Nor is conflict, despite a cultural bias against recognizing it, in any way odd. As I pointed out in Chapter 1, the coexistence of interests and scarcity make it more difficult to explain why societies hang together, rather than why they break up.

All the more, then, is it a puzzle that, at least since Culloden in 1746, despite the alarm and dramas of the revolutionary years of 1688 and 1848, the General Strike of 1926, and the violent picket lines of the miners' strike in 1984–5, and notwithstanding the Southern Irish breakaway in 1922, and the current so-called troubles in Ulster which we hesitate to name as civil war, British history and the British state have been quite outstandingly tranquil. Ever since the battle between the Parliamentary armies and the forces of the Crown, more than three hundred years ago, the outstanding fact about Britain is domestic peace. Apologists throughout the modern age and down to our own day have never tired of words like 'decency', 'tolerance', and 'restraint', and phrases like 'respect for tradition', 'innate conservatism', 'the law and the constitution', and so on through a political and social lexicon of approval for consensus and condemnation of 'extremism'. By contrast, unlike those of consensus, the ugly words of political conflict never rid themselves of their inverted commas. 'Capitalism' and 'communism', 'bourgeoisie' and 'bureaucrat', 'dialetic' and '*démarche*', 'liberation' and 'liquidation': these remain alien visitors to an unfanatical tradition of political discourse. Not only in tourist brochures is the essential England still depicted as curling wood-smoke from a Cotswold cottage against an autumn sky.

Why? How did the nation that led the Industrial Revolution somehow contrive this changelessness? How did it retain monarchic and medieval symbols of unity, absorb first a bourgeoisie and second a proletariat, turn Hadrian's Wall and the Edwardian castles into tourist attractions, and contain the eisteddfod (which, I am told, is a medieval invention of the nineteenth century) and the kilt as quaint atavistic regional colourfulness, signifying politically nothing? And why, it if it so, are these ancient manifestations of war, bloodshed, force and oppression, so long turned into harmless symbols of pacification and gentleness, now re-emerging as signals of separatism and hostility? These are the final questions for this book: the problem of fraternity which has been latent in my discussion of liberty and equality, the problem of social order which has underlain my chronicle of class, status, and party.

One thing is obvious. Neither Marxism nor economic liberalism by itself explains the central problem of order. Neither tradition ever developed a serious theory of nationalism. For the Marxist nationalism is a secondary force, more or less useful in the march of history towards world revolution, given greater or lesser emphasis according to whether the theorist prefers Lenin or Rosa Luxemburg.[2] Liberal theory, too, has a central concept of one world, evolving as rationality displaces mercantilism and other superstitions towards free trade, patterned by comparative cost advantages. Both theories come out of the early development of capitalism, both vastly overestimate the possibility of economic solutions—the Marxists by assuming that the economic power of the capitalist class is all that stands in the way of a harmonious society of free and equal men, needing no political state to organize their brotherhood; the economic liberals, by assuming that the free market generates just distribution, needing only minimal government to guard its contractual perfection.

I want to argue that there are native traditions of social and political theory, which can be of more use to those who search for a solution. If the position which I support must be labelled, its name is *citizenship*. It is a tradition of radical reform in which democracy is both a means and an end and which seeks to attain a maximum of equality between individuals in a free society. If the first enemy of social peace in Britain is the persistence of inequality, then we look to such writers as T. H. Marshall who, as I suggested in the third chapter, avoids both the Marxist and the liberal error. He stands in a tradition much influenced by Durkheim and Weber. He brings us back to politics as the arena in which the conflicting claims of class and status are fought out. As David Lockwood has pointed out,[3] his theory of citizenship offers the most cogent answer to the problem, originally posed by Durkheim, of the basis of solidarity in modern societies.

Social integration in modern society

Writing in 1893,[4] Durkheim distinguished two forms of solidarity. The first type he called 'segmental', and the second 'organic'. In pre-literate societies, solidarity is mechanical, based on substitutability and resemblance. Individuals have experience and feelings common to all. The social units of society are also similar in form and function, each family being much like any other family in the society, and each community like every other community. As society advances, it comes to depend increasingly on the division of labour. Individuals are differentiated in their feelings. They are bound together now, not by consciousness of kind, but by their interdependence, their complementarity. The question then becomes: what is the social base for organic solidarity in modern societies? Durkheim's general answer need not detain us. But before we leave him, we can note that he made an acute observation concerning late nineteenth-century Britain.

It may very well happen, that in a particular society a certain division of labour—and especially economic division of labour—may be highly developed, while the segmental type may still be rather pronounced. This certainly seems to be the case in England: major industry, big business, appears to be as highly developed there as on the continent, while the segmental system is still very much in evidence, as witness both the autonomy of local life, and the authority retained by tradition.

Local autonomy and the strength of tradition are two clues to the maintenance of social integration in Britain, despite marked inequalities of class and status. And we can add the further Durkheimian point (though one he did not specifically apply to England) that 'all external inequality compromises organic solidarity'.[5] Writers like Barbara Wootton, R. M. Titmuss, and Alan Fox have carried further T. H. Marshall's approach to a direct analysis of the relation between inequality and social integration, and I shall return to them.[6]

Societies in general are made and broken by like interests leading to cohesion or competition, and by unlike interests which bind people together or bring them into conflict. But there is another principle of social organization—domination—which has become increasingly important in modern societies in the form of the authority of rationally created rules. Authority always has two sides, force and faith: the faith of the ruled that the rulers have the right to make rules by which people must live (for example, that they must pay such-and-such amounts in taxes), and the force that the rulers have at their disposal to compel compliance with the rules. In modern societies, by far the most important source of authoritative rules is the state, and the definition of the state, at once most simple and most useful, is that it has a monopoly of ultimate force in the territory it claims. But societies are not identical with states, as the example of Scotland clearly shows. The integration of a society is based less on force and more on faith—that is, on cultural affinities of language, custom, belief, and history, which give the members a consciousness of kind and kin with each other, and a sense of cultural boundary from other peoples. These bonds are more enduring so that states and empires have risen and fallen more rapidly than have societies: a nation and people can live, politically or militarily speaking, underground through many generations of foreign rule. Faith converts force into authority and consent.

But this distinction between force and faith, though essential to understanding of social cohesion in societies and states, does not complete the analysis. What sociologists call legitimation (which gives authority to those who wield power) involves the modern state not only in enforcing and administering law but also in elaborate processes of non-coercive integration, including the display of national symbols, appeals to traditional sources of authority, selective presentation of policy, and action in terms of what is or is judged to be the preferred values of the electorate, and so on through the whole range of relations of communication between government and governed over which the state can exercise more or less control or influence.[7]

Hence faith may vary in its social bases. It may be engendered or maintained by the power of classes, status groups, or parties to influence the consciousness of those they dominate. Consequently, some may wish to distinguish a third force, and to label it 'fraud'. Fraud typically resides in the power of ruling groups to exercise calculated control over communication, and thus to impose ideas and beliefs on the majority in the interests of the minority. In this way, organized religion, schooling, and the mass media may serve to hold a society together, continually reinforcing and disseminating its established ideologies. In practice, integration by fraud is intrinsically fragile. False faith is more characteristically an unintended consequence of unequally shared power. Conspiracy theories of society cannot be convincingly applied to Britain, and those writers like Frank Parkin who interpret the problem of social order as essentially that of legitimating the control of a dominant class, none the less recognize a variety of social mechanisms, such as religious ritual, the teaching of school history, or opportunities for social mobility, as not deliberate creations of that dominant class.[8]

The forces of fusion

Despite many examples of the insecurity of consensus, no Hobbesian collapse of civil society has so far marred modern British history. On the contrary, force and faith in their varied manifestations have played their part in what has been historically, a remarkably United Kingdom. The twentieth-century inheritance was, on balance, heavily weighted towards fusion rather than fission. Some of the unifying influences are easy enough to discern. The British state, centred on the Crown in Parliament, held undisputed sway over England, Scotland, and Wales for two centuries and, more important, naval power controlled an Empire eventually covering one-quarter of the land surface of the whole earth. Britain in 1900 was still the greatest of imperial nations, a major workshop of the world, and miraculously secured at the same time by a still impregnable insularity. British society was itself the apex of a world-wide imperial dominion, and London the financial centre of world trade.

This powerful combination of industry and empire obviously afforded huge wealth and wide opportunity to its controllers. Wealth and opportunity were most unequally shared within the society, between classes, sexes, and regions. But continuing, if decelerating and unsteady, expansion, itself a supplement to integration, was further and massively reinforced by the custom and culture of a most peculiar island. It was a culture of patrician liberalism. The aristocracy and the gentry maintained a dominance over both society and state from the overthrow of absolutist monarchy in the seventeenth century, and right through the imperial and industrial developments of the next two hundred years. The continuity of cultural symbols—a constitutional monarch, a tame but titled Second Chamber, a democratized but dignified Oxford and Cambridge—was made possible by these economic and military forces and, in turn, gave venerated changelessness to the continuous adaptiveness of a dominant class.

So, as Tom Nairn has put it, and is saying, in effect, what Durkheim said:

the pioneer modern liberal-constitutional state never itself became modern: it retained the archaic stamp of its priority. Later the industrialization which it produced, equally pioneering and equally worldwide in impact, never made England into a genuinely industralized society . . . And therefore no recovery from industrial 'backwardness' has been possible, precisely because no second revolution of the state has taken place in England: only the state could have engendered such a recovery, by revolution from above—but the old patrician structure of England's political system, incapable of such radical action, has also resisted every effort at serious reform up to the present day.[9]

But, I would add, if economically weak, it was made socially strong by the culture of the gentleman.

Nairn's historical analysis has to be taken seriously. Economic liberalism as a theory of free markets in the service of economic growth is older in England than the bourgeois industrialist manufacturer. The English land-owning classes had developed it long before the Industrial Revolution.[10] The aristocracy and the gentry absorbed the bourgeoisie in the nineteenth century. This gave to the twentieth century a stratified society which, though resembling the Marxist description of polarized class society if one looked at the Northern industrial towns, was also a status hierarchy of apparent agelessness. It was rooted in a medieval agrarian past. It provided a governing class descended from pre-industrial times to which was added, especially in the Southern counties, those whose wealth and status derived from the Empire, and from the finance capitalism of the City of London.

In short, Edwardian Britain was a country of inequality, but a strongly knit nation. A legacy of feudal aristocracy had, in the course of overseas imperialism and domestic industrialization, been accepted by both bourgeoisie and proletariat. No wonder, then, that Lord David Cecil saw the sunset over his grandfather's deathbed as also the twilight of British greatness. For the fusion I have briefly sketched was gradually to be dissolved by corrosion at home and abroad. The industrial competitors abroad—America and Germany—had already ended Britain's pre-eminence. In a century of relative, though not absolute, decline there was a period of prosperity in the 1950s and 1960s. When that interlude ended, domestic discontents fanned by economic stagnation, class and status inequalities, and more recently the recrudescence of economic liberalism as 'Thatcherism', were less and less easily contained by the traditional remedies of political liberalism, gentlemanly culture, and civic incorporation. A formidable toll of human energy and resource now has to be mobilized in order to control a country hitherto frequently held up as an exemplar of urbane peace. On a Saturday in February 1978, five thousand policemen were drafted into the East London constituency of Ilford to prevent clashes between the National Front and its opponents. In Northern Ireland at the same time there were thirty-one thousand British soldiers, making a ratio of one to every forty-five of the population. This is a ratio not very different to that of teachers to schoolchildren before the Second World War. In 1984 and 1985 the massive use of police forces against massed pickets was an outstanding feature of the miners' strike.

Nevertheless, there have been strong forces making for

integration. If only because we are so accustomed now to gloomy discussion of Britain's economic decline, we should remind ourselves that it is a country which enjoyed economic growth for the first three-quarters of this century. The national bookkeeping of economists suggests a tripling of real income per head since 1900. And even if growth ended in the last quarter, prosperity is still the condition of the great majority. The average person is unquestionably better fed, better clothed, better housed, and enjoys a longer, healthier, and more leisured life than his Edwardian predecessor. Clearly allegiance to a society is more secure when these ameliorations are in train, that is, when the generations see a darker past and a brighter future.

We also do well to remind ourselves of the integrating aspects of war. It is a paradox of external conflict that it promotes equality and fraternity within the nation. This is true especially of modern 'total' war. If all must be called upon to fight for their country, all must be brought to believe that they have a stake in it. Both World Wars brought renewed promise for the future. They reinforced patriotic sentiment.

> But ever 'twixt the book and his bright eyes
> The gleaming eagles of the legions came.[11]

This was a possible reverie for a young clerk in England in the First World War and even the Second, before the bomb dropped on Hiroshima. The two Wars also softened class divisions and reduced inequality. In 1945, much more than in 1919, there was intense feeling among working men and women that the promises of English culture were about to be redeemed in their own lives. As they had sung in the shadows, so now they sang Edward Carpenter's secular hymn in the light: England is risen and day is here.

The forces of fission

Yet, although war and prosperity may tend to integrate, other twentieth-century experiences have had an opposite effect. For one thing, economic growth has had a cyclical character. Earlier slumps were increasingly forgotten in the full employment decades of the 1950s and 1960s. But their failure seriously to disturb the social and political order in the 1930s is testimony only to the power of cultural integration. As we have seen, when he came to

Jarrow in 1933, J. B. Priestley marvelled that men in such economic conditions, not under the constraint of military force, but on the contrary politically enfranchised, should nevertheless have accepted their lot.[12] That they did has to be explained largely by the strength of a consensual political culture. It inculcated belief in progress towards a more civilized society and nourished the faith that as their cause was just, so their victory was certain. Neither the consensual culture nor the belief in progress has been as strong in the face of the renewed experience of mass unemployment in the 1980s.

Again, industrial productivity in the twentienth century has been accompanied by growing alienation of labour. On his inter-war journey, Priestley reports the opinion of a craftsman that 'all our labour troubles did not come from a quarrel about distribution of the profits, but from a deeper cause, the crushing of the workman's self respect by mechanical labour in which he could not find himself'.[13] And the author returns to the theme in reflecting on a Leicester sock-making factory. He remarks the 'great distinction between the fortunate few who are outside the machine and are capable of making changes in it and the great mass of ordinary work people, mostly women, who are inside the machine, simply part of it. This distinction is so great that you feel that the two sets of people ought to belong to two different races.'[14] Of those 'inside the machine' he observes 'they are not bullied or even nagged at; their very weaknesses are elaborately taken into account; their comfort is considered, but between the time when they "clock in" and "clock out" their central human dignity which entitles them under our democratic system to a vote as good as anybody else's, has no real existence, except in that dream of life which occupies their minds as their fingers fly to do their own mysterious little task.'[15]

But above all—the factor of paramount importance—has been the essentially unprincipled inequality of distribution of wealth and income. The stubborn persistence of distributional inequality of wealth and income is such as to need no further documentation. It is true that, at least until recently, the implications of inequality have manifested themselves in the economic rather than the political sphere. Within the economic sphere, however —in industrial relations and the management of incomes policy —inequality has been corrosive. The manifestations have not been those of class warfare but rather, as John Goldthorpe has argued, 'in a situation of anomie; that is . . . a lack of moral regulation over the wants and goals that individuals hold'.[16] Consensual politics have been maintained partly by the remarkably restricted comparisons within and between classes which Runciman has analysed,[17] and partly by the political culture of democracy which I reviewed in Chapter 4.

However, the development of the social rights of citizenship generates conflict as well as consensus in such a way as to *exacerbate* anomic conditions. This unintended by-product of an otherwise integrative force takes at least three forms. First the egalitarian principle intrinsic to citizenship challenges normative approval of market inequalities. Class and citizenship are at war in the twentieth century. Second, citizenship also undermines traditional status hierarchies which, though strongly rooted in British culture, are conventionally, not legally, based. Citizenship is therefore a basis for dissent from the established social order. And third, the extension of citizenship rights into the industrial sphere—a movement towards various forms of industrial democracy—gives unions, and especially local groups of workers and their shop stewards, increased protection and power to pursue their market and work interests relatively undisciplined by traditional constraints. Attempts since 1979 to shift the balance of industrial power away from the unions by new legislation have met angry opposition in part because the citizenship ideal is outraged thereby.

So, the partial development of the principle of citizenship, under circumstances where competing distributional principles deriving from class, status, and citizenship still contend for pre-eminence, may reduce rather than increase organic solidarity. The consequences have been increasingly evident in the recent history of industrial relations. They are most dramatically illustrated in the growing bitterness of race relations in the major English cities.[18]

One feature of 'Thatcherism' is the successful exploitation of an ancient traditional belief that the economic and the political spheres should be kept separate. It is always an open question, of course, how far economic inequality, alienation, and anomy take on political forms of expression. They may be individualized or localized. Rising rates of crime, vandalism, and hooliganism are possible outcomes: and these have risen markedly in recent decades. The connections, I must emphasize, are not proven. None the less, whatever the reason for the escalation of anti-social activity, there can be no doubt that they in turn reduce confidence in the political and social order. The legitimacy of government and administration is thereby threatened. The apparently increasing frequency of corruption in government and administration—or perhaps simply the wider publicity it receives from investigative journalism—further diminishes civic trust. We cannot measure exactly the strength of these forces, and I fully appreciate that political corruption is normal rather than abnormal in the history of states. Nevertheless, solidarity in Britain in the nineteenth and early twentieth centuries depended heavily on political trust to counterbalance resentments naturally born of inequality.

Shifting balance of cohesion and conflict

Twentieth-century experience, then, has been mixed. Before the First World War, discontents springing from class divisions and stultifying industrial labour were checked by limited working-class expectations and the strong alliance of aristocrat and bourgeois. Meanwhile, the old traditions of civil liberty in which modern citizenship is rooted, though providing the legal basis for the development of class inequalities, had also begun to extend into political enfranchisement and into a set of social rights which later came to be called the Welfare State. The organization of the working class was also built on the same foundations of citizenship. These integrative forces were, however, only weakly struggling into existence, and they carried their own threats to the established order. There was also, especially on Clydeside, a serious syndicalist current flowing away from the more moderate mainstream of the trade unions, the co-operative societies, and the infant Labour party. The war itself suspended opposition and brought a primitive form of war socialism, some reduction of wage differentials, and steps towards the emancipation of women.

Return to 'normalcy', as it was then termed, shifted the balance again towards, but not quite back to, the pre-war situation. Religion had lost some of its restraining power. The expected boundaries of self-fulfilment were pushed back, educational horizons began to widen, and many intellectuals were vehemently critical of bourgeois life and values. This was the period of fellow-travelling. Nevertheless, this weakening of cultural control never showed signs of being turned into a threatening political movement. British radical politics centred on the Labour party. Bitter industrial struggles scarred the 1920s, but the rise of the Labour party after the First World War to replace the Liberal party was its incorporation into the politics of consensus, not very different from that described in the nineteenth century by Walter Bagehot. Then the slump years of the early 1930s temporarily overlaid the basic politics of belief in progress with hopelessness, fatalism, and fragmentation—a deadening and defeatist interpretation of events was universally shared: economic depression was seen as externally imposed rather than politically soluble.

Then again, partial recovery and the Second World War eased the tensions and renewed the national promise. Liberty, equality, and fraternity all made progress during the war and post-war years. Labour party philosophy dominated politics and there were even five early post-war years of a Labour government in clear majority—winning the solid allegiance of most of those who came of political age in the 1930s and 1940s. The Labour victory was never, of course, total, even among its natural supporters—the industrial working class. But, in any case, the following thirteen years of Conservative government were years of full employment, and of educational and occupational opportunity for a significant minority of the new generation of the working class. Belief in an emergent meritocracy was developing in this period, despite the evidence of continuing class inequality of conditions for fair competition, which are necessary for meritocratic principles to replace hereditary or ascriptive ones as the normative basis for an unequal society. It was a time of high net upward mobility and of slowly burgeoning mass affluence. Governments derived legitimacy, deservedly or not, from the *absolute* improvement of conditions and opportunities, not from any amelioration of relative inequality between classes, ethnic groups, or the sexes. The tide of political consensus flowed strongly for twenty years or more.

The tide began to run out in the 1960s. By this time the Empire was gone. Ideologically, all that was left was Powellite English nationalism. Economically, what remained was the overseas-oriented financial capitalism of the City, which drained talent and attention away from the needs of an ageing and sluggish industrial economy. Hope and glory faded from the land, weakening both national and local cohesion. Internal tensions became more anxiously acute with economic stagnation, quickening inflation, and rising unemployment.

Meanwhile the trade unions, fostered by the further development of citizenship rights, had become more powerfully entrenched, more able to press sectional against national interest. Indeed their successful expansion into the white-collar occupations further enlarged the sphere for competitive sectionalism in bargaining over wages and conditions. And, as I argued in my fourth chapter, the incorporation of the Labour leadership both in Parliament and in the TUC, undermined the allegiance of the rank and file, reducing the 'governability' of those officially organized into the working-class movement.

There were also ideological movements in these post-war years with strongly divisive effects. The authority of churches and chapels declined still further. Schoolteachers and parents became less effective conveyors of cultural values and traditional pieties as they too lost confidence in their right and their ability to be so. Scandals from the Profumo affair (1963) onwards dealt repeated blows to the British reputation for incorruptible government. Names like Burgess and Maclean or Blunt gradually destroyed the myth of patriotic, upright, and gentlemanly rulers schooled at Eton and Cambridge. The Poulson revelations of widespread racketeering in the Labour strongholds of the North-East were especially damaging to popular respect for the authority of both the Town Hall and Whitehall. There was a marked contrast between the moralistic Primitive Methodist Labour leaders, like Peter Lee, steeped in the proprieties of constitutional liberalism, and the political bosses like Dan Smith and Andrew Cunningham who replaced them, with their public relations networks and their eventual exposure and long gaol sentences for criminal behaviour in public office. And the adversary culture of students, intellectuals, journalists, and media men grew more strident in the 1960s. The expansion of the universities permitted the growth of social science, which emerged after 1965 as a powerful vehicle for radical criticism of established society. (Social science faculties in the expanding universities grew at three times the rate of the other faculties in the 1962–7 quinquennium.)

Then, in the 1970s, came the sudden development of nationalism in Scotland, echoed by weaker but still significant separatism in Wales. Even the detachment of Northern Ireland became a possibility. These three countries, Scotland with 5½ million, Wales with 2¾ million, and Ulster with 1½ million population, are few in numbers compared with the 46 million who dwell in England. All four peoples are intermixed, geographically and by intermarriage, to a considerable degree, but are also to a greater or lesser degree opposed to the political and cultural dominance of the London metropolis. Minorities within them aspire to political independence and, in Ulster, social tension is further and tragically compounded by conflict between the Protestant majority and the one-third minority of Catholics who receive violent, if not wholly welcomed, support from the Irish Republican Army (IRA) operating in part from Eire, south of the partition border.

In consequence, the United Kingdom faced an uncertain future, variously assessed and actively debated. One extreme, unrepresentative view was that

it depends upon one's conception of the United Kingdom. There are those who believe that this rump of the former empire will last for ever, in an essentially unchanging evolution. Their number includes virtually all England, and a still formidable mass of allies in Scotland, Wales, and Northern Ireland. On the other hand stands the growing opposition—within sight of being a majority in Scotland—which accepts the verdict a great part of the outside world passed on Britain long ago: that it is a matter of time before it founders. Its post-empire crisis is long overdue, and not even to be regretted. What else is likely to revive this polity of stultified anachronism and complacent privilege?[19]

Nairn published this judgement in 1977. The results of the general election of 1979 sharply contradicted his assessment of Scottish attitudes. But the underlying problem, more soberly stated, of social cohesion in a United Kingdom remained and was confronted by a new challenge. Thatcherism brought to an end the post-war period of consensus politics just as the crisis of West European economies ended the long post-war boom. A new period of political economy began with explicit attack on what Stuart Hall calls the historic class compromise. Neo-liberalism was to reassert the rule of the market and with it the restoration of class power. Political legitimacy was to be sought through authoritarian populism. Conviction politics and the confrontation of the enemies of the state, at home as well as abroad, were to be the basis of a renewed nation.

Frailty of authority

Whatever the balance of faith and force, cohesion and conflict, the frailty of authority is a characteristic feature of large and complex modern societies. Three types of authority are distinguished in sociology. One of these, the rational–legal in Max Weber's inelegant phrase, bids to dominate the modern world in the form of *bureaucracy*. What is rational and legal about this type of authority is that it claims to apply to particular cases. Its deeper justification comes, at least in Britain, from the fact (or at least the theory) that the general rules are arrived at by democratic legislation. Its legitimacy rests ultimately on the preferences of the majority. The danger is that bureaucrats all too easily and frequently break the chain from popular will to executive decision.

There is a second type of authority—*charisma*—the personal authority of the inspired leader who is trusted by his followers. His word is the criterion of truth and worth. This type of authority also has its frailties. It can be de-legitimized by failure to 'deliver the goods'. Public opinion polls reflect its instability. Those who aspire to it, like David Owen or David Steel, must face the ordeal of their annual party conferences. And there is a third type—tradition. Today's orders are justified on the grounds that we have always done it that way. It is ancestral wisdom. But I hardly need to explain the frailty of traditional authority in our world of rapid social change. In the village where I grew up, custom decreed that all adults, within limits well understood, could and should act *in loco parentis*. There was an intergenerational authority, legitimized by culturally stored solutions to unchanging problems. But in the shifting populations of large cities, young people are less ready to accord respect to their elders. 'Grandad' becomes a term of contempt. This is the absence of intergenerational authority.

It seems almost, once one's thoughts begin to run on these lines, that the newspapers, the radio, and the television are concerned with nothing else than authority, its legitimation, the conditions for its exercise, and the causes of its rupture. Members of Parliament defy the Speaker, young men assault old women in the street, prisoners rebel against warders in the gaols, condemned members of the Irish Republican Army refuse to recognize an Irish court.

By way of contrast, I recently saw a copy of a passport signed by Lord Palmerston in 1851.[20]

We, Henry John Viscount Palmerston, Baron Temple, a Peer of Ireland, a Member of Her Britannic Majesty's Most Honourable Privy Council, a Member of Parliament, Knight Grand Cross of the most Honorable Order of the Bath, Her Majesty's Principal Secretary of State for Foreign Affairs, request and require in the Name of Her Majesty all those whom it may concern to allow Mr. Edward Holyroyd, his wife, Mrs. Holyroyd, two daughters and three sons, travelling on the Continent, with a man and a maid servant, to pass freely without let or hindrance, and to afford them every assistance and protection of which they may stand in need. Given at the Foreign Office, London, the 10th day of July 1851.

Notice the symbols of authority here. And, perhaps even more telling, the confident description of social hierarchy from Her Majesty down through the Viscount to Mr Holyroyd and thence to sons and daughters, and finally a man and a maid servant.

Honi soit qui mal y pense, says the heraldry. No matter that, three years before, Marx and Engels in the Communist Manifesto of 1848 had, with no less confidence, announced the impending fall of the capitalist state, the overthrow of imperial authority by the rising revolutionary proletariat.

We have since seen the twentieth-century rise of *new* authorities—the TUC, and the Parliamentary Labour party—from Downing Street, Manchester, to Downing Street, London, to become what journalists described in the 1970s as the natural government of the country. But the annual conferences are a much cherished opportunity for the rank and file to belabour their masters on the platform, rather as we know many primitive tribes have annual rituals in which the chief is ceremoniously reviled and insulted by licensed warriors before the assembled people. Behind the rituals less open struggles proceed for power which can be translated into authority. Thus it is characteristic of the Russian and Chinese regimes that there have been bitter struggles for succession to the places emptied by death among the founding gerontocracy.

I choose these diverse examples partly to emphasize that the problem of authority is ubiquitous in human relationships, extending from the encounter in the street through those small human groups which are sufficiently bound by rules for us to call them institutions, like the family, or the youth club, or the office, and on up to the great political organizations of party and Parliament.

From all these instances, we can discern the three basic forms of authority—rational–legal, charismatic, and traditional—combining and contending with one another. And we can further see that social change makes each of them uncertain as legitimate sources for stable and peaceable relations between people. The examples emphasize that authority is not a synonym for law. The adults in my village had no legal authority over children: but they had the authority of long-established tradition. Neither law nor traditional authority is absolute. The young 'mugger' flouts the law. Certainly Mao exercised enormous charisma in his progress from young revolutionary in Yenan Province to the chairmanship in Peking. But charisma too has no universal writ. It may be routinized, as with Christ's authority in the institution of the papal succession. But Mao's charisma, if it did not die with him, at least could not prevent a power struggle among the survivors.

Charisma is historically like the wind which bloweth where it listeth. Churchill is thought of in Britain as having had this type of authority. He gained it at a moment of desperate external threat to a country at war. External threat does, in fact, accelerate the process whereby many are called and few are chosen. Mrs Thatcher, too, seemed to gain charismatic legitimacy during the Falklands war of 1982 and was thus rescued from an unpopularity which was undermining support for her and her party. The passing of the post-war period has carried with it a chronic political atmosphere of threatened collapse. But let us be clear that the possibility of new and dramatic leadership, which infirmity invites, is highly dangerous. Charisma is no necessary friend of democracy—*explicitly* not if it comes from the political extreme Right, and *actually* not if it comes from the extreme Left, for all its ideological clothing in rhetoric proclaiming the will of the people.

Bureaucracy

Alienation from the state apparatus is an equally widespread popular experience. Bureaucracy, like bourgeoisie, serves more often as a term of abuse than as a descriptive category. Gordon Tullock[21] has described it as a 'comprehensive criticism of politicians and civil servants for being more interested in feathering their own nests than serving the public'. Professor Tullock argues that civil servants are just like other men and that therefore 'they will make most of their decisions in terms of what benefits them, not society as a whole'. And, 'as a general rule, a bureaucrat will find that his [interests are best served] . . . if the bureaucracy in which he works expands'.

In the late 1970s the two large Civil Service unions, alarmed by what their leaders described as a 'hate campaign against civil servants', had distributed a pamphlet to MPs and other unions defending the incumbents of public offices against exaggerated rumours of their pay and pensions, and against misrepresentation of their conduct towards citizens. The Civil Service unions had also protested against cuts in public expenditure in general and public service jobs in particular. No one ought to need reminding that forced unemployment is a private tragedy and a public failure, but anyone could be forgiven, after following the public announcements of Labour and Conservative governments after 1970, for thinking that there had been a sharp reduction in the number of officials. And this was specially marked in the case of local government with its alleged reorganization for greater economy and efficiency. In fact the opposite was the case.

The Manpower Watch Survey—made jointly by central and local government—records that, between March 1975 and March 1976—a much publicized 'No Growth' period—there was an *increase* in English and Welsh local government staff of over 30,000. On a longer view it is clear that governments of either colour presided over continuous bureaucratic growth. There were $1\frac{1}{4}$ million local government employees in 1960. It was 2 million when Labour displaced the Tories in 1964. They added over 400,000 before the Conservatives came back in 1970 determined to turn the tide. But the tide flowed on. By 1975 there were 2,875,000 despite the fact that 77,000 were transferred to the NHS and Water Services in 1974 and so did not appear in the 1975 total. By 1978 there were 5 million central and local government officials, compared with 17.5 million in the private sector. No wonder that the 1979 Conservative government redoubled its resolve. There was a decrease of almost 15 per cent in the total number of industrial and non-industrial civil servants in the United Kingdom between April 1979 and April 1984, bringing the number down to 592,700. But the much larger local authority manpower was only marginally reduced (from 2,347,700 to 2,267,400).[22]

Taking a still wider view it can be seen that in the twentieth century the occupational structure has shifted its centre of gravity from basic productive employment to the tertiary sector of services and administration. One measure of the change is that between 1911 and 1966 white-collar numbers went up 176 per cent, while manual jobs rose only 5 per cent and actually decreased after 1931.

These figures reflect an increasingly organized world in which bureaucracy is the dominant working principle. Though the word 'community' also spatters its pages, the contemporary newspaper habitually looks out, sees organizations everywhere, and tells us in a more or less sensationalist way how people enter them in pursuit of their interest only to lose themselves. Paul Johnson, in the *New Statesman*[23] provides a characteristic expression of this view with an attack of spectacular verbal violence on the leaders of the TUC. For Johnson this organizational élite are the greatest threat to democracy in modern times and the closed shop the greatest blow against freedom in his lifetime.

It is the thesis of the bureaucratic brothers that they represent the people; that what they are doing, in erecting their private empires, in extending their bureaucratic control and grabbing jobs for their boys, in remorselessly driving their juggernaut over the prostrate bodies of individual men and women, that all this is done by, with, for and in the name of the people. Jack Jones, who might well be described as the Louis XIV of the trade union takeover, has seemingly convinced himself that 'Le peuple, c'est moi!' . . . But all the available evidence suggests that, at a time when so many members of the Establishment—ministers and MPs, dons, and civil servants, experts and publicists—are hurrying to pay their respects to the new totalitarianism, and sell their shares in individual liberty, the ordinary decent people of Britain are strongly opposed to rule by trade-union bureaucrats.

In common speech, of course, the word 'bureaucracy' is an established term of abuse. The word 'bureau' referred originally to the cloth covering the desks of French government officials in the eighteenth century. With its suffix added it came to refer to the rule of government, and a host of '-ocracies' have since been added to the vocabulary of politics as commentators have searched desperately to find the ultimate seat of power in modern society. The pejorative term then spread throughout Europe during the nineteenth century, at first to ridicule the high-handed arrogance of officials in absolutist regimes, and later more generally as a whip for the backs of unresponsive organizations, tortuous methods of administration, and large-scale enterprises (whether of government, business, religion, or recreation) in which power was concentrated into the hands of the administrative few.

There is, on the other hand, a technical, social-scientific use of bureaucracy to describe a type of social organization deliberately devised by men for the rational and efficient pursuit of defined purposes. No one saw more clearly than Max Weber that bureaucracy and large-scale organization were the fundamental phenomena of modern political, social, and economic life. And Weber's account of bureaucracy, from one point of view, reminds us of its virtues. Bureaucracy, he noted, was distinguished from other forms of human authority and control by its routinized rationality, its capacity to attain a high degree of efficiency, its stability, the stringency of its discipline, and its reliability. It is a matter of national pride in Britain that it showed the world how to escape from the corrupt control of administration by the privileged into uncorrupt and dedicated public service recruited on merit in open competition, by the Northcote-Trevelyan and Gladstonian reforms; and that was the acceptable face of bureaucracy.

It is true that Weber at the same time saw the tragedy of the highly organized world into which industrialization would take us—a world of disenchantment, robbed of magic and mystery. Even charisma, the gift of grace, would be routinized within it and freedom and individuality could be destroyed by it. Nevertheless, in company with both the Leftists and the Rightists of his age, Weber identified modernity with the spread of bureaucratic administration:

This is true of church and state, of armies, political parties, economic enterprizes, organizations to promote all kinds of causes, private associations, clubs, and many others. However many forms there may be which do not appear to fit this pattern, such as collegial representative bodies, parliamentary committees, soviets, honorary officers, lay judges, and what-not, and however much people may complain about the 'evils of bureaucracy', it would be sheer illusion to think for a moment that continuous administrative work can be carried out in any field except by means of officials working in offices. The whole pattern of everyday life is cut to fit this framework. For bureaucratic administration is, other things being equal, always from a formal technical point of view, the most rational type. For the needs of mass administration today, it is completely indispensable. The choice is only that between bureaucracy and dilettantism in the field of administration.[24]

Adherents of different ideological traditions than that of Weber's liberalism echoed his celebration of the inevitable march of bureaucracy as well as his ambivalence towards it. Sheldon Wolin[25] has written a subtle and scholarly account of the origin of this view in all political camps. Whatever differences there were in diagnosis and prescription, most of the major writers have been agreed on the general formula for developing wealth, welfare, and social order—organization. Thus for the nineteenth-century French conservative, de Maistre, the organization of society into a vast hierarchy of authority would reinstitute stability and peace under the command of king and pope, assisted by a public-spirited aristocracy. For his compatriot, Auguste Comte, there would be an organized hierarchy of savant-priests. For yet another compatriot, Emile Durkheim, the organization of society had to be on the basis of professional and producing groups. For the proponents of managerial élitism in the twentieth century the best organization of society is one under the control of the professional managers and administrators who alone possess the requisite knowledge for maintaining social equilibrium in the age of successive technological revolutions.

Weber himself remorselessly drove home the inference from the indispensability of bureaucracy that it made no difference whether an economic system was organized on a capitalist or a socialist basis. And he adds:

though by no means alone, the capitalistic system has undeniably played a major role in the development of bureaucracy. Indeed, without it capitalistic production could not continue and any rational type of socialism would simply have to take it over and increase its importance. Its development, largely under capitalistic auspices, has created an urgent need for stable, strict, intensive, and calculable administration. It is this need which gives bureaucracy a crucial role in our society as the central element in any kind of large-scale administration.[26]

Bureaucracy, I would stress, in theories of the Right and the Left, has been seen as an instrument not only for efficiency but also of social control. There is accordingly an élitism of the Left as well as of the Right. Lenin is perhaps the outstanding example. In Professor Wolin's phrase 'organization was to mass in Lenin's theory what idea had been to matter in Plato's: that which imparted form to the formless'. Lenin was the first to seize the implications of transferring politics to the plane of organization. He taught that politics had meaning only within an organizational setting. The trick was not to destroy the political but to absorb it into organization to create a new compound. The irony is that his prescription for revolution has also been used to preserve giant capitalism. Democracy has no meaning in such élitist thought except in so far as it is consonant with the imperatives of organization. Thus Lenin wrote:

Bureaucracy *versus* democracy is the same thing as centralism *versus* (local) democracy as opposed to the organizational principle of the opportunists of Social Democracy. The latter want to proceed from the bottom upwards . . . The former proceed from the top, and advocate the extension of the rights and powers of the centre in respect of the parts . . . My idea is 'bureaucratic' in the sense that the Party is built from the top downwards . . .[27]

Lenin's theory was the basis for Communist organization. But the historical roots of British socialism were never like that. Democracy came to Britain from the bottom upwards. The urban working classes of the nineteenth century were uprooted newcomers to the growing provincial industrial towns who responded to their circumstances with extraordinary social inventiveness to give Britain in the first half of the twentieth century its most characteristic popular organizations—the co-operative store, the trade union, and the Labour party, as well as the dance hall, the football club, and the Friendly Society. The first and the greatest three of these were experiments in democracy. This urban proletariat created its own local, communal welfare societies. Nothing could have been more democratic than the constitution of the co-op, nothing more fraternal than the miners' lodge. Nowhere could we find a more sturdy institutional protection for individuals against becoming a mass to be manipulated. Then, with political organization as its instrument, the Labour movement, dominated by the statist tradition of reform as propounded by the Webbs and the Fabians, set out to nationalize democracy and welfare; to translate fraternity, equality, and liberty from the local community to the national state.

What has been the outcome? In 1973, very near to the end of his life, R. H. S. Crossman gave an account, in the form of a review, of the Labour movement as he had experienced it. It was in essence a lament for the eclipse of voluntarism by bureaucratic organization—a disappointment in Westminster and a despair in Whitehall:

From the 1920s on, the normal left-wing attitude has been opposed to middle-class philanthropy, charity, and everything else connected with do-gooding. Those of us who became socialists grew up with the conviction that we must in this point ally ourselves with the professionals and the trade unions and discourage voluntary effort particularly since it was bound to reduce the number of jobs available to those in need.

I am now convinced that the Labour Party's opposition to philanthropy and altruism and its determined belief in economic self-interest as the driving dynamic of society has done it grievous harm. For ironically enough the Party, trade unions, and the Co-operative were all a hundred years ago inspired by a profound and passionate altruism—a belief in a new Jerusalem—linked with an urgent sense of duty—a conviction that it was an essential part of socialism to practise what one preached by volunteering to help comrades in distress.[28]

So the movement which had invented the social forms of modern participatory democracy and practised them in union branch and co-op meeting, thereby laying a Tocquevillian foundation for democracy, was ironically fated to develop through its political party the threats of a bureaucratic state. Of course, there were those who protested against these emerging tyrannies with the authentic voice of a deeply rooted English socialism. Norman Dennis has written, for example, a completely convincing demolition of British planning practices, from the standpoint of democratic socialism in the English tradition which I have described.[29] There is an authentic anti-statism of the Left.

Planning is, of course, associated with left-wing politics and the illogical 'therefore' is frequently added that criticism of it is comfort to the Right. But the 'hidden hand' is also 'a planner' with the market as its instrument. This form of 'planning', however, is vitiated by unequal distributions of power, wealth, and income between citizens; it does not accurately reflect the preferences of citizens in community as opposed to individuals in a market. Studies of planning do often turn out to be a more or less sophisticated attack on socialism and a plea to 'return to the market'. With Dennis, however, the criticism is directed to the planner's indifference to egalitarian notions of income and power, and his ignorance of the preferences and values of the community he is appointed to serve.

On what grounds can we accept or reject the theory or principle by which a bureaucracy is guided in its action? Sociologists call these grounds the 'legitimation' of the organization and its activities. Max Weber pointed out that organizations differ greatly when they come to decide whether what they are doing is 'morally right' and based upon 'the correct and relevant data'. One type of organization accepts the word of its leader on both these matters. This is charisma, the personal authority of the inspired leader—the sayings of the leader are the criteria of both truth and worth. A second type of organization rests its activities upon a piety for what has actually, allegedly, or presumably always existed and upon a belief in the everyday routine as being the inviolable norm of conduct. This is organized authority based on tradition. Thirdly, there are organizations to which Weber gave the term bureaucratic, which appeal to the rule of general laws applying to all within the jurisdiction of the organization without regard to differences of race, age, family background, or social condition. The legitimacy of such an organization's authority does not depend upon the actual benefits given to particular persons, but upon the legality of the general rule which has been purposely thought out and enacted. Authority here is based on formal as distinct from substantive justice.

This said, it is immediately apparent how enormously ambitious is the claim, scientific and moral, for a bureaucratic organization.

The task is relatively easy, and successful bureaucratic routine administrations have emerged, where the same service can (and especially where it must) be provided day after day in an identical way to large numbers of people. This is the case with, for example, gas, water, and electricity supplies, and transport and postal services. Bureaucratic administration is also appropriate, if more problematic, in the production of houses when, because of chronic shortage, large numbers of identical dwellings must be produced. It may even be appropriate to the demolition of houses where a few formal characteristics—for example, whether the house is at all damp, or possibly where a measurable amount of dampness is present—enable an official to distinguish unequivocally between a slum house and a non-slum house. But when we come to the service of more subtle and varied human needs in medicine, social security, or education, difficulties multiply and a fourth type of legitimation appears which is increasingly important in the modern world. The activities of an organization are not 'proved' right and good because they are the command of a charismatic leader, or because of tradition, or because they can be subsumed under some general rule, but because they are so certified by the trained members of the organization whose special function it is to evaluate the particular issue. This is professional authority. Decisions, characteristically in the form of 'advice', are made by those who have been appointed to a 'sphere of competence' on the basis of qualifications attested by a professional group of peers.

As long as the group of professional make claims only in the technical sphere, and as long as they merely say 'this is the given task, we know the most economical means of accomplishing it', the organization will show many acceptable bureaucratic characteristics. But it is also possible for professionals to make claims in such a way, or to such an extent, that their legitimation resembles that of the inspired leader. These claims to legitimation typically take the form of a kind of group charisma. Each case is adjudicated not by an appeal to strictly formal conceptions unambiguously established, made public, and safely recorded 'in the files', but by informal judgements rendered by the personal incumbent of the professional status in terms of concrete ethical or practical valuations. These valuations may be quite opaque to those outside the profession. The professional, by definition, is absolved from justifying his decision; he does not need to reveal his basis in theory or fact or value.

Thus the legitimacy of professional bureaucratic decisions must be judged in two ways. The first is scientific. Decisions ought to be made in the light of ascertainable knowledge. No one can read Dennis's account of planning in Sunderland and retain confidence in the professionalism of planners. Nor is this an isolated local example. Here, speaking more generally, and with examples from many branches of public policy, is R. H. S. Crossman again:

> But I was even more worried, particularly when I became a Minister and was able to see a good deal for myself, by the inexplicable decisions under which I found our social services to be operating, decisions which in themselves were inhuman and stupid. And yet as I knew full well they had been made by intelligent, well-intentioned people. How could it be possible that now we had abolished the amateurism of philanthropy and placed the administration of our welfare state in highly professional hands such decisions could be made?[30]

The second way of judging professional bureaucracies emphasizes the capacity of ordinary people to reach rational decisions about matters which directly affect them. But even more it emphasizes the moral proposition that the exercise of personal discretion is itself a social and personal good. When such discretion has to be abbreviated, as is unavoidable on countless grounds, the case of those who desire to impose restrictions must be well based in fact and convincing in terms of political, social, and moral argument. Otherwise we are all too likely to forget, in a fog of pseudo-science, that, as Dennis likes to say, 'the citizen is usually his own best expert'.

Conclusion

The outlook, some may conclude, is gloomy—the huge private businesses we have created, and the public servants we invented to realize justice, freedom, and equity will become our tyrannical masters. Even the ombudsman will turn out to be another professional bureaucrat.

What, then, is to be done? The characteristic response by the centre to peripheral unrest is further efforts at incorporation. The various forms of community development projects, initiated and controlled from Whitehall under the Urban Programme, exemplify the pattern.[31] Central direction is resented by local activists. For example, the grand national design for developing and applying a response to poverty through more effectively delivered and integrated local services degenerates into a complicated pattern of conflict between the centre and the locality, and within the locality between competing interest groups. It would be idle to pretend to an easy answer. But if there are answers, they might more readily be found in our own heritage of democracy and socialism. Our hard-won civil liberties need new defence from a radical overhaul of administrative laws. We have an unfinished programme of greater economic and social equality. But the social integration which is needed to underpin it all cannot survive the national organization we have erected.

In this context Thatcherism, if it maintains its strategy of excluding organized labour from the political process and insisting on a 'new realism' in the economic market-place, threatens the basis of social order. The renowned gentleness of British society may be jeopardized. Fraud bids to supplant faith, if necessary by the use of force. Modern states are increasingly authoritarian. Techniques of surveillance and of opinion management are increasingly built into public and private bureaucracies. In Britain, E. P. Thompson has pointed in alarm to the exploitation of the Official Secrets Act, telephone tapping, and the manipulation of the Press in the interests of the ruling party by ministerial and departmental leaks.[32] The Ponting affair of 1985 symbolizes Thatcherite government. Secrecy and restriction of information successfully resist the demands of open democratic government.

Weber saw only one escape from bureaucratic tyranny—a return to small scale. Subsequent writers following this line have been dismissed as proposing economic absurdity, as did William Morris in *News from Nowhere*, or medieval romanticism, as did G. K. Chesterton in *The Napoleon of Notting Hill Gate*. But at least this type of response to the modern conditions of state power and manipulative social integration, with its recognition of the failure of emotional bonds in large impersonal structures of authority, points forward rather than backward to the possibilities of solidarity through democracy.

If neither charisma nor rational legality is an adequate base for a viable authority, the only other recourse is to tradition, or rather to that strand of political tradition in Britain which is democracy. Democracy is the consensus of free men and women, free to assemble, to express opinion, to persuade, and to elect, but, having done so, willing to accept the will of the majority, whose rule will be tempered by consideration for the minority among whom they may at any time find themselves. Democracy so defined is always prone to exhibit the classic dilemma of conflict between the values of liberty and equality. Potential conflict, in a society with high unemployment, ethnic minorities, regional inequalities, and emergent claims to equality for women, is a strong challenge to democracy in contemporary Britain.

8

A democracy of citizens

The only way to meet the challenge of those who would dismiss any successful prospect for Britain is to turn from analysis of our present discontents to an attempt to chart the way to a brighter future. This does not mean abandoning objectivity. The determining of social ends should always be disciplined by study of the means to reach them: and that has been the burden of the earlier chapters. Exhortation alone is futile, whether to altruism or to tolerance or to recognition of the equal claim of others to share in the bounty afforded by society. The problem is to discover, to establish, and to strengthen those social institutions that will encourage and foster the kinds of relations between people that are desired.

I have asserted that liberty, equality, and fraternity are the three fundamental values in terms of which societies are to be judged. None of these ideals is fully realized in Britain. The question, then, is how each may be more fully realized. Simultaneous maximizing of them is not possible. It is a matter of finding the best balance between the revolutionary triad. Yet I believe that advance towards all three is possible, and that the limits of that advance depend upon the development of a democracy of citizens.

No theory of inevitable future history is involved in this view. Its underlying assumptions about 'human nature' and social possibility are, to be sure, reformist in a strong sense and morally committed to both libertarian and egalitarian ends and to the democratic means of their attainment.

For those who accept this tradition of social thought the past is a constraint: the future is an opportunity. That in essence is the theory of change that has underlain my discussion in this book. The peculiar constraints of British history have emerged. It is a country in which the unequal powers and advantages of a ruling minority have survived from agrarian through industrial towards post-industrial society with remarkable continuity. A long series of accommodations has been negotiated, the privileged exchanging concessions to new interests for agreement by the newcomers not to undermine the fundamentals of the inequality of the status quo.

A political culture of individualism and moderation permitted, and at each step was reinforced by, tentatively accumulated social bargains. British culture accordingly has its characteristic vocabulary of 'decency', 'the law and the constitution', 'Her Majesty's loyal Opposition' and 'custom and practice' alongside the popular suspicions of all ideals and ideologies as 'extremist'. It is a culture of gradualism, pragmatism, and appeal to common sense. The pursuit of individual liberty and sectional interest is assumed as an unproblematic law of nature. The 'national interest' is a dubious concept outside the emergency of war. Hegelian notions of an organic supra-individual entity are incomprehensible. Ancient struggles for liberties against kings and popes and potentates are seen as consensus against over-ambitious government. Localism is the natural source of authority. Individualism restricts the political power of the state and simultaneously turns the work place into the theatre if not of class warfare then at least of adversarial, arms-length bargaining over wages and job regulation. Economics and politics are thus divided by economic liberalism while the state has maintained a remarkably successful appearance or mythology of impartial even-handedness between the classes in their economic struggles. Meanwhile gradually widening opportunities, the dispensation of honours, and the slow concession of welfare rights have together adapted the status system as a continuing support to political legitimacy as well as a cushion against the harsh divisive inequalities of class.

The new Conservatism

This, on the whole, cohesive structure has faced increasing challenge since the 1960s and the end of the post-war period. Economic depression after the first oil crisis of 1973 followed its characteristic British variant—response was slower, unemployment greater, and slump longer than in the Western European economy as a whole. Balance-of-payments crises and inflation always reopen the past negotiations over the shares of the economy which should go to the complex competitors of capital and the sectional interests of labour. Class conflict is intrinsic to capitalism. In Britain the social balance has always been precarious but rescued by the culture of accommodation I have described.

These crises, on which British consensus came near to breaking-point in the early nineteenth century, have reappeared in the late twentieth century. A new Conservatism—'Thatcherism'—has resuscitated economic liberalism. The Thatcher government from 1979 resolutely set out to exclude organized labour from participation in political management, returned to a renewed emphasis on the separation of the economic from the political sphere, and did not flinch from imposing mass unemployment and failing welfare services, ostensibly as the necessary price for combating inflation and raising productivity, actually because of a conviction that the old class compromise had to be swept away if a new strong and prosperous country was to be built.

Whether or not these policies of economic liberalism will continue to be pursued in the later 1980s and 1990s and, if so, whether they will eventually strengthen the British economy, remains highly disputable. What is certain is that they are a radical departure from traditional Conservative compromise. They spell danger. If successful and leading, as promised, to a return to full employment, then the likelihood is that frustrated and resentful trade unions will renew the sectional scramble and 'pay off old scores' against management. If unsuccessful, they will encourage extremism of the Right and the Left as the legitimacy of parliamentary government is undermined. A government which pursues class war unsuccessfully is likely thereby to destroy parliamentary democracy.

Neither a triumphant return to national wealth and power through capitalist free enterprise nor a comprehensive national collapse supervened by a Fascist or Communist dictatorship are likely outcomes. But, short of total Thatcherite success or lack of it, there is an alternative, but no less dispiriting, possibility of stability which is best described as a new polarization thesis: not the class polarization envisaged by Marx for nineteenth-century industrial capitalism, but a no less fundamental dichotomy between the haves and the have-nots in a post-industrial society. It is all too readily conceivable that a political democracy with an emerging economy of increasingly white-collar employees, individualistic, privatized, and market-oriented, could be stable. The majority of the qualified, employed, and house-owning citizens could use the state to protect their interests against politically unorganized and socially fragmented minorities of the unqualified and unskilled. Control of such an unequal community would be feasible through minimal welfare and efficient police.

This is no fictional nightmare. The elements and tendencies of a new polarization can be assembled all too easily from the preceding descriptive chapters. The rich have become richer and the poor poorer in Britain since 1979. Opportunities for a career in management, enterprise, or profession are still increasing but alongside the mounting risks of serious deprivation in protracted unemployment and dependency on impoverished social services. Success in the formal economy is complemented, not substituted, by success in the informal economy.[1] The stakes of individual success or failure in school and in work are rising. Yet the odds of success or failure are lengthening along lines of social division—between the inner city and the prosperous suburb, between the North and the South, the white majority and the ethnic minorities, the privately and the publicly schooled. In short, not a simple division into two nations but a complex polarization of increasingly embittered inequalities.

If care and compassion for the weak is the mark of a good society, it is the least likely feature of an order of economic liberalism. Such an order forms classes, and liberty goes to those with power and advantage with respect to the market and the state apparatus. Such an order has the further insidiously self-fulfilling property of justifying inequality by blaming the poor for their poverty and encouraging the strong to save themselves individually at the expense of the weak. Such an order relies ultimately on individual contract enforced by the minimal state: it has no place within it for what the European tradition of reform and revolution has labelled fraternity.

Solidarity

The notion of fraternity in political discourses is a metaphorical reference to this ideal of a moral community, covering all the relationships, conjugal and consanguineous, that are entailed in the family. Indeed, it has sometimes been argued, and with force, that the fraternal metaphor impoverishes this conception: that brotherhood is more diluted and more prone to enmity than any of the other relationships; and that, in the revolutionary creed, 'brotherhood has been selected as the image of perfection, not because it represents the family at its best, but because it is the family at its least familial'.[2]

Fraternity of this kind, in reality, rejects the family. But this is not my intention. On the contrary, while recognizing that family loyalties may limit or conflict with similar civic or community ties, I assume that the fraternal loyalty of the monk or the dedicated party member can and should be an overriding creed and code of conduct only for the few. Nor is this type of human association a necessarily superior expression of moral integration. The ethical value of such a fraternity, whatever the self-sacrifice which it may entail, depends upon the treatment it gives to those who by choice or circumstance are not part of the brotherhood.

Moreover, just as the harmonious family, nuclear or extended, bears value in its own right, so too can the limited political community, even though it restricts itself to something less than the ecumenical brotherhood of man. The United Nations, the United Kingdom, England, Scotland, and Wales, can surely exist together. Of course, against those who advocate or allow particularistic forms of fraternity, the charge of 'contradiction' may be laid. Restricted definitions of community inevitably leave problems of external relations. Bounded human groups, by definition, always set such problems. But the proper reply, appealing to experience, is that the smaller group can cultivate the values to be applied in the larger. If these values are liberty and equality, then a practical meaning is given to the idea of the brotherhood of man. It is in this sense that I see fraternity, even though, and indeed because, it is rooted in small-scale organizations, as the precondition of liberty and equality. But, by the same token, the forms of fraternal association which can make up a fraternal society can vary, and communities can remain integrated while attaching different importance to liberty and equality.

However, there are two compelling arguments against the use of the term fraternity in the meaning and connotation it brings to us as a cultural inheritance. First, it is sexist. Its male and its narrowly familistic association is crippling to any future ideal of inclusion in a genuine community of citizens. Neither the addition of sorority nor any other tortuous use of kinship language can overcome the difficulty. A suitable alternative word is hard to find: 'socialist' or 'communitarian' are literally correct but ineligible for other reasons of connotation. The best alternative is 'solidarity', and I propose now to adopt it.

The second reason—nostalgia—is hardly less compelling. Fraternity, like community, so easily evokes a romantic version of the old respectable working-class district or mining-village as described by Jeremy Seabrook or Richard Hoggart. No viable policy can re-create that society even if it were desirable. Moreover, the use of the concept of community—as, for example, in 'community care' can all too easily be a disguise for forcing public responsibility on to vulnerable private individuals—in this case usually women. There is, I have argued, an authentic tradition of local collective self-help outside the state: and the best of the old tradition should indeed be retained and renewed. This means, for example, recognizing the value of what Christian socialists in the 1880s called the 'socialism of character', the belief that individuals acting both alone and in co-operation could raise the quality of themselves and their society.

Citizenship

The new Conservatism in Britain has opted for one of the two contesting alternatives for realizing the revolutionary ideals—capitalism and communism. Western industrial capitalism pioneered the market as the central mediating institution in the development of wealth and its distribution. But the market promotes neither solidarity nor equality. It was historically the means of escape from feudal community and has been the target of Marxist criticism as the mechanism of class inequality and of the substantive restriction of liberty. Industrial communism substituted a state bureaucracy for the market. But here, and especially in the Russian case, the liberal critic can point to the repressive fraternity of the party which controls the state apparatus, and the sacrifice of political liberty in exchange for a far-from-perfect equality. Out of this contention the possibilities seem to be no more than a choice between two vast historical failures.

Is there another way? I think so. The third alternative, for Britain, is to take its own traditions of citizenship and democracy seriously in all their richness and inspiration. They offer the basis for a new solidarity without which both liberty and equality are impoverished. They offer also the political and social means of progress towards a newly integrated society. They were pointed to in Durkheim's emphasis on local autonomy and respect for tradition in late nineteenth-century Britain. They are best thought of as a *radical tradition*: a willingness to change institutions under changed circumstances. But they are the radicalism of the Left rather the Right because they seek to realize more perfectly the values sought by past reform.

The relevance of capitalism and communism, in any event, has to be put in the context of actual and present British circumstances. These, briefly recapitulated, are the legacy of a 'first-world' development, post-imperialism, tentative integration with the European continent, and a resurgent economic liberalism. But they also include a tradition of solidarity which has supported the slowly developing institutions of civic, political, and social citizenship. In Britain, political solidarity is citizenship. Its seeds were sown in the civil liberties of the seventeenth and eighteenth centuries. Its roots grew in the social inventiveness of the urban working class of the nineteenth century, and in the traditions of public service which were developed by the liberal elements of the professional middle class. These have been the finest expressions of British membership one of another, but the Labour movement has faltered in its attempt to nationalize the local welfare societies of an exploited class, and the ideal of public service has been diluted in its transformation to an overpowerful bureaucracy. So the political organization of citizenship, which is democracy, and the social organization of citizenship, which is community, continue to be thwarted by class interests and bureaucratic subversions.

What, then, are the prospects for a third way, through solidarity as citizenship, between the first and second worlds of capitalism and communism? The Thatcherite answer is to dismiss the 'third way' as the failed and fudged compromise of Butskellism. Capitalist conviction is the path to a prosperous future. Against this movement, it must immediately be conceded, there is no unified powerful and coherent political movement for a third way. True, the communist alternative is even less likely to succeed by popular persuasion. But the very failure of its advocates has served mainly to weaken the political organization of the social-democratic Left, to deepen suspicions of 'socialism' as unpatriotic, and to reinforce popular disbelief that the party of nationalization and central planning has a practical solution to the problems of mass unemployment, civic disorder, and national integrity. There is, in other words, no obvious and immediately mobilizable new radicalism with a programme to match the complexity of our cumulated problems.

Indeed, the greatest danger is precisely the offer of simple solutions to our complicated plight. We have an economy that does not release our energies, a polity that does not secure our trust, and a culture which does not sufficiently attract our affections. Simple solutions can only lead to political tyranny, whether from the Right or the Left. Either would destroy that fundamental element of our social life and tradition in which we can take pride—our long-developed and tenaciously held civil liberty. Our essential predicament is that the historical conditions which allowed this liberty also permitted divisive inequalities of class and status, a stratified society held together by imperial might abroad and deference and respect for shared religious and cultural values at home. But external empire and internal social control have been losing their power to pacify without violence, leaving market success and political bureaucracy, in all their weaknesses, to justify a still markedly unequal society.

Past failures to achieve fair and equal social distribution have driven some to apathy, others to a belief in a violent seizure of power and the imposition of an authoritarian social order, and still others to denial of the possibility or even desirability of an egalitarian society. These are the roads to tyranny. Our experiences of industrial, nationalist, and racial conflict continually demonstrate the need for a new sense of equality to replace old class-restrictive liberties and status-crippled fraternities. We have still to provide a common experience of citizenship in childhood and old age, in work and play, and in health and sickness. We have still, in short, to develop a common culture to replace the divided cultures of class and status.

Equality

Our society cannot stand on such shifting foundations. To strengthen them, we need principles and practices of social distribution which are acknowledged to be just by the great majority. And in a world of growing visibility of reference groups, these principles will be seen as just only if they actually are just. The implication is that in a political democracy which secures our liberties, the paramount principle of distribution must be equality. Equality of opportunity is not enough. It is a state of affairs we have still not reached but which is, in any case, a step towards á society that could be more ruthlessly stratified than the one we live in now. Nor is it enough to eliminate all irrelevant discriminations of skin colour, sex, cultural background, or family upbringing. We need full equality of the basic material conditions of social life. If poverty remains in Britain this is not because the technical means to its abolition are missing: it is because of an inadequate sense of moral implication in the lives of compatriots. It is a failure not of economic production, but of political distribution. The guarantee of the material essentials for freedom from want does not require even a radically egalitarian policy. The altruism nurtured in the kind of family experienced by the majority, extended by standards of schooling that most parents expect, and embodied in the political definitions of citizenship which were proclaimed during and after the Second World War, would put an end to poverty, once and for all.

Nor is the end of poverty a Utopian dream. Mrs Thatcher told the House of Commons in December 1983 that 'people who are living in need are fully and properly provided for'. A subsequent national poll showed that most of the nation (57 per cent) did not agree with her. The researchers, Joanna Mack and Stewart Lansley, went further and asked their national sample to say whether they would be willing to pay extra income tax for poverty relief where poverty was what the respondents themselves had defined as minimum necessities for living in contemporary Britain.[3] Three-quarters were willing to pay a penny more on the standard rate. An increase of 5p on the income tax would have been enough to lift one-third to one-half of the poor above the level which the majority of the nation defined as minimally decent. Admittedly, five-penny philanthropists did not quite muster a majority. But they included 30 per cent of the Conservative, as well as 42 per cent of the Labour voters; and, most impressively, they included 44 per cent of the richest 10 per cent of citizens—the very people who have stood to gain most by the contrary policies of the new Conservatives.

Beyond this readily attainable minimum of a fair society, R. H.

Tawney's conception still stands: because men are men, social institutions—property rights, and the organization of industry, and the system of public health and education—should be planned, as far as is possible, to emphasize and strengthen, not the class differences which divide, but the common humanity which unites them.[4]

Unless they are shown to be relevant to needs, inequalities based on differences of personal quality are no argument against equality. Nor is the familiar argument that incentives necessitate inequality to be taken as a fundamental law of human economic nature. The incentives they assume are the products of present values and interests which arise from our existing institutions, and institutions can be changed. In a solidaristic society it could reasonably be expected that any extra rewards to effort and capacity that might be necessary for an efficient division of labour would leave the basic structure of equal citizenship unimpaired.

The outstanding example of an established solidaristic institution, one in which the most elevated familial ideal is extended voluntarily to the stranger, is the British blood donor system, which R. M. Titmuss has compared with the marketing of blood in the United States and other countries to demonstrate that large-scale solidarity is a human practicality and not merely a Utopian exhortation. From his study of American practice, Titmuss concluded that:

the commercialization of blood and donor relationships represses the expression of altruism, evades the sense of community, lowers scientific standards, limits both personal and professional freedoms, sanctions the making of profits in hospitals and clinical laboratories, legalizes hostility between doctor and patient, subjects critical areas of medicine to the laws of the market place, places immense social cost on those least able to bear them—the poor, the sick, and the inept—increases the danger of unethical behaviour in various sectors of medical science and practice, and results in situations in which proportionately more blood is supplied by the poor, the unskilled, the unemployed, negroes, and other low-income categories of exploited human populations of high blood yielders.[5]

We do not have to assume with Titmuss that, in social institutions, there is a Gresham's law of ungenerosity. But we can recognize the opposite and integrating principle, which is to seek the community of citizenship in all public organizations. To do so is to encourage, through public policy, those social motives which the blood transfusion service brilliantly exemplifies.

Family

From this point of view there is nothing more important than the policy pursued by the state towards the family. Families have unequal shares of material and cultural capital. The remedy is positive discrimination. The material base for parenthood does not measure up to democratic standards of fairness. It is true that, no thanks to government, babies now tend to be born rather more in the better-off and less in the worse-off homes. Fertility is coming to be positively correlated with family income—a reversal of the previous absurdity. But mothers, and especially working-class mothers, are still at once the most hard-worked and the least-rewarded members of our working population. They are an essential element of the social division of labour but, unlike nurses, teachers, social workers, and the like, are excluded from the paid occupational division of labour. They deserve an income which reflects their service to society. They deserve publicly provided facilities in street child centres and play groups to relieve their isolated labours in raising the under-fives. The family is our best carrier of the basic education of each new generation of citizens. An enlightened social policy should recognize this and define the experts and specialists, the schools and the child services, as agents for the support, not the replacement, of family upbringing. The implication is that we must challenge the usurpation of authority by experts (whether they appear as teachers or as administrators) and grant full citizenship to the amateur parents against the professional pedagogues. This is what is meant, for instance, by the community school. Not parent governors as tokens in a ritual, but genuine parental and community government of schools.

Education for citizens

What kind of educational policy would put solidarity into more even balance with liberty and equality? The liberal approach through slow and limited expansion is not enough. The equality of plenitude is probably an unattainable dream. We are unlikely to see the Utopia, which William Morris envisaged in *News from*

Nowhere, of a consensual restriction of consumer demands together with happy coincidences between demand and voluntary supply of services. Nor can there be firm reliance on the American hope for unrestricted supply through technological advance leading to rates of economic growth which out-distance consumer expectations. In reality, a balanced educational policy would have to deal with the equality of scarcity—which means educationally the problems of transformation from élite to mass, rather than mass to universal higher education. Such a policy is therefore bound to hurt the established vested interests of privileged minorities. Moreover, to reassert an unpalatable truth, equality can never be attained through educational policies alone.

But making the large assumption that a society which wanted equality would put through the necessary fundamental reforms for the equalization of participation in the work place and the community, the structure of schooling would be that of recurrent education, and rights of participation in it would be those of citizenship rather than those of the market-place. The selective function of education for a hierarchy of occupational positions would be transformed into one of differentiation for a complex and fluid array of jobs having roughly equal material rewards. Selection would thereby become strictly educational.

The allocation of resources to education in such a system would not substitute flat equality for the present unequal reinforcement of advantages already distributed to families in a hierarchy of class and status. It would follow the principle of positive discrimination directed against all arbitrary or accidental, and therefore unfair, disadvantages. This would mean less for the universities and more for the nurseries, less for Solihull and more for Newham, less for the 18- to 21-year-olds and more for the over-65s. The basic citizenship right to a given amount of time free from work would be universal, and its increments would accrue to everyone and not simply to those in the rising generation. This basic citizenship principle would then be linked to, and modified by, that of positive discrimination through carefully worked out and constantly revised formulas for translating measures of disadvantage into extra educational benefits in so far as these were not more appropriately dealt with through income, employment, and housing policies.

In the interests of solidarity both the organization and content of education would be centred on the idea of community schools. At all levels education would be locally governed within the national framework of citizenship rights and positive discrimination. The form of educational government would be participatory democracy, within which the role of the professional teacher would be that of community servant with all this implies for teacher training, the practice of educational administration, and the claims of teachers' unions. 'Free schools' would find their place in such a community organization, and might, incidentally, offer a more effective service of experiment and innovation than was ever given by the 'public schools'.

The idea of the community school has to be given a geographical meaning, especially for the under-fives, parents, and over-65s. In part, this would be to recognize the hidden costs of alienation, anomy, rootlessness, and isolation which are exchanged for the benefits of physical mobility. In part, it would be to recognize the costs in inhumanity of grandiose economic and political structures. In part, it would be to assert that in so far as there is a 'logic of industrialism', it does not necessarily involve the rates of migration which are presently experienced, and far less the destruction of local social networks by mindless urban planning. Educationally, it would be to assert the learning potential of all social relations and to deny the arbitrary attribution of monopoly to the formal teacher in the class-room. Culturally, it would be to assert the worth of local life, its distinctiveness, and its commonalities with other places and other times, and to deny that local experience only fosters parochialism and excludes universalism.

Higher education would become adult education, and in that sense immediately be made universal. Its organization would also be dominated by the idea of the community school, and its development would realize the principles of recurrent education. There would thus be a greater variety and flexibility of provision in community colleges and local institutions, as well as through the mass media and the Open University. Access and student finance would be provided through sabbaticals and arrangements for retirement.

Industrial democracy

Democracy is not a long tradition. It was a usurper at the end of the eighteenth century, fighting a previous tradition of feudal custom.

As I pointed out in Chapter 4, it was slow in coming. It has yet to be fully realized beyond the formalities of the polling booth in those spheres of life, particularly the work place, where it lays claim to be applied.

I am not, of course, suggesting that democracy can be applied mechanically to all forms of human association. What I am suggesting is that it can be the ultimate court of appeal for our secular lives. Families cannot be full democracies: they are not bands of brothers, and the lesser responsibility of childhood is an inescapable fact: but they can be, and can be judged as, nurseries of responsible citizenship. Schools and universities cannot be democracies, whatever is said by the National Union of Students. If you are a teacher and I come to learn, then your knowledge must have authority over my ignorance: but again, the school you run is successful precisely in so far as it brings me to competent citizenship in the trade, profession, or subject you teach me; and from that moment I can claim the right to democratic relations with you.

That is all obvious enough. But Britain is far from laying the democratic foundation for traditional authority in all the spheres to which its modern evolution points. There are two spheres of life where this is conspicuously so—the nation state and industrial organization—two areas in which the democratic principle could be more firmly applied.

The starting-point in both spheres is that a modern society organizes itself by extremely specialized division by labour. But in national affairs Britain has overreached itself. It is tied into a huge apparatus of international markets. It has given over a great deal of its effective authority to international agencies through membership of the EEC, the development of multinational companies, and its trading relations all over the world. And the island occupies a specialist position within this complex through the London money market which we call the City. Britain is very far from being an autonomous economy and, quite apart from internal dissension, the extent to which its government can control inflation, price levels, and standards of life is feeble. To domesticate authority within its shores—and so to give its people a chance to run an effective democracy—would probably entail some cost to their general standard of living.

Some would prefer to pay that material price, assuming

democratic justice in the distribution of the burden: and it must be pointed out in defence of this 'little Englandism' that no economist or politician in the current debate who seeks solutions within the international framework holds out any immediate prospect of relieving the misery of over 3 million unemployed. That is one painful and inequitably distributed cost of persistence with the large and therefore effectively undemocratic system under which Britons live.

I said, 'quite apart from internal dissension'. That brings me to the other sphere in which greater democratization is possible, and here I would point to the analyses offered by Alan Fox. Fox's main attention in *Beyond Contract* is focused on the experience of work in the office, the factory, and the workshop. Work relations in the past have given low discretion and low trust to subordinates *vis-à-vis* their superiors. This was the triumph of the so-called scientific management which reached its most extreme form in the modern factory assembly line. The low-discretion syndrome, as Fox describes it, contrasts the rank-and-file production worker with the professional. The worker on the shopfloor has little sense of being an expert; of commitment to a calling; of autonomy on the job; of obligation to produce high-quality work, and he has little or no sense of identification with the organization in which he works.

Fox has also analysed the low levels of trust which lie behind the struggles between different groups of organized workers. Obviously a more democratically integrated society would organize its work by the opposite principles of high-trust relations, both vertically and horizontally. Professional work at its best requires and involves a high level of trust between people. Rigidly hierarchical forms of industrial authority produce at best the solidarity of the resentful.

Industrial democracy is a vital element in the unfinished British programme of creating a society which commands willing and widespread allegiance. Britain has the strongest shop-steward organization in the world. Its indiscipline against corporatism is far more impressive than the corporative hierarchy of the Trades Union Council, which the mass media are quick to portray as the modern demon. What is more important than shop-steward radicalism is that this shop-floor organization is the most conspicuous form of democracy in contemporary Britain. Nevertheless, the low-discretion, low-trust principle still dominates work organization.

These tendencies could, however, be reversed. Reversal, of course, might carry its considerable price—and not only in terms of cars and television sets (at least in a transitional period). But estimates of that price must be examined with scepticism when they come from those with a private interest in maintaining the status quo. 'Scientific management' methods are not invariably the most efficient. Any argument that extension of high-trust relations must be at the expense of the expectation of affluence needs to be qualified by realistic appraisal of a country's particular conditions. However, there seems little doubt that some price would have to be paid. Moreover, there is little prospect of the bargain being eagerly sought either by those presently in authority (who have vested interests in their present power), or the workers, patients, consumers, and citizens (who are conditioned to prefer a bit more of what material benefits they already have). Only those who experience autonomy and relations of trust can fully appreciate their satisfactions.

Democratic devolution

Political organizations could be refashioned to mirror the values cultivated in home, school, and work place. The twentieth-century trends in government and industry have made size and complexity into serious obstacles to effective citizenship and threaten to replace it by oligarchic and bureaucratic power. The increase of economic co-operation over larger areas makes all the more urgent the devolution of decision. Bold advances towards a more developed citizenship—in Scotland for the Scots, in the work place for workers, in the school for parents, in the locality for the neighbour, and so on, could evoke popular support. John Osmond's elequent plea for Welsh devolution, pointing to the way in which democracy should be rooted in community, is a persuasive contemporary example:

Man needs an anchor in a particular community. It is the source of that moral power which enables him to resist the monolithic State. The nation and the community in which he seeks his roots is not an end in itself: it is man's link with eternity. 'Cadw tŷ mewn cwnwl tystion', as Waldo Williams so movingly expressed it: man's relationship to the community is 'Keeping a home amidst a cloud of witnesses'.[6]

Conclusion

These familial, educational, and industrial examples cover only a small part of the total range of the institutions of production and reproduction, all of which need to be measured and reformed in the direction which leads to a society which is integrated, because it rests on an optimal balance of what is possible to make real our traditional revolutionary dreams. My review of past progress makes it all too clear that the journey to a society of citizens is no easy one. Stratification is stubbornly resistant to change: there is bound to be opposition. There are always those who place private interest above public welfare. Yet in a society of the kind I am advocating, patient persuasion has to be our principal weapon: for persuasion is democracy in action. Only if it is given constant priority can we both guard our freedoms and override the resistance of vested interest. Only then, but certainly then, democracy has the right to enforce its will.

The attainment of a new and sound basis for social order requires political will of a strength we have hitherto lacked. No one can guarantee that either the challenge will be accepted, or the response forthcoming. After a review of the British past and present, Alan Fox concluded:

None of this offers much cheer for millenarians, but there are consolations. Life in Britain retains many decencies, and most of them are connected with painfully constructed defences against the arrogances, impertinences and corruptions of power. These decencies are under threat from different directions. An independent-spirited, independently organised working class can sometimes bring its own minor threats, but as a bulwark against the major threats its record in Britain gives hope. In other ways, too, Britain will continue to be marked by its history and its heritage, and contained in that heritage are traditions that are creative, radical and reveal a love of country that stops short of bellicose assertiveness against others. They may surface again. It is too soon to declare 'the end of an old song' and consign Britain to the category of failed enterprises.[7]

I would certainly claim that what I suggest we need is also socially and politically possible. Its elements are in our social traditions and on our political agenda. Adversity itself is now sufficient to give social response to political initiative. Here again the initiatives have to be congruent with the end in view: and that means democratic politics. Democratic politics is essentially a system in which citizens actively mould the final decisions binding on all. It works only if liberty of thought and expression is ranked first among rights and the active exercise of citizenship first among duties. Political action is inevitably carried on by imperfect people in public office. Hence the constant need for alert and knowledgeable citizens, to defeat oppression and to prevent the public services from degenerating into organizations which serve the private interests of public servants.[8]

That, all too briefly, is my view of our best way into the future. We have no paradise lost, no paradise to be regained. Yet we can, if we will, take heart from the ancient story of the departure of our primal ancestors from the Garden of Eden:

> Some natural tears they dropped, but wiped them soon;
> The world was all before them, where to choose
> Their place of rest, and Providence their guide:
> They hand in hand, with wand'ring steps and slow,
> Through Eden took their solitary way.[9]

Notes

Chapter 1: To know ourselves

1. E. Gibbon, *The Decline and Fall of the Roman Empire*, J. M. Dent and Sons, Everyman edition, 1911-13, Vol. 1, p. 5.
2. (1735-1801.) Professor of Civil Law at the University of Glasgow from 1761 to 1801.
3. (1723-90.) Professor of Logic at the University of Glasgow from 1751. He then held the Chair of Moral Philosophy from 1751 to 1763.
4. In *The Times*, 7 Oct. 1977.
5. W. Dibelius, *England*, Jonathan Cape (English edition), 1930. (First German edition 1922.)
6. Ibid. 18.
7. G. Orwell, *Collected Essays, Journalism and Letters*, Vol. II, 1940-3, Penguin, 1970, pp. 74-135.
8. Joseph Peach Lehmann, *Remember You Are An Englishman: A Biography of Sir Harry Smith*, Jonathan Cape, 1977.
9. C. Crouch, *Class Conflict and the Industrial Relations Crisis*, Humanities Press, 1977, p. 3.
10. T. Hobbes, *Leviathan*, J. M. Dent and Sons, Everyman edition, 1914, pp. 49-50.
11. M. Friedman, *Capitalism and Freedom*, University of Chicago Press, Chicago, 1962.
12. I. Berlin, *Four Essays on Liberty*, Oxford University Press, 1969.
13. R. Dahrendorf, *The New Liberty*, Routledge and Kegan Paul, 1975.
14. J. Rawls, *A Theory of Justice*, Clarendon Press, 1972.
15. R. H. Tawney, *The Acquisitive Society*, G. Bell & Sons, 1943. And *Equality*, Allen and Unwin, 1931, 4th revised edition, 1952.
16. F. Hirsch, *The Social Limits to Growth*, Harvard University Press, 1976.
17. Ibid. 11.
18. Lord David Cecil, *The Cecils of Hatfield House*, Constable, 1973, p. 267.

Chapter 2: A class-ridden prosperity

1. This division of social organization derives from Max Weber. See H. Gerth and G. W. Mills, *Essays from Max Weber*, Routledge and

Kegan Paul, 1948, pp. 180–95. See also J. H. Goldthorpe and P. Bevan, 'The Study of Social Stratification in Great Britain in 1946–76', *Social Science Information*, Vol. 16 (3/4), 1977, pp. 279–334. For a lively and recent general account of Weber, see S. Andreski, *Max Weber's Insights and Errors*, Routledge and Kegan Paul, 1984.

2. See F. Parkin, *Class Inequality and Political Order*, Paladin, 1972 (first published by MacGibbon and Kee, 1971).

3. R. Dahrendorf, *Class and Class Conflict in Industrial Society*, Routledge and Kegan Paul, 1959.

4. For example, the Oxford Mobility Study, discussed briefly in Chapter 3 and more extensively in Chapter 6 below, has made a 36- and a 7-fold classification based on J. H. Goldthorpe and K. Hope, *The Social Grading of Occupations: A New Approach and Scale*, Oxford University Press, 1974. Note is also made below of the Registrar-General's classification of five social classes (with a further division of Class III into its non-manual and manual components).

5. *Social Trends*, No. 15, 1985, p. 22

6. J. H. Goldthorpe and C. Llewellyn in their 'Class Mobility in Britain: Three Theses Examined', *Sociology*, Vol. 11, No. 2, May 1977, pp. 257–87. Table 2.1 is reproduced from this source.

7. See, for example, Daniel Bell, *The Coming of Post-Industrial Society*, Basic Books, 1973, Chapter 2.

8. R. Dahrendorf, 'Recent Changes in the Class Structure of European Societies', *Daedalus*, Winter 1964, pp. 225–70.

9. J. H. Goldthorpe, 'Women and Class Analysis: In Defence of the Conventional View', *Sociology*, Vol. 17, No. 4, 1983; N. Britten and A. F. Heath, 'Women, Men and Social Class', in E. Gamarikow, *Gender, Class and Work*, Heinemann, 1984; A. F. Heath and N. Britten, 'Women's Jobs Do Make a Difference: A Reply to Goldthorpe'; and J. H. Goldthorpe, 'Women and Class Analysis: A Reply to the Replies', *Sociology*, Vol. 18, No. 4, 1984.

10. F. Parkin, *Marxism and Class Theory: A Bourgeois Critique*, Tavistock, 1979, p. 85.

11. J. Westergaard and H. Resler, *Class in a Capitalist Society: A Study of Contemporary Britain*, Heinemann, 1975, p. 352.

12. Cf. Colin Clark, 'The Economics of Housework', *Bulletin of Oxford Institute of Statistics*, Vol. 20 (2), May 1955, pp. 205–11.

13. For details and guidance through the difficulties of measurement see A. H. Halsey, *Trends in British Society Since 1900*, Macmillan, 1972; and for later figures see *Social Trends*, a publication of the Government Statistical Service which is an invaluable source of material data on British social structures.

14. See J. Mack and S. Lansley, *Poor Britain*, Allen and Unwin, 1985.

15. Royal Commission on the Distribution of Income and Wealth, *Report,* No. 5 (Third Report on the Standing Reference), Cmnd. 6999, HMSO, 1977.
16. *Social Trends*, No. 15, 1985, p. 87.
17. See R. M. Titmuss, *Essays on the Welfare State*, Unwin University Books, 1958, pp. 34–55.
18. Westergaard and Resler, op. cit., p. 118.
19. Ibid. 119.
20. *Social Trends*, No. 15, 1985, p. 89.
21. J. B. Priestley, *English Journey*, Heinemann, 1934. Penguin edition, 1977, p. 296.
22. W. G. Runciman, *Relative Deprivation and Social Justice*, Routledge and Kegan Paul, 1966. Runciman uses the word power to mean what I refer to as party.
23. W. W. Daniel, *The PEP Survey on Inflation*, PEP Broadsheet 553, July 1975.
24. Reported in the *Guardian*, 18 Feb. 1985.
25. *Social Trends*, No. 8, 1977, Table 5. 10.

Chapter 3: The reconstitution of status

1. See G. D. H. Cole, *Studies in Class Structure*, Routledge and Kegan Paul, 1955, p. 65. His Chapter 3, 'The Social Structure of England', is a good brief summary of changes in the structures of class and status from the middle of the nineteenth to the middle of the twentieth century.
2. Robert Roberts, *The Classic Slum*. First published by the University of Manchester Press, 1971. Penguin edition, 1973 (to which my references apply).
3. Ibid. 30.
4. Ibid. 160–1.
5. Ibid. 23–5.
6. Beatrice Webb, *My Apprenticeship*, Penguin edition, 1971, p. 171.
7. Richard Hoggart, *The Uses of Literacy*, Chatto and Windus, 1957.
8. See J. H. Goldthorpe *et al., Social Mobility and Class Structure*, Oxford University Press, 1980.
9. D. V. Glass (ed.), *Social Mobility in Britain*, Routledge and Kegan Paul, 1954.
10. G. D. H. Cole, op. cit. p. 58.
11. J. Westergaard and H. Resler, *Class in a Capitalist Society*, Heinemann, 1975, pp. 324–33.
12. W. G. Runciman, *Relative Deprivation and Social Justice*, Routledge and Kegan Paul, 1966.
13. For an excellent short account, see ibid, Chapter 5. See also R. M. Titmuss, *Problems of Social Policy*, HMSO and Longmans, 1950.

14. It is often assumed that Weber's conception of status is also trivialized by liberal writers, who have identified it with the prestige of occupations. On this see F. Parkin, *Class Inequality and Political Order*, Paladin, 1972, pp. 29–32. But I think that the underestimation of class in this tradition is the more fundamental error.

15. See T. H. Marshall, *Citizenship and Social Class*, Cambridge University Press, 1950. For a brief appreciation of Marshall, see D. Lockwood, *Sociology*, Vol. 8, No. 3, Sept. 1974, pp. 363–7. See also T. Geiger, *Society in the Melting Pot*, Kiepenheuer and Witch, German edition, 1950.

16. G. M. Trevelyan, *English Social History*, Longmans, Green, and Co., 1944, p. 351 (quoted in T. H. Marshall, op. cit. p. 15).

17. T. H. Marshall, op. cit, p. 15. Marshall goes on to remark that the most celebrated actor in this drama was John Wilkes and, as he puts it, 'although we may deplore the absence in him of those noble and saintly qualities which we should like to find in our national heroes, we cannot complain if the cause of liberty is sometimes championed by a libertine'. Perhaps Marshall was thinking particularly of the occasion when Wilkes was arraigned before a posse of outraged peers of the realm, one of whom declared, 'Wilkes, you will die on the gallows or of the pox': 'That depends, my Lord,' Wilkes replied, 'on whether I embrace your principles or your mistress.'

18. This was made up of social security, £441; education, libraries, science, and arts, £314; health and personal social service, £281; housing, £195, environment services, £104; law, order, and protective services, £80; food and transport subsidies including concessionary fares, £45. (*Hansard*, 10 Nov. 1977, Written Answers, Column 186.)

19. Alan Fox, *History and Heritage: The Social Origins of the British Industrial Relations System*, Allen and Unwin, 1984, Chapter 4.

20. Anthony Giddens, *Profiles and Critiques in Social Theory*, Macmillan, 1982.

21. Frank Parkin, *Class Inequality and Political Order*, Paladin, 1972, p. 30.

22. T. H. Marshall, *Sociology at the Cross Roads*, Heinemann, 1963, pp. 87 and 115.

23. Ibid. 217.

24. Ibid. 61.

25. Ibid. 129.

26. Ibid. 135.

27. Ibid. 61.

28. Anthony Giddens, op. cit., p. 172.

29. Alan Fox, op. cit., Chapter 9.

30. Anthony Giddens (op. cit., pp. 177–8) draws attention to the extension of surveillance techniques by the modern state and points out that

the resulting threat to civil rights in both Western and socialist countries needs urgent analysis, has had little attention from Marxist or liberal political theory, and can be aided by Marshall's precise specifications of the nature of civil, political, and welfare rights.

31. *Social Trends*, No. 15, 1985, p. 23, Table 1.8.
32. *Social Trends*, No. 10, 1979, p. 102, Table 3.15.
33. Ibid. 164.
34. Michael Banton, *Race Relations*, Tavistock Publications, 1967.
35. E. J. B. Rose, *Colour and Citizenship: A Report on British Race Relations*, Oxford University Press, 1969.
36. *Guardian*, 24 Oct. 1977.
37. A. H. Halsey, 'British Black and White', *Listener*, 24 Feb. 1983, pp. 14–15.
38. J. H. Goldthorpe, 'Social Inequality and Social Integration in Modern Britain', in D. Wedderburn, *Poverty, Inequality and Class Structure*, Cambridge University Press, 1974.
39. Ibid. 221.

Chapter 4: The rise of party

1. See Colin Crouch (ed.), 'The Place of Participation in the Study of Politics', *British Political Sociology Year Book*, Vol. 3, *Participation in Politics*, 1977, Croom Helm, pp. 1–17.
2. S. E. Finer, *Anonymous Empire: A Study of the Lobby in Great Britain*, Pall Mall Press, 2nd edition, 1961 (1st edition 1958). See also J. D. Stewart, *British Pressure Groups: Their Role in Relation to the House of Commons*, Clarendon Press, 1958; and M. Kogan, *Educational Policy Making: a Study of Interest Groups and Parliament*, Allen and Unwin, 1975.
3. The relevant legislation was enacted in 1855–6.
4. Robert Price and George Sayers Bain, 'Union Growth Revisited: 1948–74 in Perspective', *British Journal of Industrial Relations*, 1976, Vol. XIV, No. 3, pp. 339–55.
5. T. H. Marshall, *Citizenship and Social Class*, Cambridge University Press, 1950.
6. Karl Marx, *Contribution to the Critique of Hegel's Philosophy of Right* (1844), in K. Marx and F. Engels, *On Religion*, Foreign Languages Publishing House, Moscow, 1957, p. 42.
7. Those juvenile thoughts, I appreciate, were neither humble nor meek.
8. A. Fox, 'Corporatism and Industrial Democracy: The Social Origins of Present Forms and Methods in Britain and Germany'. Paper prepared for the *International Industrial Democracy Conference*, July 1977 (Social Science Research Council), Cambridge, UK. The papers were published by the Social Science Research Council in

1978. Fox's general work, *History and Heritage: The Social Origins of the British Industrial Relations System*, Allen and Unwin, 1984, incorporates the earlier work.

9. Ibid.

10. See G. M. Young, *Stanley Baldwin*, Rupert Hart-Davis, 1952, pp. 93-4.

11. Ibid. 95.

12. See R. T. McKenzie and A. Silver, *Angels in Marble: Working Class Conservatives in Urban England,* Heinemann Educational, 1968; E. A. Nordlinger, *The Working-Class Tories*, MacGibbon and Kee, 1967; W. G. Runciman, *Relative Deprivation and Social Class*, Routledge and Kegan Paul, 1966. J. H. Goldthorpe *et al., The Affluent Worker,* 3 vols., Cambridge University Press, 1968-9; B. Hindess, *The Decline of Working-Class Politics,* MacGibbon and Kee, 1971; B. Jessop, *Traditionalism, Conservatism, and British Political Culture*, Allen and Unwin, 1974.

13. The Communist party used to be described by Ernest Bevin as no less the enemy of the working class than the Tory party.

14. D. Butler and D. Stokes, *Political Change in Britain*, Macmillan, 2nd edition, 1974, p. 182.

15. A. F. Heath, R. Jowell, and J. Curtice, *The British General Election 1983*, Pergamon Press, 1985.

16. Ibid.

17. B. S. Rowntree and G. R. Lavers, *Poverty and the Welfare State*, Longmans, 1951.

18. J. H. Goldthorpe *et al.,* op. cit.

19. *Report of the Committee on Financial Aid to Political Parties* (Chairman, Lord Houghton of Sowerby), Cmnd. 6601, HMSO 1976, on the basis of replies from 91 constituency Labour parties, estimated that individual membership by 1974 was down, not to two-thirds of a million, but to less than one-third of a million. The research organization, PEP, put the figure still lower at 250,000 (D. Leonard, *Paying For Party Politics*, PEP 1975). In February 1977 the Gallup organization drew a representative sample of 315 local party organizations and asked the agent, secretary, or chairman to estimate the number of individual members in his own constituency Labour party. Since the respondent's estimate was taken at its face value, the Gallup result is probably an overestimate. Even so, in Northern England, on these figures a full half of the constituency parties were reported to have 500 members or fewer, and only 12 per cent more than 1,000 members.

20. Dianne Hayter, *The Labour Party: Crisis and Prospects*, Fabian Tract 451, Sept. 1977. In only 4 per cent of the Gallup constituencies was the ratio of individual members of the Labour party to Labour

voters better than 1 in 10. In half the seats it was worse than 1 in 30, and it was worse than 1 in 30 in no less than 68 per cent of the constituencies in Labour-held seats in the Midlands, the North, and Scotland. The overall average was 1 to 26: the average for Labour-held seats in the Midlands, the North, and Scotland was distinctly worse at 1 to 35 (C. Martin and D. Martin, 'The Decline of Labour Party Membership', *Political Quarterly*, Vol. 48, No. 4 1977, p. 464). By 1977 the inability of constituencies to finance them meant that Labour had only 86 full-time agents, the fewest since 1946. About half of the constituency parties were without youth branches in the mid-1970s; even among the party members themselves who were in the age range 15–25, only about 1 in 8 were members of the Young Socialists. (Labour Party National Executive Committee Report 1977, p. 20).

21. Robert Roberts, *The Classic Slum*, Penguin, 1973.
22. David Caute, *The Fellow Travellers: A Postscript to the Enlightenment*, Weidenfeld and Nicolson, 1973.
23. S. and B. Webb, *Soviet Communism: A New Civilisation*, 2 vols., Longmans, Green, and Co. First published 1935 (2nd edition 1937).

Chapter 5: Between the generations

1. D. Bell, *Toward the Year 2000—The Trajectory of an Idea*, Beacon Press, 1969, p. 643.
2. M. Young and P. Willmott, *The Symmetrical Family*, Routledge and Kegan Paul, 1973, pp. 19 ff. For trenchant criticism of this view of economic growth, see F. Hirsch, *The Social Limits of Growth*, Harvard University Press, 1976, pp. 167 ff.
3. In a BBC Third Programme broadcast (1953), to which Lord Briggs kindly drew my attention.
4. Robert Roberts, *The Classic Slum*, Penguin, 1973, p. 74 n.
5. Arthur Waley, *The Analects of Confucius*, Allen and Unwin, 1938, p. 83.
6. E. R. Leach, *A Runaway World?*, BBC Publications, 1968, p. 44.
7. Eleanor F. Rathbone, *The Disinherited Family*, Edward Arnold, 1924, p. ix, Introduction.
8. For a detailed analysis of the history of reduction of fertility in Britain, see Michael Teitelbaum, *The British Fertility Decline*, Princeton University Press, 1984.
9. E. A. Wrigley and R. S. Schofield, *The Population History of England 1541–1871: A Reconstruction*, Edward Arnold, 1981.
10. R. M. Smith, 'Fertility Economy and Household Formation in England over Three Centuries', *Population and Development Review*, Vol. 7, No. 4, 1981, pp. 595–622. Also H. J. Hajnal in Vol. 8, No. 3, 1982, pp. 449–94.
11. D. E. C. Eversley and W. Kollman, *Population Change and Social*

Planning, Edward Arnold, 1982, and J. Ermisch, *The Political Economy of Demographic Change*, Heinemann, 1983.

12. These are graphically described by Lord Briggs in *Victorian Cities,* Odhams Press, 1963; Pelican edition, 1968.

13. See M. Teitelbaum, op. cit.; J. Habakkuk, *Population Growth and Economic Development since 1750*, Leicester University Press, 1971; J. A. Banks, *Prosperity and Parenthood: A Study of Family Planning among the Victorian Middle Classes*, Routledge and Kegan Paul, 1954; and J. A. Banks, *Victorian Values*, Routledge and Kegan Paul, 1981.

14. A. H. Halsey (ed.), *Trends in British Society Since 1900*, Macmillan, 1972, Tables 2.36, 2.37, and 2.38.

15. J. Habakkuk, op. cit., p. 69.

16. Prepared by P. R. Cox for Young and Willmott, op. cit., Appendix 4.

17. F. Engels, *The Origin of the Family, Private Property, and the State*, 1884. Reprinted in Marx and Engels Selected Works, Vol. 2, Foreign Languages Publishing House, Moscow, 1951, p. 205.

18. R. M. Titmuss, 'The Position of Women', in *Essays on 'The Welfare State'*, Allen and Unwin, 1958.

19. Eleanor F. Rathbone, op. cit., p. viii, Introduction.

20. Margaret Wynn, *Family Policy*, Penguin, 1972.

21. Frank Field, Molly Meacher, and Chris Pond, *To Him Who Hath*, Penguin, 1977.

22. A. H. Halsey (ed.), op. cit., p. 118, Table 4.7.

23. For a vivid description, see N. Dennis *et al., Coal Is Our Life,* Eyre and Spottiswoode, 1956.

24. See J. H. Goldthorpe *et al., The Affluent Worker*, Cambridge University Press, 1968.

25. *Observer*, 14 Sept. 1984.

26. J. Cheetham, *Unwanted Pregnancy and Counselling*, Routledge and Kegan Paul, 1977, p. 2.

27. *Report of the Committee on One-Parent Families,* Cmnd. 5629, HMSO, 1974, Chairman Sir Morris Finer.

28. *Social Trends*, No. 8, 1977, p. 116, Table 6.33.

29. Richard Hoggart, *The Uses of Literacy*, Chatto and Windus, 1957.

30. This, incidentally, is the basis for one interpretation of the student radicalism of the late 1960s, for example by Professor Edward Shils, 'Of Plenitude and Scarcity: The Anatomy of an International Cultural Crisis', *Encounter*, Vol. 32, No. 5, May 1969, pp. 37–57. They were the first totally indulged generation, and recruited disproportionately from the better-off families most easily placed to create for their offspring the illusion of a world from which scarcity had been banished.

31. For 1983 evidence see J. Mack and S. Lansley, *Poor Britain*, Allen and Unwin, 1985.

32. A. H. Halsey (ed.), *Educational Priority*, HMSO, 1972.

33. Richard Hoggart, p. 95.

Chapter 6: Mobility and education

1. V. Pareto, *Mind and Society*, Harcourt Brace, 1935, Vol. III, p. 2053, para. 20.

2. K. Marx, *Capital*, J. M. Dent and Sons, Everyman edition, 1936, Vol. III, p. 586.

3. See H. Braverman, *Labour and Monopoly Capital: The Degradation of Work in the Twentieth Century*, Monthly Review Press, 1974.

4. See D. Bell, *The Coming of Post-Industrial Society*, Basic Books, 1973, and J. Gershuny, *Social Innovation and the Division of Labour*, Oxford University Press, 1983.

5. A. B. Atkinson, A. K. Maynard, and C. G. Trinder, *Parents and Children: Incomes in Two Generations*, Studies in Deprivation and Disadvantage SSRC/DHSS, Heinemann, 1983.

6. See B. S. Rowntree and G. R. Lavers, *Poverty and the Welfare State*, Longmans, 1951.

7. See D. V. Glass (ed.), *Social Mobility in Britain*, Routledge and Kegan Paul, 1954.

8. J. H. Goldthorpe and C. Payne, *Trends in Intergenerational Class Mobility in England and Wales 1972–1983*, (forthcoming).

9. See J. H. Goldthorpe (with C. Llewellyn and C. Payne), *Social Mobility and Class Structure*, Oxford University Press, 1980.

10. See A. F. Heath, *Social Mobility*, Fontana, 1981.

11. The use of 'ten years after entry to the job market' as the 'destination' point had the advantage of standardizing the measure of mobility for each individual in the sample. It also may be expected to reflect the impact of education on mobility more clearly than a destination point which comes later in a man's working life. But this procedure yields a smaller amount of recorded movement into the middle class than is obtained by using 1972 occupation as the destination point. This is because the older men have a longer period in which to reach 'occupational maturity' which, for this population, means greater proportions with middle- and lower-middle-class jobs.

12. J. H. Goldthorpe and C. Llewellyn, 'Class Mobility in Britain: Three Theses Examined', *Sociology*, Vol. 11, No. 2, May 1977 p. 257–87.

13. G. Payne, 'The Lieutenant Class', *New Society*, Vol. 41, No. 772, July 1977, pp. 118–20.

14. See A. H. Halsey, 'Towards Meritocracy: The Case of Britain', in A. H. Halsey and J. Karabel (eds.), *Power and Ideology in Education*, Oxford University Press, New York, 1977.
15. J. H. Goldthorpe (with C. Llewellyn and C. Payne), 'Trends in Class Mobility', in J. H. Goldthorpe (with C. Llewellyn and C. Payne), *Social Mobility and Class Structure in Modern Britain*, Oxford University Press, 1980, Chapter 3.
16. J. H. Goldthorpe and C. Payne, op. cit.
17. See Goldthorpe and Payne for a careful discussion of the basis of the classification of occupations in this comparison.
18. A. H. Halsey, A. F. Heath, and J. M. Ridge, *Origins and Destinations*, Oxford University Press, 1980.
19. For a summary of the debate see *Oxford Review of Education*, Vol. 10, No. 1, 1984.
20. E. Ashby and M. Anderson, *The Rise of the Student Estate in Britain*, Macmillan, 1970.
21. R. Dahrendorf, *The New Liberty*, Routledge and Kegan Paul, 1975.
22. J. K. Galbraith, *The New Industrial Estate*, Hamish Hamilton, 1967.
23. For a review of the current state of the debate on this issue see M. Schiff and R. Lewontin, *Education and Class*, Oxford University Press, 1985, and A. H. Halsey (ed.), *Heredity and Environment*, Methuen, 1977.
24. See S. Ball, *Beachside Comprehensive*, Cambridge University Press, 1981, and J. Steedman, *Examination Results in Selective and Non-Selective Secondary Schools*, National Children's Bureau, 1983.
25. See A. H. Halsey, A. F. Heath and J. M. Ridge, 'The Political Arithmetic of Public Schools', in G. Walford (ed:), *British Public Schools: Policy and Practice*, Falmer Press, 1984.
26. In his foreword to the first Newsom Report, *Half our Future: A Report of the Central Advisory Council for Education (England)*, Ministry of Education, 1963.
27. UCCA, *Statistical Supplement to the 17th Report 1978-9*.

Chapter 7: Order and authority

1. See N. Glazer and D. P. Moynihan (eds.), *Ethnicity: Theory and Experience*, Harvard University Press, 1975, and J. G. Reitz, *The Survival of Ethnic Groups*, McGraw-Hill, 1980.
2. On which see T. Nairn, *The Break-Up of Britain: Crisis and Neo-Nationalism,* New Left Books, 1977, pp. 82 ff.
3. D. Lockwood, 'For T. H. Marshall', *Sociology*, Vol. 8, No. 3, Sept. 1974, pp. 363-7.

4. E. Durkheim, *The Division of Labour in Society*, translated by G. Simpson, Free Press, Glencoe, 1947.

5. Quoted by J. H. Goldthorpe in 'Social Inequality and Social Integration in Modern Britain', in D. Wedderburn, *Poverty, Inequality, and Class Structure*, Cambridge University Press, 1974, p. 232.

6. Barbara Wootton, *The Social Foundations of Wage Policy: A Study of Comparative British Wage and Salary Structure*, Allen and Unwin, 1955; R. M. Titmuss, *The Gift Relationship: From Human Blood to Social Policy*, Allen and Unwin, 1970.

7. For an excellent discussion of legitimation and ideology in Britain see S. Hall and M. Jacques (eds.), *The Politics of Thatcherism*, Lawrence and Wishart, 1983.

8. See, for example, Frank Parkin, *Class Inequality and Social Order*, Paladin, 1972.

9. T. Nairn, op. cit., p. 22.

10. See H. Perkin, *The Origins of Modern English Society 1780–1880*, Routledge and Kegan Paul, 1969, p. 187.

11. Herbert Asquith, 'The Volunteer', in *Poems of To-Day*, 2nd series, originally published separately 1922.

12. J. B. Priestley, *English Journey*, Heinemann, 1934 (Penguin edition 1977).

13. Ibid. 65.

14. Ibid. 126.

15. Ibid. 127.

16. J. H. Goldthorpe, 'Social Inequality and Social Integration in Modern Britain', in D. Wedderburn, op. cit., p. 222.

17. See his *Relative Deprivation and Social Justice*, Routledge and Kegan Paul, 1966.

18. See John Benyon (ed.), *Scarman and After: Essays Reflecting on Lord Scarman's Report, The Riots and their Aftermath*, Pergamon Press, 1984; C. T. Husbands, *Racial Exclusionism and the City: The Urban Support of the National Front*, Allen and Unwin, 1983; and J. Harris and T. Wallace (with the assistance of H. Booth), *To Ride the Storm: The 1980 Bristol 'Riot' and the State*, Heinemann, 1983.

19. T. Nairn, op. cit., p. 194.

20. Kindly sent to me by Paul Cheetham.

21. G. Tullock, *The Vote Motive: An Essay in the Economics of Politics, with Applications to the British Economy*, Institute of Economic Affairs, 1976.

22. *Social Trends*, No. 15, 1985, p. 65.

23. P. Johnson, 'Towards the Parasite State', the *New Statesman*, Aug. 1976.

24. Max Weber, *The Theory of Social and Economic Organization*,

translated by A. M. Henderson and T. Parsons, Oxford University Press, New York, 1947, p. 337.

25. S. S. Wolin, *Politics and Vision: Continuity and Innovation in Western Political Thought*, Allen and Unwin, 1961.

26. Ibid.

27. Quoted by Wolin, op. cit., from Lenin, *Selected Works,* Vol. 2, pp. 447–8, 456.

28. R. H. S. Crossman, 'The Role of the Volunteer in a Modern Social Service', in A. H. Halsey (ed.), *Traditions of Social Policy,* Blackwell, 1976, p. 278. For an interesting contrary view of the popular ideological base of the Labour movement see D. Selborne, *Against Socialist Illusion: A Radical Argument*, Macmillan, 1984.

29. N. Dennis, *People and Planning: The Sociology of Housing in Sunderland*, Faber, 1970; *Public Participation and Planners' Blight*, Faber, 1972.

30. R. H. S. Crossman, loc. cit., p. 268.

31. See D. Donnison, *Urban Policies: A New Approach*, Fabian Tract 487, 1984.

32. E. P. Thompson, *Writing By Candlelight*, Merlin, 1980, pp. 113–33.

Chapter 8: A democracy of citizens

1. R. E. Pahl's *Division of Labour*, Blackwell, 1984, is all the more interesting because social research has led him to subscribe to this aspect of the new polarization thesis from an initial standpoint which was virtually opposite.

2. Ferdinand Mount, 'The Dilution of Fraternity', *Encounter*, Vol. XLVII, No. 4, Oct. 1976, p. 20.

3. J. Mack and S. Lansley, *Poor Britain*, Allen and Unwin, 1985.

4. R. H. Tawney, *Equality*, Unwin Books, 1931 edition, p. 50.

5. R. M. Titmuss, *The Gift Relationship: From Human Blood to Social Policy*, Allen and Unwin, 1971, pp. 245–6.

6. John Osmond, *Creative Conflict: The Politics of Welsh Devolution*, Routledge and Kegan Paul, 1977, p. 251. Waldo Williams, 'Pa Beth Yw Dyn?' (What is Man?), in *Dail Pren* ('Leaves of a Tree'), Gwasg Gomer, 1956, p. 67. The quotation is in response to the question raised in the poem: Beth yw gwladgarwch? (What is patriotism?). The poem is essentially about man's search for identity. 'Adnabod' (recognition) is only attained between man and man when the common root is discovered:

> Beth yw adnabod? Cael un gwraidd
> Dan y canghennau
> (What is recognition? To find one root
> Beneath the branches.)

7. A. Fox, *History and Heritage: The Social Origins of the British Industrial Relations System*, Allen and Unwin, 1984, p. 452.
8. On this see Norman Dennis, 'Councillors, Officers and Public Participation', in Richard Rose (ed.) *The Management of Urban Change*, Sage Publications, 1974. See especially pp. 169–70: 'England has created for herself a civil service of municipal officers entirely subordinated to the popular will in law and in fact . . . The control of the expert by the amateur representing his fellow citizens is the key to the whole of our system of government.' When one considers that the literature of English local government, early and late, is full of such statements, it is apparent that, if councillors can be coped with and controlled with ease and with their acquiescence, there is little to be feared from participants with no *locus standi*, or whose *locus standi* is in no way comparable with that of the local government councillor. Indeed, from the point of view of 'correct' decisions being arrived at in the field of urban renewal, in so far as these lie within the jurisdiction of the English local authority, there is a great deal to be said for deflecting attention from the local government councillor. If he did not exist he would be regarded as an impossibly hopeful panacea, extravagantly Utopian, by exponents of 'power and the people'. His weaknesses and the weaknesses of his position are either shared by or exacerbated among any alternative contenders for influence on behalf of residents in areas of urban renewal. They have none of his strengths. While it is true, therefore, that officers are able to operate with a good deal of confidence on the assumption that the 'correct' decision will be made by councillors, they can be even more confident that neighbourhood councils, residents' panels, and any other arrangements yet suggested which aspire to the councillor's functions without giving them the councillor's power, will also, save in the most exceptional circumstances, have their views accepted if they are 'correct', and if they are not, ignored. Like the roar going round Sunderland when Roker Park is full, the officers can chant in chorus: 'Easy! Easy!'
9. John Milton, *Paradise Lost*, Book XII, ll. 645–9.

Further reading

General

To read more deeply into the subject of this book is a twofold task. On the one hand it involves further study of theories derived from the social sciences, and on the other hand it calls for wider knowledge of the social, economic, and political history of Britain in the twentieth century. Relevant sources of social and political theory are mentioned in the suggestions for further reading under each chapter heading below. As a general introduction there is J. Plamanatz, *Man and Society*, 2 vols., Longmans, 1963. On the side of historical sources, a compilation of social trends from the beginning of the twentieth century to the end of the 1960s is made in A. H. Halsey (ed.), *Trends in British Society Since 1900*, Macmillan, 1972. Then from 1970, there is a convenient official source, *Social Trends*, published by the Central Statistical Office annually. This covers much the same ground as *Trends in British Society Since 1900* from 1951 and has added further 'social indicators' of particular interest in each year, for example in No. 15 (1985) an essay on 'British Social Attitudes: The 1984 Report' by R. Jowell and C. Airey. This is itself a valuable new source.

Economic Trends is a companion publication, and B. R. Mitchell and P. Deane, *Abstract of British Historical Statistics*, Cambridge University Press, 1962, contains a useful long-run series. David Butler and Gareth Butler, *British Political Facts 1900–1984*, Macmillan, 1985, is a parallel and invaluable source of political information.

There are bibliographies of work on British twentieth-century history in C. L. Mowat, *Britain between the Wars*, Methuen, 1955; *British History Since 1926: A Select Bibliography*, Historical Association, 1960; and A. J. P. Taylor, *English History 1915–1945*, Oxford University Press, 1965. H. J. Perkin, *The Origins of Modern English Society 1780–1880*, Routledge and Kegan Paul, 1969, and A. Marwick, *British Society Since 1945*, Allen Lane, 1982, are useful social histories of Britain.

To know ourselves

Further reading on the study of society in general, and of British society in particular, could well begin with J. Rex, *Approaches to Sociology*, Routledge and Kegan Paul, 1974, which is accurately described by its own subtitle as 'An Introduction to Major Trends in British Sociology'.

E. Butterworth and D. Weir, *The New Sociology of Modern Britain*, Fontana, 1984, is a more empirical introduction to the study of British society. K. Popper, *The Poverty of Historicism*, Routledge and Kegan Paul, 1957, is the best modern book on methodology, and C. A. Moser and G. Kalton, *Survey Methods in Social Investigation*, Heinemann, 2nd edition, 1971, the best introduction to survey methods.

The next step is to read more deeply into contemporary political argument. B. Barry, *Political Argument*, Routledge and Kegan Paul, 1965, is an excellent introduction. M. Friedman, *Capitalism and Freedom*, University of Chicago Press, 1962, is a powerful exposition of libertarian theory. R. H. Tawney, *Equality*, Allen and Unwin, 1952, remains the best statement of egalitarianism: but see also W. Letwin (ed.), *Against Equality*, Macmillan, 1983. R. M. Titmuss, *The Gift Relationship: From Human Blood to Social Policy*, Allen and Unwin, 1971, is an eloquent plea for fraternalism which might be read alongside Ivan Illich, *Tools for Conviviality*, Fontana, 1973. Brian Barry, *The Liberal Theory of Justice*, Clarendon Press, 1973, is a good summary and criticism of John Rawls, *A Theory of Justice*, Clarendon Press, 1972. R. Dahrendorf, *The New Liberty*, Routledge and Kegan Paul, 1975, is an excellent modern discussion of current social development from a liberal standpoint. F. A. Hayek, *The Constitution of Liberty*, Routledge and Kegan Paul, 1960, is a classic source. A. Macfarlane, *The Origins of English Individualism*, Blackwell, 1978, is indispensable for understanding of the British case.

Finally, H. Gerth and C. W. Mills, *Essays from Max Weber,* Routledge and Kegan Paul, 1948 (particularly Weber's essay on 'Class Status and Party'), is an essential theoretical starting-point for the ground covered by the next three chapters.

A class-ridden prosperity

A general introduction to sociological research and writing on stratification in Britain is provided by H. Newby, *The State of Research into Stratification in Britain*, Economic and Social Research Council, 1982. Discussion of the general character of class in advanced societies is provided by A. Giddens, *The Class Structure of the Advanced Societies*, Hutchinson University Library, revised edition, 1981; and F. Parkin, *Class Inequality and Political Order*, Paladin, 1972, and *Marxism and Class Theory: A Bourgeois Critique*, Tavistock, 1979. W. G. Runciman's *Relative Deprivation and Social Justice*, Routledge and Kegan Paul, 1966, is an important interpretation of the history of class and status in twentieth-century Britain in terms of the theory of relative deprivation. W. W. Daniel in his PEP *Survey on Inflation*, 1975, brings Runciman's 1962 survey up to date. J. Westergaard and H. Resler, *Class in a Capitalist Society*, Heinemann, 1975, presents a detailed account of

British class structure from the Marxist standpoint. An outstanding empirical study of stratification in Britain is John Goldthorpe, David Lockwood, Frank Bechhofer, and Jennifer Platt, *The Affluent Worker*, Cambridge University Press, 1968-9. All three volumes are relevant: Vol. 1, *Industrial Attitudes and Behaviour*, 1968, Vol. 2, *Political Attitudes and Behaviour*, 1968, and Vol. 3, *The Affluent Worker in the Class Structure,* 1969.

For more detailed analysis of inequalities in income and wealth, there is A. K. Sen, *Poverty and Famines*, Clarendon Press, 1982, and A. B. Atkinson, *The Economics of Inequality*, Clarendon Press, 1975, which expounds the relevant methods of economic analysis. The most up-to-date information on the distribution of income and wealth in Britain is to be found in the Royal Commission on the Distribution of Income and Wealth (Chairman Lord Diamond), *Report*, No. 7, 1979. Peter Townsend's *Poverty in the United Kingdom*, Penguin, 1979, is a monumental study. There are also useful essays published in D. Wedderburn (ed.), *Poverty, Inequality, and Class Structure*, Cambridge University Press, 1974. The best recent work is J. Mack and S. Lansley, *Poor Britain*, Allen and Unwin, 1985.

The reconstitution of status

There is no comprehensive modern study of status in British society. There are, however, useful studies of particular groups. Though very different in style, Richard Hoggart, *The Uses of Literacy*, Chatto and Windus, 1957, and J. H. Goldthorpe *et al., The Affluent Worker in the Class Structure*, Cambridge University Press, 1969, give authoritative accounts of the status aspects of working-class life in two different times and places. To these two works should be added R. Roberts, *The Classic Slum*, Manchester University Press, 1971, with its graphic description of status distinction within a working-class district of Salford in the first quarter of the century. Two examples of status in more narrowly defined occupational groups are Norman Dennis *et al., Coal is our Life*, Eyre and Spottiswoode, 1956, especially Chapter 5, and A. H. Halsey and M. Trow, *The British Academics*, Faber, 1971, Chapter 10. The status of coloured immigrants in Britain is well treated in the massive sociography by E. J. B. Rose, *Colour and Citizenship: A Report on British Race Relations*, Oxford University Press, 1969. For more recent discussion see J. Benyon (ed.), *Scarman and After: Essays Reflecting on Lord Scarman's Report, The Riots and their Aftermath*, Pergamon, 1984.

The essential source on citizenship as a special form of status is T. H. Marshall, *Citizenship and Social Class*, Cambridge University Press, 1950, and his later work, *Social Policy in the Twentieth Century*, Cambridge University Press, 1967, should also be read. Professor

R. Pinker has put together some of T. H. Marshall's best later essays in *The Right to Welfare*, Heinemann, 1981. W. G. Runciman, op. cit., contains the best general account of changes in status in Britain since the First War. A new and powerful theoretical development of citizenship theory and social policy is Graham Room's *The Sociology of Welfare: Social Policy, Stratification and Political Order*, Martin Robertson, 1979.

Reference is made in this chapter to the role of religion in maintaining the status system. For further reading on this question see B. Wilson, *Contemporary Transformations of Religion,* Blackwell, 1976, and R. Towler, *The Need For Certainty: A Sociological Study of Conventional Religion*, Routledge and Kegan Paul, 1984.

The rise of party

An illuminating introduction to British twentieth-century politics is S. Beer, *Modern British Politics*, Faber, 2nd edition, 1969, and his *Britain Against Itself*, Faber, 1982, placing politics in 'the age of organization'. The authoritative source on electoral history in Britain in the twentieth century is D. Butler and D. Stokes, *Political Change in Britain*, Macmillan, 1974. C. Crouch, *Class Conflict and the Industrial Relations Crisis*, Humanities Press, 1977, is a difficult but extremely worthwhile book on the relation betwen government and working-class organization. S. E. Finer, *Anonymous Empire: A Study of the Lobby in Great Britain*, Pall Mall Press, revised edition, 1966, is indispensable for the further study of 'party' as the term is used in this chapter.

The definitive work on the sociology and history of British industrial relations is A. Fox, *History and Heritage*, Allen and Unwin, 1984. See also C. Crouch, *Trade Unions: The Logic of Collective Action*, Fontana, 1982.

The best recent account of British political organization from the point of view of electoral behaviour is A. F. Heath, R. Jowell, and J. Curtice, *How Britain Votes*, Pergamon Press, 1985.

Three studies of élites and power may be recommended: J. Fidler, *The British Business Elite*, Routledge and Kegan Paul, 1981; P. Stanworth and A. Giddens, *Elites and Power in British Society*, Cambridge University Press, 1974; and W. Guttsman, *The British Political Elite*, MacGibbon and Kee, 1963. Changes in working-class organization are discussed in B. Hindess, *The Decline of Working-Class Politics*, MacGibbon and Kee, 1971, and B. Jessop, *Traditionalism, Conservatism, and British Political Culture*, Allen and Unwin, 1974. R. T. McKenzie and A. Silver, *Angels in Marble*, Heinemann, 1968, is a good historical study of working-class Conservatism. A good recent survey of modern literature on power is Dennis Wrong's *Power: Its Forms, Bases and Uses*, Blackwell, 1979.

Between the generations

Further exploration of this field might well begin with a general book on demography such as P. R. Cox, *Demography*, 4th edition, Cambridge University Press, 1970. A good history of demographic development in Britain is J. Habakkuk, *Population and Economic Development Since 1750*, Leicester University Press, 1971, and the beginnings of the decline in fertility among the upper-middle-class Victorians are well studied in J. A. Banks, *Prosperity and Parenthood*, Routledge and Kegan Paul, 1954. An excellent history of the evolution of the modern family in Europe and North America is Edward Shorter, *The Making of the Modern Family*, Collins, 1975. F. Mount, *The Subversive Family*, Jonathan Cape, 1982, is an interesting controversial account. J. R. Goody, *The Development of the Family and Marriage in Europe*, Cambridge University Press, 1983, is an important anthropological account. Two worthwhile empirical studies of the family in Britain are C. Rosser and C. G. Harris, *The Family and Social Change*, Routledge and Kegan Paul, 1965, and M. Young and P. Willmott, *The Symmetrical Family*, Routledge and Kegan Paul, 1973. G. Gorer's *Sex and Marriage in England Today*, Nelson, 1971, is worth reading, and H. Gavron, *The Captive Wife*, Routledge and Kegan Paul, 1966, is a well-known book on the role of the housewife. See also A. Oakley, *Housewife*, Allen Lane, 1974, and E. Roberts, *A Woman's Place*, Blackwell, 1984. Childhood is well treated in M. Pringle, *The Needs of Children*, Hutchinson, 1980, and a modern treatment of the problems of family policy is M. Wynn, *Family Policy*, Penguin, 1972. A collection of essays by S. B. Kumerman and A. J. Kahn, *Family Policy: Government and Families in Fourteen Countries*, Columbia University Press, 1978, includes a study of Britain by R. A. Parker and H. Land which argues that public policies assume and support a traditional form of family organization. A bibliography of recent work is R. Chester, *The Family: A Register of Research in the United Kingdom*, Economic and Social Research Council, 1984.

Mobility and education

A recent survey and appraisal of the sociology of education may be found in A. H. Halsey and J. Karabel (eds.), *Power and Ideology in Education*, Oxford University Press, 1977, and an excellent textbook is O. Banks, *The Sociology of Education*, Batsford, 1968. On meritocracy the indispensable source is M. Young, *The Rise of Meritocracy 1870–2033*, Thames and Hudson, 1958. On comprehensive schools see C. Benn and B. Simon, *Half Way There*, McGraw-Hill, 1970, S. Ball, *Beachside Comprehensive*, Cambridge University Press, 1981, and P. Willis, *Learning To Labour*, Saxon House, 1977. The best historical treatment of the problem of equality in education is H. Silver (ed.),

Equal Opportunity in Education, Methuen, 1973, and Birmingham Centre for Contemporary Cultural Studies, *Unpopular Education: Schooling and Social Democracy in England Since 1944*, 1981. An empirical study of educational disadvantage is A. H. Halsey, *Educational Priority: Vol. 1: E.P.A. Problems and Policies*, HMSO, 1972.

The classic study of social mobility in Britain is D. V. Glass (ed.), *Social Mobility in Britain*, Routledge and Kegan Paul, 1954. More recent work is reported in J. H. Goldthorpe and K. Hope, *The Social Grading of Occupations: A New Approach and Scale*, Oxford University Press, 1974, J. H. Goldthorpe (in collaboration with C. Llewellyn and C. Payne), *Social Mobility and Class Structure in Modern Britain*, Oxford University Press, 1980; and A. H. Halsey, A. F. Heath and J. M. Ridge, *Origins and Destinations*, Oxford University Press, 1980. A lucid exposition of the general state of research on mobility is A. F. Heath's *Social Mobility*, Fontana, 1981.

Order and authority

A good general and valuable set of essays on social order is E. Shils, *Tradition*, Faber, 1981. An empirical study of the division of labour in Britain now is R. E. Pahl, *Division of Labour*, Blackwell, 1984.

In the literature on problems of devolution and disintegration in the United Kingdom, J. Osmond, *Creative Conflict: The Politics of Welsh Devolution*, Routledge and Kegan Paul, 1977, is outstanding, but see also T. Nairn, *The Break-Up of Britain*, New Left Books, 1977.

Criticism of the traditional British social order and proposals for its reform along egalitarian lines are to be found in R. H. Tawney, *Equality*, Allen and Unwin, 1952, and *The Acquisitive Society*, Bell, 1943. See also R. Williams, *Culture and Society*, Chatto and Windus, 1959, and *The Long Revolution*, Chatto and Windus, 1961; and Julian Le Grand, *The Strategy of Equality*, Allen and Unwin, 1982.

For criticism of the basis of income distribution, a classic source is B. Wootton, *Social Foundations of Wages Policy*, Allen and Unwin, 1955, but see also J. H. Goldthorpe in D. Wedderburn (ed.), *Poverty, Inequality, and Class Structure*, Cambridge University Press, 1974.

Analysis of the social order from a fraternitarian point of view is carried further by A. Vincent and R. Plant, *Philosophy, Politics and Citizenship*, Blackwell, 1984. Also highly relevant is A. MacIntyre, *After Virtue*, Duckworth, 1981. Altruism is analysed in the context of contemporary Britain in M. Ignatieff, *The Needs of Strangers*, Chatto and Windus, 1984; R. M. Titmuss, *The Gift Relationship*, Allen and Unwin, 1971; and also the essay by R. H. S. Crossman in A. H. Halsey (ed.), *Traditions of Social Policy*, Blackwell, 1976. A more general introduction to the study of social policy in Britain is Julia Parker, *Social Policy and Citizenship*, Macmillan, 1975.

A powerful study of social integration and anomy in the work place is A. Fox, *Beyond Contract: Work, Power and Trust Relations*, Faber and Faber, 1974. Norman Dennis's analysis of the relation between people, local government bureaucracies, and local politicans may be found in his *People and Planning*, Faber, 1970, and *Public Participation and Planners' Blight*, Faber 1972. See also D. E. C. Eversley and E. Evans, *The Inner City*, Centre for Environmental Studies, 1980, D. Donnison, *Urban Policies: A New Approach*, Fabian Tract 487, 1984, and J. Seabrook, *What Went Wrong*, Gollancz, 1978.

Finally, three excellent works on social integration in England, Scotland, and Wales are B. H. Harrison, *Peaceable Kingdom: Stability and Change in Modern Society*, Oxford University Press, 1982, C. Harvie, *No Gods and Precious Few Heroes: Scotland 1914-1980*, Edward Arnold, 1981, and K. O. Morgan, *Rebirth of a Nation: Wales 1880-1980*, Oxford University Press, 1981.

Index